■ The Louisiana State Constitution

The Oxford Commentaries on the State Constitutions of the United States
G. Alan Tarr, Series Editor

Professor G. Alan Tarr, Director of the Center on State Constitutional Studies at Rutgers University, serves as General Editor for this important new series which in its entirety will cover each of the 50 states. Each volume of The Oxford Commentaries on the State Constitutions of the United States contains a historical overview of the state's constitutional development, plus a section-by-section analysis of the state's current constitution. Other features included in the volumes are the text of the state's constitution, a bibliographic essay, table of cases, and index. This series provides essential reference tools for those investigating state constitutional development and constitutional law.

The Louisiana State Constitution

Lee Hargrave

THE OXFORD COMMENTARIES ON THE STATE CONSTITUTIONS OF THE UNITED STATES
G. Alan Tarr, Series Editor

OXFORD
UNIVERSITY PRESS

OXFORD
UNIVERSITY PRESS

Oxford University Press, Inc., publishes works that further Oxford University's objective of excellence in research, scholarship, and education.

Oxford New York
Auckland Cape Town Dar es Salaam Hong Kong Karachi Kuala Lumpur Madrid Melbourne Mexico City Nairobi New Delhi Shanghai Taipei Toronto

With offices in
Argentina Austria Brazil Chile Czech Republic France Greece Guatemala Hungary Italy Japan Poland Portugal Singapore South Korea Switzerland Thailand Turkey Ukraine Vietnam

Previously published in 1990 by Greenwood Press

Published by Oxford University Press, Inc.
198 Madison Avenue, New York, New York 10016

Library of Congress Cataloging-in-Publication Data

Hargrave, W. Lee.
The Louisiana state constitution / Lee Hargrave.
p. cm. — (The Oxford commentaries on the state constitutions of the United States)
Includes bibliographical references and index.
ISBN 978-0-19-977903-1 (hardback)
1. Constitutions—Louisiana. 2. Constitutional law—Louisiana.
I. Louisiana. Constitution (1974) II. Title. III. Series.
KFL4011974.A6 H367 2011
342.76302—dc22 2011001735

Note to Readers
This publication is designed to provide accurate and authoritative information in regard to the subject matter covered. It is based upon sources believed to be accurate and reliable and is intended to be current as of the time it was written. It is sold with the understanding that the publisher is not engaged in rendering legal, accounting, or other professional services. If legal advice or other expert assistance is required, the services of a competent professional person should be sought. Also, to confirm that the information has not been affected or changed by recent developments, traditional legal research techniques should be used, including checking primary sources where appropriate.

(Based on the Declaration of Principles jointly adopted by a Committee of the American Bar Association and a Committee of Publishers and Associations.)

CONTENTS

SERIES FOREWORD

In 1776, following the declaration of independence from England, the former colonies began to draft their own constitutions. Their handiwork attracted widespread interest, and draft constitutions circulated up and down the Atlantic seaboard, as constitution-makers sought to benefit from the insights of their counterparts in sister states. In Europe, the new constitutions found a ready audience seeking enlightenment from the American experiments in self-government. Even the delegates to the Constitutional Convention of 1787, despite their reservations about the course of political events in the states during the decade after independence, found much that was useful in the newly adopted constitutions. And when James Madison, fulfilling a pledge given during the campaign for the ratification of the Constitution, drafted the Federal Bill of Rights, he found his model in the famous Declaration of Rights of the Virginia Constitution.

By the 1900s, however, few people would have looked to state constitutions for enlightenment. Instead, a familiar litany of complaints was heard whenever state constitutions were mentioned. State constitutions were too long and too detailed, combining basic principles with policy prescriptions and prohibitions that had no place in the fundamental law of a state. By including such provisions, it was argued, state constitutions deprived state governments of the flexibility they needed to respond effectively to changing circumstances. Indeed, Louisiana's constitution was often cited as a prime example of an unwieldy state charter.

The state constitutions' impediments to effective government encouraged political reformers to look to the federal government, which was not plagued by such constitutional constraints, thereby helping to shift the locus of political initiative away from the states. Meanwhile, civil libertarians concluded that state bills of rights, at least as interpreted by state courts, did not adequately protect rights and therefore looked to the federal courts and the Federal Bill of Rights for redress. As power and responsibility shifted from the states to Washington, so too did the attention of scholars, the legal community, and the general public.

During the early 1970s, however, state constitutions were "rediscovered." The immediate impetus for this rediscovery was former President Richard Nixon's appointment of Warren Burger to succeed Earl Warren as Chief Justice of the United States Supreme Court. To civil libertarians, this appointment seemed to signal a decisive shift in the Supreme Court's jurisprudence, because Burger was expected to lead the Court away from the liberal activism that had characterized the Warren Court. They therefore sought ways to safeguard the gains they had achieved for defendants, racial minorities, and the poor during Warren's tenure from erosion by the Burger Court. In particular, they began to look to state bills of rights to secure the rights of defendants and to support the other civil liberties claims that they advanced in state courts.

This "new judicial federalism," as it came to be called, quite quickly advanced beyond its initial concern to evade the mandates of the Burger Court. Indeed, less than two decades after it originated, it has become a national phenomenon. When judges and scholars turned their attention to state constitutions, they discovered an unsuspected richness. They found not only provisions that paralleled the Federal Bill of Rights but also constitutional guarantees of the right to privacy and of gender equality, for example, that had no analogue in the U.S. Constitution. Careful examination of the text and history of state guarantees revealed important differences between even those provisions that most resembled federal guarantees and their federal counterparts. Looking beyond state declarations of rights, scholars and jurists discovered affirmative constitutional mandates to state governments to address such important policy concerns as education and housing. Taken altogether, these discoveries underlined the importance for the legal community of developing a better understanding of state constitutions.

Yet the renewed interest in state constitutions has not been limited to judges and lawyers. State constitutional reformers have renewed their efforts with notable success: since 1960, ten states—among them, Louisiana—have adopted new constitutions, and several others have undertaken major constitutional revisions. These changes have usually resulted in more streamlined constitutions and more effective state governments. Also, in recent years political activists on both the left and the right have pursued their goals through state constitutional amendments, often enacted through the initiative process, under which policy proposals can be placed directly on the ballot for voters to endorse or reject. Scholars too have begun to rediscover how state constitutional history can illuminate changes in political thought and practice, providing a basis for theories about the dynamics of political change in America.

Lee Hargrave's fine study of the contemporary Louisiana Constitution and its several predecessors, like earlier volumes in this series of The Oxford Commentaries on the State Constitutions of the United States, reflects this renewed interest in state constitutions and will contribute to our knowledge about them. Because the constitutional tradition of each state is distinctive, the volume begins with the history and development of Louisiana's constitutions. It then provides the full text of the current constitution, with each section accompanied by commentary that explains the provision and traces its origins and its interpretation by the courts and other governmental bodies. For readers with a particular interest in a specific aspect of Louisiana constitutionalism, the book offers a bibliography of the most important sources dealing with the constitutional history and constitutional law of the state. Finally, the book concludes with a table of cases cited in the constitutional history as well as a subject index.

G. Alan Tarr

PREFACE

The scope of coverage provided in this book is the result of a number of compromises. The Louisiana Constitution of 1974, though shorter than its predecessor, is nonetheless longer and more detailed than most other state constitutions, and subsequent amendments have also added to its length. Given the need to incorporate the entire text of the document in this book, the historical introduction, the commentary, and the bibliography have of necessity been kept brief so that the book stays within manageable proportions. Completeness in the commentary has been sacrificed, but I have attempted to examine the most important subjects.

Since this volume is part of a series designed to accommodate the needs of a wide audience, I have avoided my normal emphasis on technical legal analysis. I have attempted to explain case developments without excessive legal language and have also avoided the copious (many would say absurdly excessive) footnoting of the usual law review style. I have included a complete table of cases with citations.

My history could not have been done without substantial reliance on Alden L. Powell's *A History of Louisiana Constitutions*. Out of print, this history was drafted during the early 1950s for the Louisiana State Law Institute as part of its research materials for a new constitution for the state.

My commentary is illuminated by my service as a member of the research staff of the Louisiana Constitutional Convention of 1973. I served as coordinator of legal research and later was also involved with the editing of the documents of the convention as a member of the Louisiana Constitutional Convention Records Commission. To the extent that a reader might find that the documentation of some of my conclusions about the 1973 convention is wanting, I must often rely simply on my having been there. Also at the convention and also helpful to me over the years in matters relating to the convention were David Poynter and Edward Hardin, the clerk and assistant clerk, respectively, of the convention. Hardin was also the editor of the convention documents. Numerous delegates to the convention have been helpful over the years, especially delegates (and Justices) Albert Tate, Jr., and James Dennis. I acknowledge the summer research support for this work provided by the Louisiana State University law center.

PART ONE

The History of the Louisiana Constitution

Louisiana's eleven constitutions—eight in the nineteenth century and three in the twentieth—were the result of profound political changes and intense partisan struggles that occurred during the state's complex history. Louisiana developed from French and Spanish colonialism into a melting pot that incorporated American Anglo-Saxon immigrants, blacks (slave and free), and more recent European immigrants. The state developed into a more democratic society, then moved from slave holding to secession to reconstruction. It moved from radical reconstruction to conservatism and then into a progressive era capped with Huey Long's rise to power.

A rich mixture of political influences not only shaped basic policy and governmental structure. The desire of each new group to protect its reforms was accomplished by putting those reforms in a new constitution. More than in any other state, "the constitution was increasingly viewed as a statutory bank vault within which favored schemes, phobias, and interests of the prevailing elite could be secured into the future beyond the reach of fickle legislatures and ungrateful governors."[1]

[1] Mark T. Carleton, "Elitism Sustained: The Louisiana Constitution of 1974," *Tulane Law Review* 54 (1980): 560,561.

In the twentieth century, as amendment became easier, the focus switched to change by amendment rather than by convention. From 1921 to 1974, voters approved 536 amendments.

The Constitution of 1974 was drafted by a convention that attempted to bring Louisiana into the mainstream of American state constitutionalism. To a large extent, it succeeded. Still, the constitution contains more limitations on the legislature and more detailed provisions than do most other state constitutions. Moreover, the tradition of cementing reforms in the constitution is still alive. A "reform" governor in 1989 proposed and the people adopted an amendment to establish a constitutional trust fund to prohibit future legislatures from allocating the proceeds of a gasoline tax to uses other than highway construction.

CONSTITUTION OF 1812: ARISTOCRATIC BEGINNINGS

The people of Louisiana in 1812 had lived under French and Spanish colonial rule, authoritarian government that did not produce the experimentation with democracy and constitutions that characterized the British colonies. As it approached statehood, Louisiana was an aristocratic society, and its first constitution reflected an elitist view of government. The requirements of the congressional legislation with respect to democratic institutions were met, but the drafters took for a model the conservative Kentucky Constitution of 1797. Two of the drafters, James Brown and Allan B. Magruder, came to Louisiana from Kentucky.[2] Indeed, the document was drafted in the language of the French elite, and it was only "a duly authenticated English translation" that was sent to Washington to comply with the enabling act. This was so although another provision of the document declared that English would be the official language.

Under the constitution's "government by gentlemen," [3] suffrage was confined to free white males 21 years or older who owned property or paid taxes (Art. II, sec. 8). The property requirement alone had the effect of barring two-thirds of the adult freemen from voting.

The governor was chosen by the legislature from the two candidates who received the highest popular vote and had to "hold in his own right a landed estate of five thousand dollars value" (Art. III, sec. 4), a fortune in those days. The governor had broad powers of appointment. With senate approval, he appointed "all Judges, Sheriffs and . . . all other Officers . . . whose appointments are not otherwise provided for," including local officials (Art. III, sec. 9).

Although the constitution accommodated Anglo-American criminal law institutions, including the jury system, it preserved the French-Spanish civil law

---

[2] Cecil Morgan, *The First Constitution of Louisiana* (Baton Rouge: Louisiana State University Press, 1975), 10.

[3] The phrase is the title of chapter five in Roger W. Shugg, *Origins of Class Struggle in Louisiana* (Baton Rouge: Louisiana State University Press, 1968).

in the private realm. Reacting to an earlier attempt by territorial governor William C. C. Claiborne to adopt the common law, the drafters in Article IV, section 11 provided "the legislature shall never adopt any system or code of laws, by general reference." This provision, one of the few additions to the Kentucky model, was introduced by Creole aristocrat Bernard Marigny, but it was also praised by the Anglo-American lawyer Edward Livingston who said the people of Louisiana "dreaded the Common Law of England. They feared another attempt to introduce it."[4]

The 1812 Constitution could be amended only by a convention that was called after approval of the call by the legislature and by a majority of the qualified voters. That constitution was never amended.

The constitution did protect some civil rights as required by the Enabling Act, but it did not contain a separate bill of rights. Interestingly, though, Article I, section 2 required separation of powers: "No person or Collection of persons, being one of those departments, shall exercise any power properly belonging to either of the others; except in the instances hereinafter expressly directed or permitted." Presumably the Francophone drafters were guided to specify the principles of Montesquieu that had influenced but were not specified in the federal constitution rather than specifying a catalog of rights. The separation of powers provisions has remained in all subsequent constitutions.

The 1812 document stated simply that the judicial power was vested in a supreme court and "such inferior courts as may be convenient to the administration of justice" (Art. IV, sec. 4). The constitution did require, however, that the supreme court ride a specific circuit. It would sit in New Orleans from November to July and hold sessions in Opelousas and Alexandria from August through October (Art. IV, sec. 3).

New Orleans was designated the capital, but it could be removed by law. Local government was left to legislation, but the trend for constitutionalizing New Orleans local government was begun, as the "citizens of the town of New Orleans shall have the right of appointing the several public officers necessary for the administration and police of the said city" (Art. VI, sec. 23).

Representation in the general assembly was based on the numbers of qualified voters in each county, but the constitution itself enumerated the apportionment in the first legislature. Such a constitutional enumeration remained common in succeeding constitutions. The assembly met in regular annual session in January, "before spring work had begun on the plantations. The social season of New Orleans, in full swing by midwinter, may have furnished an added attraction for solons who were not unwilling to combine a bit of pleasure with public service."[5]

---

[4] Robert H. Marr, "A Historical Review of the Constitutions of Louisiana," *Proceedings of the Louisiana Bar Association* (1913): 229, 232.

[5] Alden L. Powell, *A History of Louisiana Constitutions* (Baton Rouge: State of Louisiana, 1954), 281.

The predominantly French Catholic society chose to adopt strong separation of church and state. No state office could be held by a person "while he continues to exercise the functions of a clergyman, priest or teacher of any religious persuasion, society or sect" (Art. II, sec. 22).

Overall, however, that constitution was free of many defects of the state's modern constitutions, particularly the statutory detail. Except for its suffrage provisions, it might have served the state well for years longer.

CONSTITUTION OF 1845: JEFFERSONIAN DEMOCRACY

Responding to the influx of poor, Anglo-American immigrants and their Jacksonian democratic ideals, the legislature called a constitutional convention in 1845 designed to expand the suffrage, reapportion the legislature, and enlarge the appellate jurisdiction of the supreme court. The convention, however, did not limit itself to these items and made substantial revisions and additions to the constitution.

Delegates represented a close political balance, with 39 Whigs and 38 Democrats, and not surprisingly, the convention produced a compromise document. Democratic reforms included abolition of property qualification for voting and holding office. Suffrage was extended to white males 21 or older who had been U. S. citizens for two years and residents of the state for two years. A few delegates sympathetic to the anti-immigrant Know-Nothing Party were responsible for limiting the vote to persons who had been citizens for two years. Also ineligible to vote were persons who had moved from the state for more than 90 consecutive days. During the busy summer months, New Orleans had a large transient population which deserted the city in the fall when yellow fever began raging, and perhaps returned in the following spring. The majority was unwilling that this transient population have any claim to residence for voting purposes. The effect of the provision in practice was "to make the 'baptism of yellow fever' a qualification for voting in New Orleans."[6] The time of electing legislators was changed from July to November, reducing the political power of New Orleans because of the transients there in the summer. Substantial debate was devoted to placing the system of registration of voters, a means of lessening corruption, in the constitution. That effort failed. In the end, the electorate was enlarged by about one-third, leaving the franchise in the hands of two-fifths of the adult freemen.

Other democratic changes were implemented. Most local offices were made elective, and the governor's appointment powers were limited. District judges remained appointed but for fixed terms rather than for life. Terms of supreme court justices were reduced to eight years.

---

[6] Ibid., 303.

Representation in the senate, however, was designed to give the conservative planters a strong position. Representation in the upper house was based on total population, slave and free, giving the slaveholding parishes a veto over legislation they opposed. Representation in the house was based on the numbers of qualified voters. In this compromise between the planters and the small farmers, New Orleans lost out; the city remained underrepresented. According to the 1840 census, its population had increased to about 102,000 out of a total population of 352,000 for the state, but the constitution limited it to a maximum of four senators (of 32) and twenty representatives (of 100). The convention did form a Committee on the Bill of Rights, which was successful in obtaining adoption of most of its recommendations, but in Title VI, General Provisions, and not as a separate bill of rights.

As a precursor, the convention reforms in the judiciary resulted in more detail. Qualifications, terms, and minimum salaries for district judges were provided. Justice of the peace courts were established, and parish courts that had been established by legislation were abolished. The new justices of the peace were to be elected, as were clerks of the district courts, sheriffs and coroners. Often repeated is the quotation from Creole aristocrat, Bernard Marigny, who complained, We have an election for almost everything, from a sheriff down to an inspector of porks: [7] The appellate jurisdiction of the supreme court was described in detail, and for the first time it was given jurisdiction "in criminal cases on questions of law."

The constitution directed the legislature to establish free public schools and to provide means for their support (Art. 134). A superintendent of public education was established. Revenue dedication appeared also: Article 135 requiring that proceeds from the sale of lands donated by the United States be treated as a loan to the state, with 6 percent interest on those funds being used to support the schools and for no other purpose. Article 137 provided that a university "shall be established in the city of New Orleans." The constitution gave it a name, the University of Louisiana, and designated its four faculties: law, medicine, natural sciences and letters.

Marigny, "as much of a Frenchman in 1845 as he had been in 1812," was responsible for the provision that senate and House officers speak both French and English and that members could address either house in French or English.[8] Another unique "statutory" addition reflected the changing mores of the aristocracy: suffrage and the right to hold office were denied to anyone who shall "fight a duel with deadly weapons . . . or send or accept a challenge . . . or act as second"(Art. 89, 130).

[7] Debates, Constitutional Convention of 1845, p. 844, quoted in ibid., 297.

[8] Marr, "A Historical Review," 235.

The territorial legislative council, following a pattern of other states, had divided the state into twelve counties in 1804, but the influence of the former ecclesiastical parishes would not die. They became the units of local government, and counties were finally abolished in the Constitution of 1845. Policy mandates abounded, ranging from requiring the legislature to provide for change of venue in civil and criminal cases, to requiring taxes to be equal and uniform throughout the state. More limitations on the legislature appeared: no legislative divorces; no pledge of the "faith of the state" for debts of persons, corporations or body politic whatever"; state debt limited to $100,000; no privilege or monopoly could be granted for more than twenty years; no corporations established by special law; the state could not subscribe to stock of private corporations; lotteries were prohibited.

Another innovation was an easier amendment procedure under which amendments could be proposed by three-fifths of the two houses. Before submission to the voters, however, the next session of the legislature had to approve them again by majority vote.

CONSTITUTION OF 1852: MORE DEMOCRACY AND INTERNAL IMPROVEMENTS

The Constitution of 1852 has been described as a peculiar document, both more radical and more conservative than previous ones. The convention, composed of 85 Whig delegates and 45 Democratic delegates, would spur the demands for internal improvements as well as extend democratic reforms.

The document provided for election of virtually all offices, including judges. Terms of office were shortened, and residence requirements were reduced to one year in the state and six months in the parish. Residents who moved within the state would not lose a right to vote in the former parish until a similar right was acquired in the new parish. An attempt was also made to lessen election fraud in New Orleans through a new registration law.

Apportionment in both houses, however, was based on total population, giving the planter parishes with slaves an important voice. A tendency toward more democracy was more apparent than real. Under the new constitution, the twelve parishes in the black belt had as many representatives as twenty white parishes with twice the number of freemen.

Most important, and a portent of developments, were constitutional provisions for grants to private corporations and commercial interests as part of a movement for internal improvements. A whole new Title VII, Internal Improvements, was added. The alliance between the commercial interests in New Orleans and the black belt planters was aimed at raising capital to be used in expanding plantations and building railroads. These groups needed each other's assistance also to check the flood of paper money and halt other agrarian legislation that had threatened them since 1845. The Internal Improvements

Code that the Whigs incorporated in the constitution "called for state economic aid to banking, railroad and other transport companies. It was written into the state constitution to become selfoperating to protect this kind of special interest legislation from being curtailed or repealed by Democratic legislatures in the future."[9] It was an important step in the expansion of constitutional provisions that would grow and provide Louisiana with the longest state constitution.

A board of public works was established, with its four members elected from districts. The limitation on the use of state credit for private purposes was reduced so that the state might subscribe to stock and make loans to any company "formed for the exclusive purpose of making works of internal improvement, wholly or partially within the state" (Art. 109). The provisions against monopolies were discontinued.

With its new authority, the legislature in 1853, still under Whig control, adopted legislation to aid banks, railroads, and other businesses, appropriating millions of dollars for those purposes.

A startling change in the judiciary was in the provisions for popular election of judges. The chief justice of the supreme court was to be elected at large in the state and associate justices from supreme court districts. In a mild concession to Anglo-American views, the constitution allowed the legislature to restrict the court's jurisdiction in civil cases to questions of law alone instead of allowing review of the facts also, as had been allowed. The attorney general, the district attorneys, and the judges of the inferior courts were to be elected for the first time (Art. 81–84).

Amendment of the constitution was simplified. Amendments could be Proposed in one legislative session only, by two-thirds vote of each house, and required a majority approval of those voting. Gone were the requirements that the amendments be proposed by two legislatures and approved of a majority of all qualified voters.

Little change was made in the rights of citizens, though clergymen were given the right to hold public office. Office-holders who participated in duels, however, were to be removed from office (Art. 126). The governor's powers were virtually unchanged, though the minimum age for the office was dropped from 35 to 28 and the residence requirement reduced from fifteen to four years.

Baton Rouge was made the state capital, and the legislature was forbidden to remove it without consent of three-fourths of the members elected to both houses.

---

[9] Mark T. Carleton, "History of Louisiana Constitutions," in Louis E. Newman, ed., *Focus on CCI73* (Baton Rouge: LSU Institute of Government Research, 1973), 5.

CONSTITUTION OF 1861: SECESSION

Although an unresolved debate continues about whether a majority of Louisianians favored secession, about 20,000 adult white males voted to elect delegates to a convention that adopted, on January 26, 1861, an ordinance of secession. The convention continued the 1852 Constitution and made only cosmetic changes in reference to allegiance to the Confederate States of America.

CONSTITUTION OF 1864: EARLY RECONSTRUCTION

The Constitution of 1864 became enmeshed with the complexities of the end of the Civil war and was never put into effect. It was drafted while General Nathaniel P. Banks was still trying to secure control over northern areas of the state. New Orleans supplied 63 delegates, and only 35 came from the country parishes, still largely held by Confederates. General Banks issued the call for the convention, which produced delegates who for the most part were not well-known men. "The debates were desultory and quite dull generally, lacking the eloquence, sparkling wit, and clear analysis of issues which had characterized those of 1845. The Convention spent much of its time in a tangle of parliamentary procedure."[10] Working-class whites and some black groups gained ascendancy, and the convention went so far as to adopt a minimum wage provision.

Not men of wealth, the delegates voted themselves a per diem of ten dollars, a large sum in 1864 dollars. Total cost of the convention was more than $364,000 and expenses included $9,400 for liquor and cigars. "Neither carpetbaggers nor corrupt Negroes were present."[11] The excesses were those of white Louisianians.

City merchants were able to protect their interests, but the planters were not. Small fanners were able to redress some of their grievances. Surprisingly, little support for black suffrage emerged. Pressured by General Banks, the delegates did adopt a provision that allowed the legislature to extend suffrage to blacks in the future, but this was not likely so long as the legislators were elected by whites.

Among the major provisions of the document were several that repudiated the Whig Constitution of 1852. All white males were entitled to vote after a one-year period of residence in the state. Apportionment was based on the numbers of qualified voters. Restrictions on banks and corporations were revived, and the emphasis on internal improvements was halted.

A foreboding provision did away with the prohibition against lotteries, and the legislature was authorized to allow sale of lottery tickets and to permit

[10] Powell, *A History*, 351 n. 1.

[11] Ibid., 353, citing Shugg, Origins, 200–202.

gambling houses. As to the latter, they "in all cases shall be on the first floor and kept with open doors" (Art. 116).

A progressive income tax was provided for. Public schools for blacks as well as whites were to be established, the expansion of the proposal to include blacks, coming again from pressure from General Banks.

Slavery was abolished, this occurring in Louisiana one year before ratification of the Thirteenth Amendment abolished slavery nationally. The convention also defeated a proposal to compensate slave owners for their losses.

Additional detail continued to creep in. The salaries of the governor and lieutenant governor were fixed in the constitution (respectively, $8,000 and $5,000 per year); those specific amounts would prevent political strife. Judges were again to be appointed rather than elected. The supreme court regained its power to review matters of fact in civil cases.

Reflecting the fact that residents of the city dominated the convention, the constitution contained a new title dealing with New Orleans that included detailed provisions governing the police, even down to the minimum salary of privates in the force.

All during this period, however, doubt existed as to the validity of the new document since the convention had been called by an army general rather than by legitimate state authorities. More important, the document did not satisfy the national authorities, who were now imposing the Reconstruction Acts.

CONSTITUTION OF 1868: RADICAL RECONSTRUCTION

As the Civil War waned, Confederate veterans returning to the state joined with small farmers in opposing Negro suffrage and northern radicalism. Under conditions of general unrest, race riots occurred in New Orleans in 1866. The proposed Fourteenth Amendment was rejected in 1867. Federal military reconstruction was inevitable.

The Reconstruction Acts declared that no legal government existed in Louisiana and called for the adoption of a new constitution. The South was divided into five military districts, with Louisiana and Texas comprising the Fifth District under the authority of General Philip Sheridan. Enforcing the Reconstruction Acts, he issued a call for a constitutional convention under which all adult males, black or white, who swore they had not aided the Confederacy were to vote for delegates. Half the white voters were thus excluded. The convention that resulted was made up of equal numbers of black and white delegates. It met during 1867–1868 and produced a constitution that adopted the state's first full-fledged bill of rights and provided for black suffrage.

Representation in both houses was on the basis of total population. Integrated public schools were to be established. Discrimination based on race in public places was prohibited. Slavery was abolished, and citizenship was open to all. Freedom of assembly and worship were provided. All persons were granted equal rights and privileges on "any conveyance of a public character." Places of public accommodation were to be open without racial discrimination.

Substantial changes in the judiciary were made again. District courts were regulated in the constitution, and the parish court system was revived. District judges were to be elected, and the Orleans district courts were subject to special regulations. Justices of the peace were also to continue.

For the first time, the legislature was directed to adopt a poll tax of $1.50 per year and to provide pensions for veterans.

To cover its expenses the convention, lacking financial support from the state, issued warrants, which were made valuable by the provision they could be used to pay taxes in the future.

Among the convention's unique provisions was one reducing the age require ment for the governor to 21 (any qualified voter) so that 25-year-old Henry Clay Warmoth could qualify. In the ensuing elections, Warmoth was elected governor and Oscar J. Dunn, a Negro, was elected lieutenant governor. The Republicans had thus secured control of the state's government. The Whigs ceased to function, and the new political division was between the new Republicans and the more conservative Democrats.

As the Republican carpetbaggers exerted their political influence, backed by the newly enfranchised black voters, the state entered a period of corruption and misrule. Corruption attended grants to private corporations to undertake canals, railroads, drainage, and other public improvements projects. The infamous Louisiana lottery came into prominence and began exerting influence on state government.

The 1868 Convention reflected the policies of a temporarily dominant faction: the Radical Republicans and freedmen. Supported by federal military power, they sought to destroy the planter-merchant elite. This set the stage for another pendulum swing, when the conservatives would again strive for power. While historian Allan P. Sindler admits racial politics were to come to the fore later, he concludes, "While the battle for racial supremacy clearly alienated the mass of whites from Republican rule, the upper classes resented more the economic ills and the looting of public funds occasioned by Radical government. It was only after their serious attempts to enlist the Negro in common cause met with failure that the upper classes adopted white supremacy as the rallying cry in the struggle for self-government."[12] And just as the radicals had tried to cement their policies in a constitution, the victorious Democrats in the next pendulum swing would try to cement theirs.

[12] Alan P. Sindler, *Huey Long's Louisiana: State Politics, 1920–52* (Baltimore: Johns Hopkins University Press, 1956), 13.

CONSTITUTION OF 1879: CONSERVATIVES AND THE LOTTERY

Founded in 1868, the Louisiana Lottery Company collected money from throughout the United States—between $20 million and $30 million annually. It paid less than 50 percent of that in prizes and paid the state only $40,000 a year for the right to operate. Its political agent, Major E. A. Burke, was the political boss of Louisiana. An antilottery movement began to gain some ground, and Governor Francis T. Nicholls in 1879 signed a bill abolishing the company. Federal court restraining orders halted the state's action, and a state constitutional convention followed, the call being supported by the lottery company. The convention "met, gave the lottery a twenty-five year charter, and shortened the terms of all state officials except Burke by one year. Burke's term [as state treasurer] was extended until 1884."[13]

In other areas, conservative forces were in control. The convention was composed of 98 Democrats and 32 Republicans. The majority wanted to establish white supremacy, end high taxation and spending, and curb corruption. With the resurgence of the Bourbon planter-merchant elite, the rights of the freed blacks were limited, and jim crow legislation was coming to the fore.

The constitution imposed many restrictions on the legislature and on local officials while enlarging the powers of the governor. Indeed, the 1879 Constitution has been referred to as the state's first "long constitution," a document of 40 odd pages. Excessive taxation was a target of the reformers. Innovations that survived into the 1921 Constitution included the item veto, a pardon board, limited special legislative sessions, segregated schools, and detailed provisions for Orleans parish. New Orleans ceased to be the state capital, and Baton Rouge once again became the seat of government.

The equal rights articles of the 1868 Constitution and the provisions against fixing the price of manual labor were discontinued. Women, on the other hand, were given a small measure of recognition; women 21 years of age were "eligible to any office of control or management under the school laws" (Art. 232).

Reacting to legislative corruption, the constitution regulated the organization and procedure of both houses in detail as never before, extending to the style of the enacting clause, the requirements of minutes, recording votes in a journal, signing of bills in open session, amendments, conference committees, and no appropriations for contingencies. For the first time, the scope of the legislative power in special sessions was limited by the call issued by the governor.

The attempts to control taxation and loan of the state's credit were expanded. No bonds could be issued by the legislature except to repeal invasion or

---

[13] Joe Gray Taylor, *Louisiana: A Bicentennial History* (New York: Norton, 1976), 134; Taylor, *Louisiana Reconstructed*, 1863–1876 (Baton Rouge, Louisiana State University Press, 1975), 197.

suppress insurrection. (Art. 44) No excess compensation was to be paid to public officers or contractors (Art. 44). The list of improper local and special laws was increased to fifteen subsections (Art. 46). The legislature was mandated to provide a system to ensure equality in assessments (Art. 203). License taxes were provided, and the local authorities were forbidden to impose such taxes in amounts greater than imposed by the state (Art. 206). The list of exemptions from tax was long.

Farmers, plagued by high interest and low prices, were able to obtain some relief in the form of homestead exemption provisions in the constitution. Homesteads were exempt from seizure and sale, up to $2,000.

Gambling was declared a vice, and the legislature was mandated to pass laws to suppress it (Art. 172); however, the legislature was also given authority to grant lottery charters but for not less than $40,000 per year "in money." Only after January 1, 1895, could no lotteries exist. The Louisiana Lottery Company was thus able to look forward to at least fifteen more profitable years.

Gone were the previous prohibitions against segregation in public education. Instead a mandate was added to establish a separate university "for persons of color" in New Orleans. Parish public schools were mandated, and numerous detailed provisions regulating them were adopted. English was to be the language of instruction, "but in parishes where French was the predominant language, the exercises might also be taught in French if it could be done without extra expense" (Art. 226). Louisiana State University and Agricultural and Mechanical College was mentioned for the first time and some funds dedicated to it (Art. 230).

The title on the judiciary was expanded and completely revised. It contained 68 articles, an increase from the 22 articles in the prior document. The title covered regulation of the courts, the attorney general, sheriffs, coroners, clerks, district attorneys, justices of the peace, constables, and the Orleans courts of limited jurisdiction. The detail of the provisions was such that seven different articles had to be amended within three years of adoption.

Even the militia was regulated in detail; conscientious objectors could be excused from service upon payment of an equivalent amount in money for their services (Art. 183). New provisions governing corporations amounted to a code on corporations and corporate rights. Most were attempts to limit the sale of watered stock and otherwise to guarantee the proper management of private corporations.

CONSTITUTION OF 1898: MORE JIM CROW

The 1898 Constitution made few structural changes in government organization Basic political forces were at work, however, and were aimed at limiting the right to vote. The Bourbon Democrats sought to consolidate their power, eliminating the black vote and reducing the voting strength of poor, uneducated whites as well. Led by Governor Murphy Foster, the 1896 legislature adopted a registration law designed to reduce the votes of the uneducated of both races. It also called for the Constitutional Convention of 1898 to make the restriction permanent. Although the people ratified the call for the convention, the document drawn up was to go into effect without a popular vote.

Restrictions were placed on voting, including residence requirements of two years in the state, one in the parish, and six months in the precinct. This provision "eliminated [from the voting rolls] those sharecroppers who demonstrated independence by moving each year."[14] Literacy requirements and requirements of ownership of property of at least $300 were imposed. Grandfather clauses were adopted to protect the vote of illiterate whites. Black voter registration, about 130,000 in 1897, decreased to 5,320 in 1900 and to 1,342 in 1904; corresponding figures for whites indicated a reduction from 164,000 to 125,000 to 92,000.

Another important issue facing the convention was the state penal system. The abuses of the convict lease system had been acknowledged, and provision was made in the basic document to prohibit leasing of convicts to private interests after 1901.

Innovations in public schools were adopted, making segregation of the races mandatory (Art. 248). A state board of education was established, and property tax revenues were dedicated to public schools (Art. 254). Authorization for taxation of inheritances not to exceed 10 percent was added, with the limitation that the revenues be used exclusively for school purposes (Art. 236). Here again the recipe for a lengthening constitution was evident: authorization to tax in the constitution, a limitation on the amount of the tax in the constitution, and a dedication of the proceeds of the tax in the constitution.

Another popular reform was to increase the power of the state to control corporations. No local or special laws were to be adopted. The 1898 Constitution also created a number of new state agencies, including the Railroad Commission. The legislature had refused to adopt such a body, but the convention went ahead with its own policy of rate regulation.

Attention was given to the detail of governing New Orleans. Mandates for retirement of city debt were adopted, as well as authorization to appoint seven tax assessors and seven tax collectors for the city (Art. 309–320).

Populist unrest had been growing, and the convention Democrats made some effort to ameliorate some of the economic conditions that were driving the small farmers to the Populist party. The Board of Agriculture and Immigration was formed to promote agriculture and foster settlement of fertile farmland. An examiner of state banks was established, with the duty of examining all state banks at least twice each year (Art. 194). Speculation in grain futures was to

---

[14] Taylor, *Louisiana: A Bicentennial History*, 143.

be controlled, and the convention called for laws to forbid "persons or corporations . . . to combine or conspire together . . . for the purpose of forcing up or down the price of any agricultural product or article of necessity, for speculative purposes" (Art. 190).

CONSTITUTION OF 1913: DETAIL BREEDS DETAIL

The legislature called a constitutional convention primarily to refund the state debt and to enlarge the powers of the New Orleans Sewerage and Water Board. As early as 1913, matters of local concern were becoming regular items in the state constitution. The convention call was quite limited, and the convention was empowered to adopt the new constitution without submitting the final document to the voters. It met for less than two weeks. It went beyond the call, however, precipitating supreme court decisions that called into question whether the constitution itself was constitutional.

The 1913 document was longer than its predecessor because the drafters included the 66 amendments to the 1898 Constitution that had been adopted in the intervening years. Fifteen of those amendments affected the judiciary, among them a return to elected supreme court judges. Five different amendments to the article on Confederate pensions were accommodated, and more money was dedicated to education. One state tax collector replaced the seven tax collectors in Orlcans, but the seven Orleans tax assessors remained.

In the process of incorporating the amendments, the drafters also revised some provisions and added a few others, especially with respect to the port of New Orleans and the juvenile courts. These few changes, however, were annulled by the supreme court, which concluded that the convention was bound by the enabling act calling the convention (*State v. American Sugar Refinery Co.*, 1915; *Foley v. Democratic Parish Committee of the Parish of Orleans*, 1915).

CONSTITUTION OF 1921: MORE DETAIL

With the uncertainty over the validity of provisions of the 1913 Constitution, the need for a new constitution was the major topic at the annual session of the Louisiana Bar Association in 1919. A leader in the movement for a new consituation was Dean Robert Lee Tullis of the recently founded Louisiana State University Law School. The 1920 legislature proposed a convention, and the call, approved by the voters, empowered the convention to adopt a constitution without further voter approval.

Reform was needed, but the convention took place after Governor John M. Parker's modest attempts at reform in the legislature had floundered. Also, no preparatory studies had been made, and the convention had no research staff. It "was a prolonged, well-lobbied and confused affair. . . . Its product was a lengthy mish-mash of organic and statutory law, with the customary restraints upon the legislature."[15] No basic changes in governmental structure were adopted, although numerous public policy issues and detailed proposals were tackled. A long, detailed document not very different from the 1879 Constitution was adopted, and constraints on the power of the legislature to legislate in many fields were added.

The 1921 Constitution was not the result of intense partisan political bickering as many of its predecessors were. For the most part the delegates were conservative white supremacists. There was virtually no Republican opposition to the Democratic power structure in the state, and no black delegates were present at the convention. Now that the population of New Orleans was proportionally reduced (one-fifth of the state), the city-country forces were not as contentious as in the past, and the city was given its full representation in the legislature for the first time. The Long and anti-Long divisions that were to shape the future of Louisiana politics were a few years away.

Most of the substantive limitations on legislature were carried over, and the convention added new ones as well. One significant addition was a reaction to grants or sales of valuable mineral-producing land owned by the state. The legislature could not "alienate, or authorize the alienation of, the fee of the bed of any navigable stream, lake or other body of water, except for purposes of reclamation" (Art. IV, sec.2). The mineral rights on all state lands sold had to be reserved by the state.

Conservative civilian jurists prevailed and limited the power of the legislature to allow establishment of common law trusts. That provision (Art. IV, sec. 16) also enshrined a traditional Louisiana Civil Code provision guaranteeing children a right to inherit a percentage of the deceased's estate by specifying, "No law shall be passed abolishing forced heirship"-a typical example of how detail bred more detail. Section 16 was amended in 1944, 1952, 1958, and 1962 to liberalize the types of trusts allowed and to regulate the rights of adopted children as forced heirs. In this regard, the constitution went into the detail not only of providing that adopted children would be forced heirs of the adopting parents but that they "shall retain their rights as heirs of their blood relatives."

More state officers sought to be constitutionally protected from the reach of the legislature. The register of the state land office, the commissioner of agriculture and immigration, and the commissioner of conservation were successful in being included in the constitution, but the legislature was authorized to consolidate any of these offices. The consolidation provision (Art. V, sec. 1) was amended in 1958, 1960, and 1962. Again, a compromise provision that provided little real protection was adopted, but one that occupied more space and prompted more detail.

[15] Carleton, "History," 7.

A renamed Public Service Commission was provided, but no change was made in its organization. A proposal for appointed rather than elected commissioners was an apparent attempt to remove Huey P. Long as commissioner from the third district, but it failed.

The judiciary was overhauled again, this time by an especially interested group, since 91 lawyers were among the 146 delegates. The final draft of the judiciary article contained more than 35 printed pages.

A touchy question involved the right to vote. Because the grandfather clause had been ruled unconstitutional, the convention sought subtler ways of limiting black suffrage. They decided that prospective voters would be required to read and provide "a reasonable interpretation" of any clause of the state or federal constitution. An exception was made for persons unable to read who were of "good character"; they could register if they understood the obligations of citizenship in a republican form of government and were able to interpret any constitutional provision (Art. VIII, sec. 1). It was expected that registrars would use their discretion in making these decisions in a way designed to preserve white supremacy.

Substantial time was spent debating a severance tax. By this time, Louisiana's oil and gas development was underway, but the state was collecting little revenue from its token severance tax. Attempts by Governor Parker in 1920 to raise the tax by legislation were unsuccessful; he had allowed lawyers for Standard Oil to draft the legislation.[16] Strong sentiment existed in the convention to increase it to 3 percent; Governor Parker appeared before the convention to oppose an increase beyond the 2 percent provided by his "gentleman's agreement" with the oil companies. Ultimately the document did not specify the rate of severance tax but simply allowed the legislature to determine the matter.

Much detail was provided to develop policies on levee construction. Early land grants on the Mississippi River put the burden of levee construction on riparian landowners. By 1921, levee districts were being promoted to build levees, and for the first time, compensation was to be provided for landowners whose property was appropriated for levee purposes (Art. XVI, Sec. 1–6).

By 1947, 219 amendments to the 1921 Constitution had been adopted. The document's structure had made it almost impossible to use effectively. Kimbrough Owen of Louisiana State University, who would direct the Louisiana State Law Institute's project for a new constitution, identified these structural problems as the plethora of detail, confusing terminology, inconsistencies, references to other legal documents, informal amending procedure, duplication of material, contradictions, and omissions.[17]

---

[16] T. Harry Williams, *Huey Long* (New York: Knopf, 1969), 142.

[17] Kimbrough Owen, "The Need for Constitutional Revision in Louisiana," *Louisiana Law Review* 8 (1947):4–16.

Attempts at constitutional reform were confounded by the transfers of power between the Long and anti-Long factions. Anti-Long governor Sam Houston Jones attempted to reform the executive department, but his attempts at reorganization were invalidated by the supreme court. *Graham v. Jones*(1941) held the constitutional amendment that was adopted to reorganize the executive branch violated a constitutional prohibition against submitting more than one amendment in the same proposal. During the administration of anti-Long governor Jimmie Davis, the legislature instructed the Louisiana State Law Institute to prepare a draft or projet of a new constitution. With the aid of an academic staff drawn primarily from Louisiana State University, it completed the projet, along with elaborate notes and studies, in the summer of 1950. However, Earl Long, Huey's brother, was elected governor in 1948, and he sought to change the constitution primarily to remove the prohibition against the governor's serving successive terms. He was encouraged in his aspirations by the landslide vote that Russell Long, Huey's son, had received in the 1950 senatorial election. The 1950 leg-islature proposed a referendum of the voters to decide whether to call a consti-tutional convention. The second extraordinary session that year modified the proposal to accommodate some of the opposition by limiting the governor's powers over the product. Controversy continued, however, even among members of the Long faction, and Governor Long abandoned the convention as opposition mounted. A third extraordinary session was called, in which the legislature met for one day and voted unanimously to suspend the call.

The movement for reform continued, though, and funds were provided for the law institute projet to be printed and widely distributed. These documents were submitted to anti-Long governor Robert F. Kennon in 1954. By 1956, however, when the election to call a new constitutional convention was held, Earl Long had been elected governor once again. This time it was the voters who refused to call a constitutional convention. The vote was nearly 6-1 against the call.

The fate of Act 166 of 1956, which provided for the call, indicates some of the complexities of the forces that united against the change. Originating from a bar association committee that emphasized the necessity for committee organization and research staff, the proposal was first revised to increase substantially the number of delegates appointed by the governor. Then amendments proposed by the segregationist bloc were adopted to require the continuation of the existing bill of rights, as well as designated articles relating to suffrage. Paying the usual attention to detail, the legislation designated the seven working committees of the convention.

Two prominent Baton Rouge attorneys who qualified as candidates for the convention also indicated their opposition to the call. R. Gordon Kean, parish attorney and law partner of anti-Long governor J. Y. Sanders, stated, "I do not believe present conditions would permit proper deliberation of the fundamental rights of the people which will be involved."[18] Carlos Spaht, often a Long supporter and a Longite candidate for governor, was opposed to the call, adding that if a constitution were to be drafted, the power of the governor had to be curbed: "Our constitution cannot be a short one containing only the basic fundamental law."[19]

Spaht also stated that the civil service provisions must remain in the constitution, providing another good example of how the constitution kept growing. Civil service had been adopted by the anti-Long forces of Governor Sam Houston Jones during his 1940–1944 term. After his 1948 victory for the governorship, Earl Long succeeded in pushing legislation that weakened the system. When Robert F. Kennon, the anti-Long candidate, became governor in 1952, he re-stored the civil service provisions, this time cementing them by placing the whole text of the provisions in the constitution. That attitude on civil service has prevailed, and the 1974 Constitution continues to contain lengthy, detailed reg-ulations of the civil service system.

Between 1921 and 1972, the legislature proposed 802 constitutional amendments. Voters ratified 536 of those proposals.[20] Then the people reacted: they refused to approve constitutional amendments. In 1970, when the constitution had grown to more than 250,000 words, voters rejected all 53 proposed amendments, 19 of which concerned only New Orleans. In 1972, 36 of 42 proposed amendments were defeated. Only a small part of the electorate was even voting on the proposed amendments. The pressure for a new constitution was increasing, and this time the popular new governor supported the move. Reapportionment had also produced significant changes in the legislature. With the support of Governor Edwin W. Edwards, along with numerous "good government" groups, the legislature in 1972 called for selection of delegates to a convention. This time the convention was to submit its proposal to popular ratification. During the course of the Constitutional Convention of 1973, dubbed CC/73 by its public relations staff, a newspaper poll revealed that 69 percent of the people favored a new constitution, with 9 percent opposed and 22 percent undecided. [21]

CONSTITUTION OF 1974: TECHNICAL, MODEST REFORM

CC/73 consisted of 105 elected delegates and 27 delegates appointed by the governor to represent various interests. All of the initial appointed delegates were from more liberal south Louisiana. Legislators were well represented, with 25 current and 9 former members chosen as delegates. Ten women and 12 blacks

[18] *Baton Rouge State Times*, Sept. 14, 1956, p. 1.

[19] Ibid., Sept. 15, 1956, p. 4a.

[20] Carleton, "Elitism Sustained," 563.

[21] *Baton Rouge Sunday Advocate*, May 13, 1973, p. 1.

were among the group. The governor chose not to exert direct con troll over the convention and intervened only at the end on a narrow list of matters. Convention committees drafted the preliminary proposals themselves rather than allocating that work to staff members, as had been envisioned by the legislature. A large staff, using members of the legislative council as well as a number of college and law school faculty, was assembled and did assist the committees.

Delegates were allowed to choose their committee assignments, resulting in substantial expertise, as well as substantial self-interest, in each of the substantive committees. Twelve of seventeen members of the Judiciary Committee were lawyers, including a Supreme Court justice and a district judge. Also on the committee were two sheriffs, a clerk of court, and a city court marshal. Four delegates were parish tax assessors; all served on the Committee on Revenue, Finance and Taxation. As one might expect, this structure led to a document that made few radical changes.

Little substantive change resulted, but the document was superior technically. It was simplified, shortened, and made more consistent. It was more of a triumph of the legal technicians than of the reformers. Substantial limits on the flexibility of the legislature remain, and more detail than would be desirable exists. In the end, the word count was a victory-down from 250,000 to 30,000 words. But as the Public Affairs Research Council indicated in its voter guide, that was not a great deal shorter than the 1921 Constitution, which contained 49,200 words before 536 amendments were added over the years.

CC/73 committees were not always linear in their path to a short (or shorter) constitution. The director of the Public Affairs Research Council described the case of the "iris lady," a little lady this spring who sold one of our convention committees on making the wild iris our state flower by constitutional mandate. Put that in the constitution and the com-mittee dutifully said yes. Later they had to reverse themselves when they learned it would cost millions to chip away all the marble magnolias that we have all over the state and replace them with iris. [22]

The people reflected the convention's inclination to give the legislature some additional latitude but not too much. A newspaper poll indicated that two-thirds of the population favored a requirement for a supermajority vote in the legislature for raising taxes; a majority favored dedications of funds in the constitution. [23]

Reluctance to change was also demonstrated by the election results. Given a choice between a more radical Proposition B that provided one board system to govern higher education or Proposition A, with three management boards and one policymaking board with limited authority, the voters adopted the latter by a larger vote than they adopted the constitution. Overall the new constitution was approved by a vote of 360,980 (58 percent) to 262,676 (42 percent).

---

[22] Edward J. Steimel, "Interest Representation in the Constitution," in Newman, *Focus on CC173*, 101.

[23] *Baton Rouge State Times*, May 16, 1973, p. 1–B.

Proposition A prevailed by a vote of 331,339 (62 percent) to 199,985 (38 percent). A sobering note came from the low turnout: 64 percent of the registered voters had not taken part in the referendum.

The success in shortening the constitution was achieved in part by continuing parts of the old constitution as statutes rather than simply repealing them. These constitution ancillaries would continue protecting some of the interest groups that had supported them. Another device was to continue some provision (for example, the number of judges in a judicial district) and provide for change only by supermajority votes.

In terms of substance, the bill of rights incorporated for the first time an equal protection clause and a public accommodations provision, prompting the National Association for the Advancement of Colored People to support the document, as well as stronger guarantees for payment for expropriated property to the full extent of the loss.

The legislature was given more independence, with the senate electing its leader instead of having the lieutenant governor preside over it. Substituting for the alternating short fiscal sessions were annual sessions. Many limitations were weakened, but flexibility is still limited by the requirement of supermajority votes on numerous matters. Executive reorganization into no more than twenty departments was required, but the constitution did little to reduce the number of statewide elected officials. The judiciary article changed little, though it did clear the way for the legislature to do so without the necessity of constitutional amendments.

Home rule was strengthened, with provisions allowing local governments, if they choose, to exercise any power not prohibited by state law or by the constitution. Although some improvement in revenue and finance was provided, as in eliminating several constitutional tax rates and constitutional dedications, it still continued stringent limitations on raising taxes. Income tax rates remain embedded in the constitution, as are provisions to limit property taxation of homesteads. The Public Affairs Research Council predicted that the document "reflects policies which may be considered politically expedient today but which will almost certainly place Louisiana in a financial bind in the future and cause harmful shifts in the tax burden." [24]

By 1989 Louisiana voters faced 36 proposed amendments to the 1974 Constitution; 21 were adopted. The constitutional provisions touching on revenue and finance, as predicted, caused the most difficulties and have been most amended. History is repeating itself as more constitutional dedications of funds and limitations on taxation are being adopted. Tinkering with the judiciary article has also occurred, primarily transferring criminal appellate jurisdiction to the courts of appeal from the supreme court.

---

[24] Public Affairs Research Council, *Voters Guide* (Baton Rouge: The Council, 1974), 28.

PART TWO

The Louisiana Constitution and Commentary

PREAMBLE

> We, the people of Louisiana, grateful to Almighty God for the civil, political, economic, and religious liberties we enjoy, and desiring to protect individual rights to life, liberty, and property; afford opportunity for the fullest development of the individual; assure equality of rights; promote the health, safety, education, and welfare of the people; maintain a representative and orderly government; ensure domestic tranquility; provide for the common defense; and secure the blessings of freedom and justice to ourselves and our posterity, do ordain and establish this constitution.

The preamble to Louisiana's constitution is a philosophical sermon that lacks the force of law, explained Alphonse Jackson, chairman of the Committee on Bill of Rights and Elections, which drafted it. Considering the limited effects of the preamble, it is surprising that the 1963 Constitutional Convention devoted substantial time to it. The debate on the preamble, however, became a preliminary skirmish to test the strength of the opposing views that would clash more intensely in the debate on the controversial sections of the declaration of rights.

The committee proposed a preamble similar to that of the Illinois Constitution of 1970-one that would expand Louisiana's existing preamble to include the aspirations of more progressive forces in the state. Included were references to equality of rights and promoting health and welfare. The convention defeated three attempts to delete some of the new statements, and the proposal of the committee was adopted. That vote set the pattern for convention action on the declaration of rights, which expanded individual rights.

Article I

Declaration of Rights

SECTION 1
Origin and Purpose of Government

All government, of right, originates with the people, is founded on their will alone, and is instituted to protect the rights of the individual and for the good of the whole. Its only legitimate ends are to secure justice for all, preserve peace, protect the rights, and promote the happiness and general welfare of the people. The rights enumerated in this Article are inalienable by the state and shall be preserved inviolate by the state.

Virtually a second preamble, this section continues the first section of the 1921 Constitution. One can expect the same dearth of litigation under the new section as under the prior provision. The committee did propose to add a last sentence stating that the rights in the declaration are "inalienable and shall be preserved inviolate." To indicate clearly that a person may waive rights, the convention changed the language to provide that the rights are "inalienable by the state and shall be preserved inviolate by the state."

SECTION 2
Due Process of Law

No person shall be deprived of life, liberty, or property, except by due process of law.

The due process guarantee continues Article I, section 2 of the 1921 Constitution. It is a flexible doctrine that gives the courts significant discretion to develop standards of reasonableness and fundamental fairness that government must follow in limiting the rights of individuals. It is not a static concept but one that evolves in tandem with the society's concept of fundamental rights. Like its federal counterpart, the Louisiana guarantee has a procedural as well as a substantive component.

Procedural Due Process. The Louisiana courts have long held that life, liberty, or property cannot be taken without a fair proceeding. The supreme court made a significant expansion of the procedural due process guarantee in *Wilson v. City of New Orleans*(1985), finding improper the immobilizing of parked automobiles by a device known as the Denver boot because of outstanding traffic citations. The liberty interest in the use of one's automobile was protected against deprivation by a scheme that was inadequate. It denied due process because it did "not provide for a neutral decision maker to decide whether a vehicle owner should be classed as a scofflaw and targeted for booting, notice to an owner that such action is about to be taken against him, or an opportunity to respond at least informally to a summary of adverse evidence."

Louisiana is a community property state in which the earnings of both husband and wife normally become community assets (assets owned by them in indivision) and can be seized by the creditors of either spouse. The supreme court in *Magee v. Amiss*(1987) suggested, however, that due process required at least notice to the spouse who did not contract the debt before seizure of community assets. Even in the area of economic rights, where court standards are often less stringent than in other areas, the court in *Haughton Elevator Division v. Division of Administration*(1979) held that a bidder on a public contract could not be disqualified without being given an opportunity to respond to allegations of irresponsibility.

Substantive Due Process. In substantive matters, the Louisiana Supreme Court has used the due process clause to invalidate unreasonably vague criminal statutes. Included were a provision making it a crime to fail "to take all usual and all reasonable measures" to ensure operation of a sewage system (*State v. Dousay*, 1979) and an ordinance forbidding "indecent, vile, and profane language" (*City of Baton Rouge* v. *Ewing*, 1975). In *State v. Spooner*(1988), the supreme court also disallowed a presumption in a statute providing for forfeiture of currency used in the commission of the crime. The presumption that money "in close proximity" to illegal contraband was used in the crime was held to be improper. A taking of the money based on that presumption was a denial of due process.

Statutes of limitations that extinguish rights to sue after the passage of time are upheld if a reasonable time is allowed for exercise of the right. Protection of architects and contractors against claims arising more than ten years from completion of their work was approved in *Burmaster v. Gravity Drainage District No. 2*(1978). *Crier v. Whitecloud*(1986) approved a statute immunizing physicians from claims arising more than three years from their treatment of a patient. When periods of limitation are shortened, application of the new period to existing claims is permissible only if the person has a reasonable time after the change to assert the right (*Reichenphader v. Allstate Insurance Co.*, 1982). Six months is usually considered a reasonable time.

Louisiana has been a leading state in finding state constitutional rights to be broader than their federal analogs, especially under substantive due process. It was not unusual for the supreme court to decide in 1915 that regulating hours of workers was an unreasonable restriction of freedom of contract (*State v. Legendre* 1915), but in holding a junkyard fence ordinance unconstitutional in 1939, the court did not follow the federal trend toward less court scrutiny of economic legislation. The ordinance was found to be unduly restrictive because it required the fence to be made of wood (*City of New Orleans v. Southern Auto Wreckers*(1939)). It was indeed a departure from orthodox cases to decide in *Schwegmann Bros.* v. *Louisiana Board of Alcoholic Beverage Control*(1949) that a statute requiring a minimum markup on liquor sales was an unreasonable regulation of economic freedoms. More recently the court has used substantive due process to overturn some spot zoning ordinances (*Four States Realty v. City of Baton Rouge*, 1974) and to invalidate an ordinance prohibiting frog gigging (a method of catching frogs with a mechanical device) on a local lake for eleven months of the year (*City of Shreveport v. Curry*, 1978). In these cases, the court examined governmental interests in some depth instead of simply relying on presumptions of rationality.

State Action. The state due process protects, as it does in the federal Constitution, against governmental action. The Louisiana concept of state action is at least as expansive as under the federal guarantee, extending in *Bodker v. Louisiana State High School Athletic Association* (1985) to the actions of the high school athletic association, a voluntary, nonprofit organization composed of private and public high school members. The organization regulated high school athletic competition, was funded in part by public money earned by state schools at athletic events, and adopted rules that affected athletes at public schools.

SECTION 3
Right to Individual Dignity

No person shall be denied the equal protection of the laws. No law shall discriminate against a person because of race or religious ideas, beliefs, or affiliations. No law shall arbitrarilly, capriciously, or unreasonably discriminate against a person because of birth, age, sex, culture, physical condition, or political ideas or affiliations. Slavery and involuntary servitude are prohibited, except in the latter case punishment for crime.

The 1921 Constitution contained no equal protection clause. This section repeats and then expands the equal protection guarantee of the Fourteenth Amendment to the U.S. Constitution. The Louisiana protection against discrimination goes beyond the federal decisions construing the federal provisions. Like the federal guarantee, citizens are protected against discrimination by governmental action. Private action, however, is reached by the slavery and involuntary servitude clause of the last sentence and by the guaranteed access to public accommodations provided in Article I, section 12.

The 1973 convention rejected a simpler committee proposal that paraphrased the Fourteenth Amendment equal protection clause. Rather than leave the development of the law to the courts, the delegates chose to list a number of types of discrimination that are prohibited: race, religion, age, sex, culture, physical condition, and political views. That listing, adopted in response to the demands of various minority groups, is not exclusive. The first sentence of the section provides the general rule and gives the courts the basis to expand the equal protection guarantee to other types of classifications.

The second sentence (which uses absolute language) in comparison with the third sentence (which employs the arbitrary, capricious, or unreasonable formula) permits no discrimination whatsoever with respect to race or religion. The level of scrutiny for the classifications listed in the third sentence is not directly apparent. Justice James L. Dennis, a delegate to the 1973 convention, suggested in *Sibley v. Board of Supervisors of Louisiana State University* (1985) that more than a minimal rational basis be required to support such a classification and that the burden of proving the acceptability of the classification was on the state. He stated:(1) When the law classifies individuals by race or religious beliefs, it shall be repudiated completely; (2) When the statute classifies persons on the basis of birth, age, sex, culture, physical condition, or political ideas or affiliations, its enforcement shall be refused unless the state or other advocate of the classification shows that the classification has a reasonable basis; (3) When the law classifies individuals on any other basis, it shall be rejected whenever a member of a disadvantaged class shows that it does not suitably further any appropriate state interest.Cases since *Sibley*, however, are not precise on the point, and it appears that the inquiry by the courts into the reasonableness of classifications is essentially not susceptible of precise quantification.

Birth. The reference to birth encompasses prohibition of discrimination against illegitimate children. The supreme court has invalidated several inheritance laws that favored legitimate children, including laws prohibiting a parent from willing separate property to adulterous illegitimate children (*Succession of Robbins*, 1977), prohibiting illegitimate children from inheriting from their mother if legitimate children survived her (*Succession of Thompson*, 1979), laws that favored the legitimate heirs of the father and excluded the illegitimates (*Succession of Brown*, 1980), and laws limiting illegitimates to one-quarter the parents' estate when legitimate children existed (*Jordan v. Cosey*, 1983).

Court decisions recognizing these rights have been applied retroactively to January 1, 1975, the effective date of the 1974 Constitution.

Recent amendments to the Louisiana Civil Code have also virtually done away with the differences in the inheritance rights of legitimate and illegitimate children. Article 888 now provides, "Descendants succeed to the property of their ascendants."

Age. Debates during the 1973 Constitutional Convention support the view that some age classifications are permissible and that the prohibition against age discrimination is to be tempered with the concept that the young and the old can be given preferential treatment,[1] The constitution itself draws several lines based on age. One has a right to vote at 18 years of age (Art. I, sec. 10) and is eligible for legislative office at 18 (Art. III, sec. 4) and statewide elected office at 25 (Art. IV, sec. 2). Waiver of juvenile court procedures is allowed for those 15 or older (Art. V, sec. 19). Mandatory retirement of judges is at age 70 (Art. V, sec. 23).

A court of appeal has held that this section does not limit private employers from imposing mandatory retirement at 65 (*Baynard v. Guardian Life Insurance Co.*, 1981). Another court found a violation of the provision when a municipal police department fired a 55-year-old employee in part because of her age (*Mixon v. City of New Orleans Police Department*, 1983).

Sex. The mention of sex was designed to establish equal rights for women, a subject of intense interest in the Committee on Bill of Rights and Elections. The Louisiana Supreme Court, however, did not use this section as an important basis to establish equality of rights for men and women. Substantial declines in sex-based or gender-based (new term) discrimination have occurred in Louisiana, but the impetus for change has been the federal courts and the state legislature.

In *State v. Corky* (1984), the supreme court found no constitutional violation in a statute forbidding bars from hiring "B-girls" but allowing the hiring of men to solicit drinks from patrons. In *Williams v. Williams* (1976), it found no defect in alimony statutes that provided payments to needy wives but not to needy husbands. Statutes that made it a crime for a husband to fail to support his wife but did not make the wife similarly responsible were upheld (*State v. Barton*, 1975),[2] and the court approved the law that confined the offense of prostitution to females engaging in indiscriminate sex with males for compensation (*State v. Devall*, 1974). Most of these statutes, however, have been changed by the legislature to make them gender neutral.

The court refused to hold unconstitutional the provisions that made the husband the sole manager of community property (*Corpus Christi Parish Credit*

[1] VI *Records of the Louisiana Constitutional Convention of 1973* (Baton Rouge, State of Louisiana, 1977), Aug. 30, 1973.

[2] State v. Barton, 315 So. 2d 289 (La. 1975); overruled in State v. Fuller, 377 So. 2d 335 (La. 1979) in light of the decision in Orr v. Orr, 440 U.S. 268 (1979).

Union v. Martin 1978). The U. S. Supreme Court, however, held the community property management system unconstitutional in *Kirchberg v. Feenstra* (1981). A 1979 revision of the Louisiana Civil Code provisions governing community property (Art. 2325–2437) was also adopted, providing for equal management of community assets.

Culture. The reference to culture was designed to prohibit discrimination of persons who choose to "preserve, foster, and promote their respective historic, linguistic and cultural origins" (Art. XII, sec. 4). The section was included in response to Francophone groups interested in protecting the Louisiana French heritage and the use of the French language. Little litigation has resulted from this provision, and the convention record is clear that keeping English as the official language is permissible.

Physical Condition. Prohibition of discrimination because of physical condition was a response to a number of handicapped individuals who lobbied the convention. Although the provision has not been applied often, a strong minority of the supreme court has suggested it prohibits the limiting of tort recoveries of victims of medical malpractice when other tort victims are not so limited (*Sibley v. Board of Supervisors of Louisiana State University*, 1985).

Political ideas or affiliations refers to basic rights to freedom of beliefs and associations with respect to government.

Other Classifications. The first sentence of the section prohibits unreasonable classifications on any grounds, even if not listed in the third sentence. The supreme court invalidated legislation in *Clark v. Manuel* (1985) because it classified on the basis of mental condition. Involved were laws that conditioned location of group homes for the mentally handicapped on approval of the local governing authority while not subjecting other uses of property to such approval.

The supreme court has sustained civil procedure laws that treat the state differently than private persons, allowing jury trials of suits against private defendants but not against governmental defendants (*Rudolph v. Massachusetts Bay Insurance Co.*, 1985).

Although the prohibition against involuntary servitude is seldom invoked, it was applied in *Callaghan v. Department of Fire* (1980) to invalidate a civil service commission's penalty that disciplined an employee by making him work 24 hours without pay.

SECTION 4
Right to Property

Every person has the right to acquire, own, control, use, enjoy, protect, and dispose of private property. This right is subject to reasonable statutory restrictions and the reasonable exercise of the police power. Property shall not be taken or damaged by the state or its political subdivisions except for public purposes and with just compensation paid to the owner or into court for his benefit. Property shall not be taken or damaged by any private entity authorized by law to expropriate, except for a public and necessary purpose and with just compensation paid to the owner; in such proceedings, whether the purpose is public and necessary shall be a judicial question. In every expropriation, a party has the right to trial by jury to determine compensation, and the owner shall be compensated to the full extent of his loss. No business enterprise or any of its assets shall be taken for the purpose of operating that enterprise or halting competition with a government enterprise. However, a municipality may expropriate a utility within its jurisdiction.

Personal effects shall never be taken. But the following property may be forfeited and disposed of in a civil proceeding, as provided by law: contraband drugs; property derived in whole or in part from contraband drugs; property used in the distribution, transfer, sale, felony possession, manufacture, or transportation of contraband drugs; property furnished or intended to be furnished for contraband drugs; property used or intended to be used to facilitate any of the above conduct; or other property because the above described property has been rendered unavailable.

This Section shall not apply to appropriation of property necessary for levee and levee drainage purposes. [As amended by Acts 1989, No. 840, effective November 6, 1989]

Protection of property rights continues to be specified in detail in addition to the due process clause. The first sentence of this section is virtually another due process clause, giving courts flexibility in determining the scope of property rights with regard to matters not covered in detail in the remaining parts of the section. Although this section refers to a right to dispose of property, that right is limited by Article XII, section 5, which requires continuation of some type of forced heirship laws.

The author of the provision, Delegate Louis Jenkins, recognized in debate that the permitted statutory regulations can be given a broad ambit. He described the police power as "the authority of the state to do virtually anything in furtherance of the common welfare in the nature of regulation of property, so long as property rights are not denied entirely."[3] The supreme court determined it was reasonable for an ordinance to limit use of facilities for charitable bingo to two days each week (*Theriot v. Terrebonne Parish Police Jury*, 1983). It also found no constitutional violation in a statute that allowed summary destruction of slot machines (*Brown v. State*, 1980).

The remainder of the section deals with expropriation and forfeitures, in contrast to the first paragraph's concern with regulation. More limits were placed on the power to. expropriate than under the prior constitution, though the fourth paragraph does continue "appropriation" for levees. Under this doctrine,

---

[3] VI Records, Sept. 13, 1973.

preserved in Louisiana Civil Code Article 665, riparian land historically subject to the levee servitude can be taken without compensation. Recent statutes have gone beyond the constitutional requirements, however, and provide for actual cash value compensation in such appropriations. (Louisiana Revised Statutes 38:301).

In all expropriation proceedings, both parties have a right to trial by jury to determine the compensation due. The committee had proposed giving only the landowner that right; the convention extended it to any party. With this addition, a private landowner can be put at a disadvantage if the state demands a jury trial in an expropriation for a popular public project. Jury awards of compensation, like all other jury determinations, continue to be subject to appellate review of facts (Art. V, sec. 5, 10) and thus to reduction or increase by appellate courts. Indeed this section is the only guarantee of jury trial in civil cases. Reflecting the state's civil law background, the constitution has no parallel to the federal Seventh Amendment, which guarantees jury trial in most civil cases.

An important aim of the supporters of section 4 was to increase the level of compensation paid to landowners for property taken—hence the change from the 1921 Constitution's language ("just and adequate compensation") to the new phrase ("compensated to the full extent of his loss"). The new formula comes from the 1972 Montana Constitution and according to committee comments was "intended to permit the owner whose property has been taken to remain in equivalent financial circumstances after the taking."

The author explained that compensation would extend to costs of litigation and attorney fees, moving costs, and the cost of re-establishing a business whose premises had been taken.[4] The courts have indeed increased the types of losses for which compensation is provided. The supreme court in *State v. Constant* (1979) required compensation for business losses resulting from the taking of land where a boat landing business was conducted even though the amount of those losses was greater than the market value of the expropriated land. A landowner is also entitled to the loss of future rentals if the loss can be proved (*State Department of Transportation and Development v. Davis*, 1981).

Changing the justification for exercise of the eminent domain power from the 1921 word formula (public purposes, purpose of public utility) to a higher standard (public and necessary purpose) provoked intense controversy resolved only in a final compromise that applies the higher standard exclusively to takings by private entities and continues the old standard to takings by public agencies. Also only private entities are subject to the provision that "in such proceedings, whether the purpose is public and necessary shall be a judicial question." The aim of this expression was to leave the question to the courts to determine,

[4] Lee Hargrave, "The Declaration of Rights of the Louisiana Constitution of 1974," *Louisiana Law Review* 35 (1974): 16.

without the aid of a presumption of constitutionality. That presumption remains, however, with governmental takings.

Statutes allowing "quick taking" by public entities are allowed. Such proceedings allow preliminary ex parte orders to transfer title to the property if the taker deposits with the court funds equal to appraisals of the property. Subsequent litigation over the amount due can then be continued but without delaying the public project for which the land is to be used. Quick takings by private entities, however, are not allowed. Compensation resulting from inverse condemnation is also addressed in this section; the text provides that property need not be taken to invoke the section. It applies only if the property is only damaged.

The prohibition against taking "a business enterprise or any of its assets . . . for the purpose of operating that enterprise or halting competition with a government enterprise" is an innovation seen by its backers as important in maintaining the institution of private property. An exception allows a municipality to expropriate a utility within its jurisdiction and to operate it.

A final limitation added by the 1973 convention was that personal effects, other than contraband, shall never be taken, no matter how public or necessary the purpose. The term *personal effects* was used with the knowledge that it was not precise; it is a flexible concept open to court construction on a case-by-case basis. Committee comments did not provide a definition but gave examples: "Personal effects are intended to include money, stocks, bonds, objects of art, books, papers, essential tools of trade, and clothing."

The last sentence of paragraph 2 originally stated, "Personal effects, other than contraband, shall never be taken." The supreme court extended the concept of contraband beyond specific items whose possession is made illegal by statute to include the broad concept of derivative contraband—things normally susceptible of private ownership that are used in criminal activities (*State v. Manuel*, 1983), such as automobiles, weapons, and currency. The court, however, did require that the state prove the connection with criminal activity beyond a reasonable doubt, imposing a higher standard of proof than under similar federal requirements (*State v. Spooner*, 1988).

In response to these court developments, voters approved a constitutional amendment in 1989 that added paragraph 3 to allow forfeiture of drug-related contraband in a civil proceeding, presumably with a lesser burden of proof. The listing in the amended legislation, however, allows forfeitures only as to drug-related contraband. It would appear to disallow forfeiture of any other types of contraband.

Read literally, the prohibition against taking personal effects would prevent taking such effects as evidence in criminal cases. Section 5, however, recognizes the power to seize "things" pursuant to a reasonable search and seizure. Sections 3 and 5 can be reconciled by allowing the temporary detention of things to be used as evidence in criminal proceedings, provided they are returned to the owner after the proceedings are completed.

SECTION 5
Right to Privacy

> Every person shall be secure in his person, property, communications, houses, papers, and effects against unreasonable searches, seizures, or invasions of privacy. No warrant shall issue without probable cause supported by oath or affirmation, and particularly describing the place to be searched, the persons or things to be seized, and the lawful purpose or reason for the search. Any person adversely affected by a search or seizure conducted in violation of this Section shall have standing to raise its illegality in the appropriate court.

Article I, section 7 of the 1921 Constitution guaranteed that persons would be secure in their persons, houses, papers and effects against unreasonable searches and seizures. This section extends the older text to add protection of property and communications and to specify that these things are also protected against unreasonable invasions of privacy. The ancestry of this last phrase can be traced to the reference of an expanded federal right to privacy in *Griswold v. Connecticut* (1965) and to fears of unrestrained gathering and dissemination of information on individuals through use of computer data banks.

The protection of privacy must be balanced with the right to examine public documents established in Article 12, section 3. Appellate courts allowed the public to examine records of disciplinary hearings before the Board of Professional Engineers and Land Surveyors (*Amoco Production Co. v. Landry*, 1982) and ordered disclosure of the names and addresses of city employees to a union organizer (*Webb v. City of Shreveport*, 1979). A closely divided supreme court did not keep private information about royalties paid to private persons out of oil and gas produced from public lands. The information had been provided during discovery procedures as part of a civil lawsuit, and the court in *Plaquemines Parish Commission Council v. Delta Development Co.* (1985) allowed the information to be released to newspaper reporters.

Free press guarantees are also to be considered in determining the scope of protection of privacy. The supreme court in *Roshto v. Hebert* (1983) did not grant damages for invasion of privacy after a newspaper published, 25 years after the event, information about plaintiff's conviction of cattle theft.

In *Hondroulis v. Schumacher* (1989), the supreme court extended the notion of privacy to some aspects of personal autonomy, including the right to choose to obtain or reject medical treatment. Inherent in this concept is the right to be informed of the risks associated with the treatment. Consequently a statute that presumed a written consent to surgery was valid was not consistent with the constitution when the patient was not adequately informed.

Although the prior constitution provided in Article VII, section 7 that "no such search or seizure shall be made except upon warrant," the courts allowed warrantless searches and seizures. The new provision omits the old language and instead paraphrases the federal guarantee in an implied recognition of the permissibility of warrantless searches and seizures so long as they are reasonable.

An important expansion beyond the federal protections came in *State v. Church* (1989), a 4-3 decision of the supreme court that held unconstitutional roadblock checkpoints for drunk drivers in which all motorists driving by a particular point were stopped. The court stated, "Although this Shreveport DWI [driving while intoxicated] roadblock may meet federal constitutional standards, as viewed by the present United States Supreme court, the seizure occurred without reasonable suspicion or probable cause to believe that defendant Church had violated some law and was therefore unconstitutional under Article I, Section 5, of the Louisiana Constitution of 1974. Evidence of Church's intoxication was correctly suppressed by the trial court."

An early draft that prevented any wiretapping and bugging was replaced with a provision that does protect communications but only against unreasonable interception. The supreme court in *State v. Reeves* (1983) concluded that it was not unreasonable to allow a participant to record secretly a conversation to which he was a party. A federal court applying state law also determined that the provision does not protect against interception by private persons of radio telephone conversations (*Edwards v. State Farm Insurance Co.*, 1987).

Convention debate indicated a desire by some delegates to prevent the use of evidence improperly obtained by private persons and not to apply the exclusionary rule only to state action. The committee documents are not so clear on the point. The supreme court in *State v. Nelson* (1978) held inadmissible statements made to private guards in stores when their conduct was unreasonable and a statute allowed them to use only reasonable force to detain shoplifters. The guards in a jewelry store grabbed a suspected thief's throat to prevent him from swallowing a ring they thought was in his mouth. The supreme court has yet to rule on searches by private individuals in other contexts. A court of appeal, however, in *State v. Clark* (1984), held that evidence (weapons and an illegally killed deer) obtained by a landowner from hunters on his land was not covered by the prohibition.

An innovation is the expansion of the class of persons given standing to contest improper searches and seizures and to have evidence so secured excluded from use at trial. The last sentence of the section was designed to abolish the federally developed standing requirement by which a defendant asserting a Fourth Amendment violation was required to show he or she was the "victim of a search or seizure, one against whom the search was directed, as distinguished from one who claims prejudice only through the use of evidence gathered as a consequence of a search or seizure directed at someone else."[5] Any person

[5] Jones v. United States, 362 U.S. 257, 261 (1960).

adversely affected by the search can raise it under this section, including anyone whose guilt it would tend to prove. The supreme court has not applied this provision with the breadth the drafters intended. While the court recognizes that it requires exclusion of evidence at trial against a defendant if the privacy rights of another person were violated in obtaining the evidence, that evidence can be used for other purposes. In *State v. Culotta* (1976), the court allowed the evidence to be used to establish probable cause necessary to obtain a search warrant directed at the defendant.

Although the exclusionary rule is not explicitly stated, it is implicit. In fact, the last sentence of the section, which gives standing to persons denied it in federal cases, is an implicit recognition of the broadening of the right to suppress evidence obtained in violation of the constitutional guarantee. The Louisiana courts have not departed, however, from the view of the federal cases that illegally seized evidence may nonetheless be used against a person in a civil proceeding. The evidence was allowed by the supreme court to be used in a disciplinary proceeding before the Louisiana State Racing Commission (*Pullin v. Louisiana State Racing Commission*, 1986) and in a proceeding to deny an employee unemployment compensation because of misconduct (*Lamartiniere v. Department of Employment Security*, 1979).

Another innovation was the requirement that the warrant specify "the lawful purpose or reason for the search." The policy objective was to require what the case law had not clearly required; that a person whose privacy is invaded by the state must be told of the state's proper basis for making that invasion. In this way, the subject of the invasion is less likely to resist it. It also gives the person information that may be helpful in later legal proceedings contesting the search.

SECTION 6
Freedom from Intrusion

No person shall be quartered in any house without the consent of the owner or lawful occupant.

The former prohibition was against quartering any "soldier, sailor or marine" in any house; this section covers quartering any person. The prohibition applies at any time—not just in time of peace. Consent of the lawful occupant, not just that of the owner, is required.

SECTION 7
Freedom of Expression

No law shall curtail or restrain the freedom of speech or of the press. Every person may speak, write, and publish his sentiments on any subject, but is responsible for abuse of that freedom.

Constitutional convention debates on this section concerned form more than substance. The delegates rejected a more precise and particularized provision and adopted instead a slight recast of the 1921 constitutional provision, a very general one that was conceived as reflecting the existing state of the law under the First Amendment to the U. S. Constitution. In terms of substance, the delegates rejected an attempt to narrow the freedom of expression by voting down a proposal for a right of reply to a person whose character was "assailed" by the press.

The Louisiana Supreme Court has tended to be protective of free speech, often citing both the federal and state constitutional guarantees to support its decisions. In *Economy Carpets Manufacturers and Distributors v. Better Business Bureau* (1976), the court upheld the free speech rights of a litigant who sued the Better Business Bureau for treble damages in a case asking for a jury trial and about the same time placed portable advertising signs critical of the bureau, the attorney general, and the judge near the company's suburban office and in the downtown area across the street from the bureau's office. A unanimous supreme court found no danger to the administration of justice and the conduct of a fair trial resulting from the signs.

Reflecting the state's interest in good food, the court extended the fair comment principles to include a caustic restaurant review in *Mashburn v. Collin* (1977). A New Orleans restaurant critic had referred to one dish as "trout á la green plague" and to one sauce as "yellow death on duck."

The supreme court in *Roshto v. Hebert* (1983) held that free speech policies prevented the award of damages for invasion of privacy because a newspaper published, some 25 years after the event, information about plaintiffs' conviction of cattle theft. The paper ran a regular feature, "Page from Our Past," which reproduced the front page of old issues. The issue publicizing the plaintiffs' trial in 1973 and the affirmation of their conviction in 1977 were both run, the second occurring after protests against the first publication.

In an odd use of the press guarantee, a court of appeal reasoned that since a state college had no power under that guarantee to censor the student newspaper, it could not be held liable for defamation published by that paper (*Milliner v. Turner*, 1983).

SECTION 8
Freedom of Religion

No law shall be enacted respecting an establishment of religion or prohibiting the free exercise thereof.

The convention adopted this paraphrase of the First Amendment to the U. S. Constitution by a 104-0 vote, deleting the 1921 Constitution's provisions, which were more stringent and more precise in prohibiting use of state money for parochial schools. Three provisions of the former document had been relied upon in *Seegers v. Parker* (1970) to prohibit aid to teachers of secular subjects in church-operated schools. To reverse that decision and adopt instead the more flexible federal standard, which allows some aid to parochial schools, two of the provisions were deleted entirely,[6] and the language of this section was adopted in place of the third.

Free exercise of religion did not extend to protecting an elaborate outdoor Christmas display in a suburban residential area, a display that attracted thousands of spectators in vehicles, much to the dislike and inconvenience of neighbors (*Rodrigue v. Copeland*, 1985). The court upheld injunctions that the display be limited in size, time, and sound volume.

In *State v. Morgan* (1984), the probation of a criminal defendant was conditioned on his regularly attending an organized church of his choice. The court of appeal determined that such a condition violated both the state and federal prohibition of laws respecting an establishment of religion.

SECTION 9
Right of Assembly and Petition

No law shall impair the right of any person to assemble peaceably or to petition government for a redress of grievances.

Paraphrasing the First Amendment to the U. S. Constitution and Article I, section 5 of the previous state constitution, this section continues existing principles and the existing construction of the law that protect peaceful assemblies and petitions for redress but not those that are violent.

SECTION 10
Right to Vote

Every citizen of the state, upon reaching eighteen years of age, shall have the right to register and vote, except that this right may be suspended while a person is interdicted and judicially declared mentally incompetent or is under an order of imprisonment for conviction of a felony.

This section replaced the 1921 Constitution's broad limitations on suffrage with a strong statement of a right to vote, a right not conditioned on residency

[6] Article IV, section 8: "No money . . . in aid of any church . . . or in aid of any priest, preacher, minister or teacher thereof." Article XII, section 13: "No appropriation of public funds shall be made to any private or sectarian school."

requirements, character and literacy tests, or a 21-year-old threshold for voting. The only limitations on the right that are allowed are stated in the section.

Establishing a right to register, as well as to vote, recognizes the state's power to require registration as a prerequisite to voting. In fact, Article XI, section 1 requires the legislature to adopt an election code that provides "for permanent registration of voters." Implicit in such a procedure is the requirement of some time to prepare voting lists, depending on the available technology. The right adheres to state citizens, those persons being defined in the Fourteenth Amendment to the U. S. Constitution as citizens of the United States who reside in Louisiana. Residence is thus a related issue but not in terms of durational residency requirement.

Suspension of the right in case of mental incompetency requires both interdiction as provided in the Louisiana Civil Code and a judicial declaration of mental incompetence. Interdiction, which can be for reasons other than mental incompetence, is not enough, nor is commitment in an institution under a court order.

SECTION 11
Right to Keep and Bear Arms

The right of each citizen to keep and bear arms shall not be abridged, but this provision shall not prevent the passage of laws to prohibit the carrying of weapons concealed on the person.

Omitted in section 11 is a reference to the militia, unlike the related 1921 constitutional provision and the similar federal provision. The reference instead to the "right of each citizen" indicates that the right exists without regard to a person's participation in a militia.

A floor amendment would have added: "No law shall require the licensing or registration or impose special taxation on the ownership" of firearms. The amendment was rejected, suggesting that registration should be allowed.

Prior constitutions contained a proviso that allowed punishment of "those who carry weapons concealed." This section was amended to limit that power to "weapons concealed on the person." The author of the amendment conceived of his proposal as prohibiting statutes forbidding the carrying of concealed weapons "in an automobile, or in a boat, or in an airplane," or anywhere else but on the person.[7]

The convention debates contain a statement by a strong supporter of the right to keep and bear arms that carrying of weapons is not a right of citizenship as conceived of in section 29, which automatically restores to persons convicted of

[7] VI Records, Sept. 12, 1973 at 6.

crime full rights after their sentence is completed.[8] Louisiana has adopted legislation making it a crime for certain convicted felons to possess firearms, a statute upheld in *State v. Amos* (1977).

SECTION 12
Freedom from Discrimination

In access to public areas, accommodations, and facilities, every person shall be free from discrimination based on race, religion, or national ancestry and from arbitrary, capricious, or unreasonable discrimination based on age, sex, or physical condition.

This section, new in the 1974 Constitution, was inspired by public accommodations sections of the federal Civil Rights Act of 1964. It goes beyond regulating state action to prohibiting private discrimination. In some respects it goes beyond the federal legislation, which enumerates covered establishments. This provision uses more general references to "public areas, accommodations, and facilities," makes no exceptions based on the size of the establishment, and requires no showing of affecting interstate commerce. The section implicitly excludes from its coverage institutions that are true private clubs since they would not be "public" areas, accommodations, or facilities.

Borrowing the formula of section 3, this section establishes an absolute prohibition of discrimination based on race, religion, or national ancestry. Discrimination on other bases is permitted so long as it is not "arbitrary, capricious, or unreasonable."

SECTION 13
Rights of the Accused

When any person has been arrested or detained in connection with the investigation or commission of any offense, he shall be advised fully of the reason for his arrest or detention, his right to remain silent, his right against self incrimination, his right to the assistance of counsel and, if indigent, his right to court appointed counsel. In a criminal prosecution, an accused shall be informed of the nature and cause of the accusation against him. At each stage of the proceedings, every person is entitled to assistance of counsel of his choice, or appointed by the court if he is indigent and charged with an offense punishable by imprisonment. The legislature shall provide for a uniform system for securing and compensating qualified counsel for indigents.

---

[8] Ibid.

Cautions at Arrest. A deliberate choice was made during the 1973 convention to add to the constitution the requirement of warnings to persons arrested or detained similar to those required by *Miranda v. Arizona* (1966). The cautions include not only the standard right to remain silent, the right against self-incrimination, and the right to counsel but also the right to be informed fully of the reason for the arrest or detention. This last reference constitutionalizes and expands a provision of the Code of Criminal Procedure, which had required an officer to advise one of the cause for an arrest.

This section does not state the means of enforcing the requirements, just as the entire declaration of rights catalogs numerous guarantees without providing specific means of enforcement. However, the convention's virtual incorporation of *Miranda* as construed in 1973 assumes continuation of the exclusionary rule then in effect for enforcement of its provisions. The supreme court in *In re Dino* (1978) applied the requirements to juveniles accused of conduct that would be a crime for an adult and conditioned effective waivers of these rights on consultation with an adult interested in that juvenile's welfare. A similar concern for the mentally retarded was shown in *State v. Welch* (1976), in which the court noted that "refusal by the police to honor the request of the parent of a mentally retarded semi-literate defendant to confer with a lawyer . . . was in violation of Article 1, Section 13 and Miranda even though the defendant was a major." The court also determined that the waiver of counsel by a person in custody was not effective when, although unknown to that person, his attorney was available to counsel with him and was seeking to advise him, but the police did not inform the defendant of that fact. In that case, *State v. Matthews* (1982), the attorney had requested that the police refrain from questioning his client.

Specific Accusations. The right of an accused to be informed of the nature and cause of the accusation is a continuation of the language of the prior constitution. The committee proposal attempted to require that the accused be precisely informed in an attempt to raise the requirements of specificity, but the convention rejected the proposed change, continuing the existing interpretation of the language, which allowed brief, short form indictments and bills of information.

Right to Counsel. The right to counsel includes effective assistance. The supreme court in *State v. Myles* (1980) extended the principle to the penalty phase of a capital murder case. There the conviction was upheld, but the death sentence was reversed because the attorney did not make an adequate presentation to the jury during the penalty phase of the trial.

The final sentence, mandating the legislature to provide for compensating counsel for indigents, was added by floor amendment. The committee proposal concentrated on establishing judicially enforceable rights and did not propose unenforceable mandates to the legislature. The convention, however, in an effort to prod state efforts in this regard, adopted the mandate by an overwhelming 99-11 vote. No enforcement device exists to require the legislature to comply with the mandate. The supreme court so held in *State v. Campbell* (1975) and *State v. Bryant* (1975).

SECTION 14
Right to Preliminary Examination

The right to a preliminary examination shall not be denied in felony cases except when the accused is indicted by a grand jury.

An innovation, this section was proposed by a floor amendment with the expressed goal of changing the statutory provision that made a preliminary hearing discretionary with the judge once a bill of information (accusation of a crime) had been filed by a district attorney. Citizens now have an absolute right to the preliminary examination in all felony prosecutions except when an indictment has been returned by a grand jury. The district attorney can no longer cut off the right by simply filing a bill of information.

The contemplated purpose and scope of the preliminary examination is the traditional one of judicial intervention to determine whether probable cause exists to hold an individual rather than leaving that decision to law enforcement agencies. Also envisioned was the requirement that the state produce witnesses and the right of a defendant to call witnesses. The supreme court, however, in *State v. Sterling* (1979) determined that the state could choose to present no witnesses, thus failing to show probable cause and allowing the accused to be released from jail without bail. In effect, the prospective defendant has no right to use the preliminary hearing as a means to discover the state's evidence.

SECTION 15
Initiation of Prosecution

Prosecution of a felony shall be initiated by indictment or information, but no person shall be held to answer for a capital crime or a crime punishable by life imprisonment except on indictment by a grand jury. No person shall be twice placed in jeopardy for the same offense, except on his application for a new trial, when a mistrial is declared, or when a motion in arrest of judgment is sustained.

Most criminal prosecutions in Louisiana continue to be instituted by bills of information filed by a district attorney. An attempt to expand the required use of grand jury indictments to all felonies necessarily punishable at hard labor failed. Only offenses punishable by death or life imprisonment require screening by a grand jury.

The committee proposal also recommended granting an accused person a right to counsel in grand jury proceedings, a right to compulsory process to present witnesses to the grand jury, and a right to the transcribed testimony of witnesses before the grand jury. All of these objectives were rejected by the convention.

SECTION 16
Right to a Fair Trial

Every person charged with a crime is presumed innocent until proven guilty and is entitled to a speedy, public, and impartial trial in the parish where the offense or an element of the offense occurred, unless venue is changed in accordance with law. No person shall be compelled to give evidence against himself. An accused is entitled to confront and cross-examine the witnesses against him, to compel the attendance of witnesses, to present a defense, and to testify in his own behalf.

Presumption of Innocence. Added by the 1973 convention was the explicit requirement that a defendant be "presumed innocent until proven guilty." The statement incorporates both the presumption of innocence and the requirement that the state has the burden of proving a defendant's guilt, constitutionalizing two principles that have long been basic assumptions of criminal procedure and due process. The presumption guarantees "that the accused may insist that he be brought into court with the appearance, dignity, and self-respect of a free and innocent man and not garbed in prison clothes" (*State v. Brown*, 1978).

Speedy Trial. The section guarantees the right to a speedy, public, and impartial trial. The supreme court found a denial of the right to a speedy trial in *State ex rel. Miller v. Craft* (1976), a case in which a person of limited mental capacity was incarcerated for 22 months without assistance of counsel and without being charged with an offense. The delay resulted primarily because of the state's failure to conduct a mental examination it had requested. Relief was dismissal of the charge pending against the accused.

Venue. The section continues the basic policy that an accused person is to be tried in the parish in which the offense occurred. The manner of expressing the guarantee is changed, however. It is a right of an accused person rather than an absolute jurisdictional requirement. It is clear now that an accused can waive that right.

Self-Incrimination. This section establishes the right of an accused person not to incriminate himself. The right is not limited to questions of guilt or innocence. In *State v. Johnson* (1983), the supreme court held that it applied in a proceeding after defendant's conviction to sentence him as a habitual offender. He could not be compelled to testify whether he was the person who was convicted of an earlier felony.

Confrontation. Continued is the right of an accused to confront the witnesses against him or her. Added was language to specify clearly that cross-examination of the witnesses is included. In *State v. Brady* (1980), the supreme court held that a defendant had a right to ask a witness if he had made a deal with the district attorney.

Right to Testify. Also added was the right of an accused person to testify in his or her own behalf. The supreme court in *State v. Shoemaker* (1987) found a violation of this section when the defendant was not allowed to present his version of the facts surrounding a sale of marijuana to an undercover agent, facts important to an entrapment defense.

SECTION 17
Jury Trial in Criminal Cases

> A criminal case in which the punishment may be capital shall be tried before a jury of twelve persons, all of whom must concur to render a verdict. A case in which the punishment is necessarily confinement at hard labor shall be tried before a jury of twelve persons, ten of whom must concur to render a verdict. A case in which the punishment may be confinement at hard labor or confinement without hard labor for more than six months shall be tried before a jury of six persons, five of whom must concur to render a verdict. The accused shall have the right to full voir dire examination of prospective jurors and to challenge jurors peremptorily. The number of challenges shall be fixed by law. Except in capital cases, a defendant may knowingly and intelligently waive his right to a trial by jury.

The 1974 Constitution made a number of changes in the jury trial guarantee. In the trial of noncapital major felonies, the jury continues to consist of twelve persons, but ten must concur to render a verdict instead of the nine required under the prior constitution.

Juries for the lesser felonies were enlarged from five to six, but the former requirement of jury unanimity was abandoned. Consent of five of the six was to be sufficient for a verdict. The U. S. Supreme Court, in *Burch v. Louisiana* (1979), held that this provision violated the federal Constitution and that unanimity of the six jurors was required. The state law provision in the smaller jury has thus been superseded; however, the federal courts have allowed the less-thanunanimous requirement for the twelve-person jury.

The provision continues the prior constitution's guarantee of a right to challenge jurors peremptorily, with the number of challenges to be fixed by law. The innovation in the selection process is the right "to full voir dire examination of prospective jurors." The purpose of the provision is to continue the traditional Louisiana practice of allowing the defense to examine prospective jurors at some length. It prevents adoption of a jury selection procedure as used in the federal system where the defense's ability to examine prospective jurors can be substantially circumscribed. In a number of cases, the Louisiana courts have reversed convictions because of the failure to allow the wide latitude on voir dire the constitution demands, especially if the lower court judge curtails questions about how prospective jurors react to a defendant who does not take the witness stand, as in *State v. Frith* (1982).

Consistent with Louisiana's civil law heritage, the constitution does not contain a right to a jury trial in civil cases. Article V, section 5(C) also continues prior provisions that allow the appellate courts in civil cases to review facts found by a jury, this review extending to reversing or revising such jury determinations.

SECTION 18
Right to Bail

Excessive bail shall not be required. Before and during a trial, a person shall be bailable by sufficient surety, except when he is charged with a capital offense and the proof is evident and the presumption of guilt is great. After conviction and before sentencing, a person shall be bailable if the maximum sentence which may be imposed is imprisonment for five years or less; and the judge may grant bail if the maximum sentence which may be imposed is imprisonment exceeding five years. After sentencing and until final judgment, a person shall be bailable if the sentence actually imposed is five years or less; and the judge may grant bail if the sentence actually imposed exceeds imprisonment for five years.

This section goes beyond the federal limitation on excessive bail and establishes a right to bail. A person "shall be bailable," before and during trial in all cases, unless charged with a capital offense in which the proof is evident and the presumption of guilt is great.

After conviction and before sentencing, one has a right to bail if the maximum possible punishment is five years or less; after sentence and pending appeal, one has the right to bail if the actual punishment imposed is five years or less. Bail is discretionary in other instances.

SECTION 19
Right to Judicial Review

No person shall be subjected to imprisonment or forfeiture of rights or property without the right of judicial review based upon a complete record of all evidence upon which the judgment is based. This right may be intelligently waived. The cost of transcribing the record shall be paid as provided by law.

Not part of the committee proposal, this section resulted from a floor amendment designed to cure what its author conceived as a hiatus in the previously adopted judiciary article. Under that article, a convicted person has a right of appeal if convicted of a felony or if a fine exceeding $500 or six months imprisonment was imposed. In minor criminal matters, however, no right of appeal was provided. By virtue of this provision, such defendants have a "right of appeal or review, as provided by law." The provision allows the legislature to provide the review by courts of appeal or, in the case of courts of limited jurisdiction, by trial de novo in district courts.

The review, based on "a complete record of all evidence," has been enforced by the courts. The supreme court held in *State v. LeBlanc* (1979) that the defendant in a misdemeanor case is entitled to a record even if he or she did not specifically request in advance that the record be made. In *State v. Bizette* (1976), a conviction was overturned because of the lack of a record due to a failure of the recording equipment.

SECTION 20
Right to Humane Treatment

> No law shall subject any person to euthanasia, to torture, or to cruel, excessive, or unusual punishment. Full rights of citizenship shall be restored upon termination of state and federal supervision following conviction for any offense.

This section not only prohibits cruel or unusual punishment but adds the prohibition against excessive punishment. This addition, an expansion of the prior prohibition of excessive fines, has been the basis for development of appellate review of sentencing to determine whether the severity of the punishment imposed is warranted. Since the supreme court first applied this prohibition in *State v. Sepulvado* (1979), finding excessive a three and a half year prison sentence imposed on a teenage defendant convicted of consensual carnal knowledge of a juvenile, the courts have been routinely examining sentences for excessiveness.

Another innovation is the prohibition of laws subjecting a person to euthanasia. The language was modified on the convention floor to make clear that the prohibition is directed to laws requiring that the hopelessly ill be killed and that it does not prevent private persons from halting extraordinary life continuation treatments of a dying patient.

An important addition is contained in the last sentence: "Full rights of citizenship shall be restored upon termination of state and federal supervision following conviction of any offense." The committee had proposed that "full rights" be restored, but an amendment changed it to "full rights of citizenship" after a debate indicating a desire not to prohibit the application of multiple offender laws providing for stronger punishment upon subsequent convictions. Indeed, the author of the provision stated his proposal would not prevent legislation prohibiting carrying of weapons by convicted felons or restricting the issuance of liquor licenses to such persons. He explained he had in mind basic rights, "as the right to vote, to work, to hold office and to be employed by the state."[9] Restoration of the right to vote is provided for in the more specific wording of Article I, section 10.

SECTION 21
Writ of Habeas Corpus

The writ of habeas corpus shall not be suspended.

The 1921 provision was changed to refer to a right rather than a privilege. The exception, which allowed suspension of the writ in case of rebellion or invasion, was deleted; it was thought "that emergencies and other times of disorders are precisely the time when the writ is most needed by the citizens."[10] In effect, the right to the writ exists as long as the courts are in operation to grant the writs.

SECTION 22
Access to Courts

All courts shall be open, and every person shall have an adequate remedy by due process of law and justice, administered without denial, partiality, or unreasonable delay, for injury to him in his person, property, reputation, or other rights.

This section generally repeats Article I, section 6 of the 1921 Constitution. It is essentially a second due process clause and not a substantial expansion of flexible due process rights. Attempts have been made to use this section as the basis for prohibiting statutes from limiting amounts of damage awards to injured plaintiffs, but they have been unsuccessful. The supreme court upheld the constitutionality of legislation requiring mandatory review of medical malpractice claims by a medical review panel before the institution of damages suits in *Everett v. Goldman* (1978). The limitation of awards under workers' compensation laws was upheld in *Bazey v. Tortorich* (1981). Also not prohibited by this provision were laws that capped medical malpractice awards in suits against the state (*Sibley v. Board of Supervisors of Louisiana State University*, 1985), although one member of the court suggested otherwise in *Williams v. Kushner* (1989). Allowed too were grants of tort immunity to sheriffs and their employees (*Martinez v. Reynolds* 1981).

---

[9] Hargrave, "Declaration of Rights," 64.

[10] VI Records, Sept. 12, 1973.

SECTION 23
Prohibited Laws

No bill of attainder, ex post facto law, or law impairing the obligation of contracts shall be enacted.

Traditional prohibitions against ex post facto laws and laws impairing the obligation of contracts were continued from the 1921 Constitution. New is the prohibition against bills of attainder, incorporating the federally inspired guarantee against legislative acts inflicting punishment without judicial trial.

SECTION 24
Unenumerated Rights

The enumeration in this constitution of certain rights shall not deny or disparage other rights retained by the individual citizens of the state.

A section such as this is more appropriate to a government of enumerated powers than to a state government, which has residual power to legislate in all fields except as limited by the constitution. This section, however, continues Article I, section 15 of the prior constitution and is derived from the Ninth Amendment to the U. S. Constitution. It is, in effect, another broad due process clause that allows courts to expand individual rights through recognition of other rights that are fundamental. Little development has occurred in this regard.

Article II

Distribution of Powers

SECTION 1
Three Branches

The powers of government of the state are divided into three separate branches: legislative, executive, and judicial.

SECTION 2
Limitations on each Branch

Except as otherwise provided by this Constitution, no one of these branches, nor any person holding office in one of them, shall exercise power belonging to either of the others.

Article II continues the separation of powers truism in language that originated with Thomas Jefferson in the Kentucky Constitution, which was the pattern for the Louisiana Constitution of 1812. The noncontroversial nature of the article during the Constitutional Convention of 1973 was demonstrated by the fact that the two sections passed by votes of 100-0 and 107-1 in a debate that takes up less than half a page in the convention transcripts. While the principle is still an important one, Louisiana in modern times has swayed from a strict separation of powers.

The 1974 Constitution blurs the distinction as to which powers are executive, legislative and judicial. Article V, section 5 gives the supreme court power to adopt "procedural and administrative rules not in conflict with law." Article X grants some judicial powers to civil service commissions. Article IV, section 5(G)(2) grants the governor substantial discretion over appropriations by granting the power to "veto line items or use means provided in the bill so that total appropriations for the year shall not exceed anticipated revenues for that year." That power was upheld in *Bruneau v. Edwards* (1987).

Louisiana courts have moved with the national trend in their reluctance to use separation of powers limits as a basis to abrogate legislation. The supreme court upheld, in *State ex rel. Guste v. Legislative Budget Committee* (1977), legislation granting the governor power to appoint 24 of 28 members of the powerful Joint Legislative Committee on the Budget. The court in *Guidry v. Roberts* (1976) held that campaign finance laws could be enforced by a committee that included legislators. The supreme court in *State v. Green* (1990), on rehearing, held by a 4-3 vote that the selection procedure for the Board of Ethics for Elected Officials was constitutional. The composition of the board did not violate the separation of powers doctrine, though the board was composed of members selected by the house and senate. The board members "are not subject to such significant control that the Legislature can be deemed to be performing executive functions through its control of the members of the board in the executive branch."

The separation of powers principle is invoked in extreme cases to invalidate legislation, especially in case of delegation of power to administrative agencies without adequate specificity. Also, in *Cross v. Alexander* (1986), the supreme court invalidated a procedure for reducing the numbers of state employees, primarily in the executive branch. That procedure required consent of the Joint Legislative Committee on the Budget before vacant positions were filled. The court reasoned that separation of powers of each branch be "so constituted that the members of each have as little agency as possible in the appointment of the members of the others." In the 1930s, *Saint v. Allen* (1930) held that members of the legislature who were lawyers could not be employed by the highway department to represent it.

In the definition of crimes especially, the supreme court has been willing to find violations of the nondelegation of power doctrine. *State v. Broom* (1983) held invalid the designation as a felony the violation of regulations of the Department of Public Safety regarding the handling of explosives. *State v. Rodriguez* (1980) held it was an improper delegation to require the Department of Health and Human Resources to add to its list of controlled dangerous substances any substance so classified by the U. S. Drug Enforcement Administration.

These articles are also used to support the doctrine that courts have inherent powers that cannot be limited by the legislative and executive branches. Cases applying this doctrine are discussed in the commentary after Article V, section 5.

Article III

Legislative Branch

SECTION 1
Legislative Power; Composition; Continuous Body

(A) Legislative Power of State. The legislative power of the state is vested in a legislature, consisting of a Senate and a House of Representatives. The Senate shall be composed of one senator elected from each senatorial district. The House of Representatives shall be composed of one representative elected from each representative district.
(B) Continuous Body. The legislature is a continuous body during the term for which its members are elected; however, a bill or resolution not finally passed in any session shall be withdrawn from the files of the legislature.

Section 1(A) made little change, continuing the senate and the house of representatives as existing. Section 1(B) was an innovation in the 1974 Constitution designed to allow the legislature, and especially its committees, to continue more activities during the interim between annual sessions.

SECTION 2
Sessions

(A) Annual Session. The legislature shall meet annually in regular session in the state capital for not more than sixty legislative days during a period of eighty-five calendar days. A legislative day is a calendar day on which either house is in session. No such session shall continue beyond the eightyfifth calendar day after convening. The legislature shall convene at noon on the third Monday in April. No new matter intended to have the effect of law shall be introduced or received by either house after midnight of the fifteenth calendar day, except by a favorable record vote of two-thirds of the elected members of each house. No measure levying a new tax or increasing an existing tax shall be introduced or enacted during a regular session held in an odd-numbered year.

(B) Extraordinary Session. The legislature may be convened at other times by the governor and shall be convened by the presiding officers of both houses upon written petition of a majority of the elected members of each house. The form of the petition shall be provided by law. At least five days prior to convening the legislature in extraordinary session, the governor or the presiding officers, as the case may be, shall issue a proclamation stating the objects of the session, the date on which it shall convene, and the number of days for which it is convened. The power to legislate shall be limited, under penalty of nullity, to the objects specifically enumerated in the proclamation. The session shall be limited to the number of days stated therein, which shall not exceed thirty calendar days.

(C) Emergency Session. The governor may convene the legislature in extraordinary session without prior notice or proclamation in the event of public emergency caused by epidemic, enemy attack, or public catastrophe.

(D) Organizational Session. The legislature shall meet in an organizational session in the state capitol to be convened at ten o'clock in the morning on the day the members are required to take office. No such session shall exceed three legislative days. The session shall be for the primary purpose of judging the qualifications and elections of the members, taking the oath of office, organizing the two houses, and selecting officers. No matter intended to have the effect of law shall be introduced at an organizational session. [Paragraph D added by Louisiana Acts 1989, No. 841]

The 1921 Constitution provided for alternating annual sessions of 60 and 30 days, the shorter sessions being confined to fiscal matters. The fiscal sessions were implemented after a long period during which the legislature met only in biannual regular sessions. Section 2(A) changed the system, providing for annual 60-day sessions. A remnant of the old limitations on the fiscal sessions remains, however: no tax increases or new taxes are allowed during sessions held in an odd-numbered year. *Audubon Insurance Co. v. Bernard* (1983) dealt with legislation assessing insurers a fee to be transferred to the firefighters' retirement system. The court construed the charge to be a tax, and thus invalid, in part because it was adopted in the regular session of an odd-numbered year.

The governor may call the legislature into an extraordinary session at any time, and the houses can call themselves into extraordinary sessions upon petition of a majority of the members of each house. Nothing in the constitution prevents these special sessions from enacting or raising taxes. In a special session, the legislature is confined to legislating with respect to the objects stated in the call.

The section prohibits the introduction of bills ("new matter") after the fifteenth day of the session without a two-thirds vote. This limitation was applied by the court of appeal in *Casey v. Southern Baptist Hospital* (1988), a case in which a bill dealing generally with strict liability in tort was drastically amended to provide immunity from liability to blood providers. The court concluded this was the type of "gutting of bills in order to 'introduce' new proposed legislation" that the section was designed to prohibit. Under this same rationale, the once-common practice of introducing bills by title only, and then amending them later to pour substantive content into them, is constitutionally flawed.

Hainkel v. Henry (1975) held that legislative committees may meet and take action when the legislature is not in session without such a day being counted as a legislative day within the limitations of this section.

Paragraph D was added by amendment in 1989 to allow organizational sessions when new legislators are elected every four years. Legislators take office the second Monday in January following their election (Art. III, sec. 5; Art. IV, sec. 3), the same time statewide elected officials are sworn in. The organizational session is limited to seating the members, electing officers, and otherwise organizing the bodies.

SECTION 3
Size

The number of members of the legislature shall be provided by law, but the number of senators shall not exceed thirty-nine and the number of representatives, one hundred five.

The existing numbers of both chambers were stated here as the maximum size for each house. Reductions in size are allowed.

SECTION 4
Qualifications; Residence and Domicile Requirements; Term; Vacancies

(A) Age; Residence; Domicile. An elector who at the time of qualification as a candidate has attained the age of eighteen years, resided in the state for the preceding two years, and been actually domiciled for the preceding year in the legislative district from which he seeks election is eligible for membership in the legislature.

(B) Domicile; Special Provisions. However, at the next regular election for members of the legislature following legislative reapportionment, an elector may qualify as a candidate from any district created in whole or in part from a district existing prior to reapportionment if he was domiciled in that prior district for at least one year immediately preceding his qualification and was a resident of the state for the two years preceding his qualification. The seat of any member who changes his domicile from the district he represents or, if elected after reapportionment, whose domicile is not within the district he represents at the time he is sworn into office, shall be vacated thereby, any declaration of retention of domicile to the contrary notwithstanding.

(C) Term. A member of the legislature shall be elected for a four-year term.

(D) Vacancy. A vacancy in the legislature shall be filled for the remainder of the term only by election by the electors of the respective district as provided by law.

The voting age was set at 18, and that same age was adopted as the minimum for service in the legislature. This section, however, also continues some residence requirements: two years' residence in the state and a year of domicile in the district. Paragraph B allows flexibility in the domicile requirement when reapportionment occurs. The four-year term was continued, and the vacancy provision makes clear that the person filling a vacant seat is not entitled to a complete four-year term.

SECTION 5
Taking Office

(A) Full Term. Members of the legislature shall take office on the same day as the governor and other officials elected statewide.

(B) Filling Vacancy. A person elected to fill the remainder of an unexpired legislative term shall take office within thirty days after the secretary of state promulgates the election returns.

This section borrows the provisions of Article IV, section 3. As last amended in 1986, that section provides for taking office on the second Monday in January following the previous fall's statewide elections.

SECTION 6
Legislative Reapportionment; Reapportionment by Supreme Court; Procedure

(A) Reapportionment by Legislature. By the end of the year following the year in which the population of this state is reported to the president of the United States for each decennial federal census, the legislature shall reapportion the representation in each house as equally as practicable on the basis of population shown by the census.

(B) Reapportionment by, Supreme Court. If the legislature fails to reapportion as required in Paragraph (A), the supreme court, upon petition of any elector, shall reapportion the representation in each house as provided in Paragraph (A).
(C) Procedure. The procedure for review and for petition shall be provided by law.

The requirement of decennial reapportionment is stated in Paragraph A. The innovation in this regard, however, is Paragraph B, which provides an enforcement mechanism if the legislature fails to reapportion itself. Any elector is given standing to request reapportionment by the supreme court, and the court is required to do so upon such a request.

SECTION 7
Judging Qualifications and Elections; Procedural Rules; Discipline; Expulsion; Subpoenas; Contempt; Officers

(A) Judging Qualifications and Elections; Procedural Rules; Discipline; Expulsion. Each house shall be the judge of the qualifications and elections of its members; shall determine its rules of procedure, not inconsistent with the provisions of this constitution; may punish its members for disorderly conduct or contempt; and may expel a member with concurrence of two-thirds of its elected members. Expulsion creates a vacancy in the office.
(B) Subpoena Power; Contempt. Each house may compel the attendance and testimony of witnesses and the production of books and papers before it, before any committee thereof, or before joint committees of the houses and may punish those in willful disobedience of its orders for contempt.
(C) Officers. Each house shall choose its officers, including a permanent presiding officer selected from its membership. The presiding officers shall be the president of the Senate and the speaker of the House of Representatives. The clerical officers shall be the clerk of the House of Representatives and the secretary of the Senate, each of whom may administer oaths.

The prior constitution made the lieutenant governor the presiding officer of the senate. The 1973 convention sought to increase legislative independence from the executive branch by allowing the senate to select its own president. Paragraph C incorporates that change in its requirement that both houses elect their own presiding officers. This change leaves the lieutenant governor, a statewide elected official under Article IV, section 6, with virtually no constitutional duties.

Paragraph B grants both houses the power to compel testimony and to punish disobedience with its orders through proceedings for contempt of the legislature. The supreme court in *House of Representatives v. Bernard* (1979) affirmed this power in allowing the legislature to hold in contempt the commissioner of insurance who refused to comply with a subpoena to appear before a house committee.

The power provided in Paragraph A to punish members or even expel them was recognized in *Gerald v. Louisiana State Senate* (1981), the court affirming the expulsion of a senator convicted of a federal felony. The court found that the legislature's procedures in that expulsion proceeding complied with due process even though the senator was not present at the session and not all the procedures of criminal trials were met.

SECTION 8
Privileges and Immunities

A member of the legislature shall be privileged from arrest, except for felony, during his attendance at sessions and committee meetings of his house and while going to and from them. No member shall be questioned elsewhere for any speech in either house.

Similar provisions in nine previous constitutions repeated this privilege designed to immunize members from trivial arrests during sessions. Virtually no reported cases have dealt with the provision.

SECTION 9
Conflict of Interest

Legislative office is a public trust, and every effort to realize personal gain through official conduct is a violation of that trust. The legislature shall enact a code of ethics prohibiting conflict between public duty and private interests of members of the legislature.

Article X, section 21 mandates in more general terms the adoption of a code of ethics for all officials and employees of the state and its political subdivisions. Louisiana Revised Statutes 42:1101 *et seq.* adopted such a code of ethics, and the Board of Ethics for Elected Officials was established to enforce the code.

SECTION 10
Quorum; Compulsory Attendance; Journal; Adjournment with Consent of Other House

(A) Quorum. Not less than a majority of the elected members of each house shall form a quorum to transact business, but a smaller number may adjourn from day-to-day and may compel the attendance of absent members.

(B) Journal. Each house shall keep a journal of its proceedings and have it published immediately after the close of each session. The journal shall accurately reflect the proceedings of that house, including all record votes. A record vote is a vote by yeas and nays, with each member's vote published in the journal.
(C) Adjournment. When the legislature is in session, neither house shall adjourn for more than three days or to another place without consent of the other house.

These detailed requirements of a majority for a quorum, a journal of proceedings, open voting, and prohibited adjournments are in keeping with the constitutional detail of nine prior constitutions.

SECTION 11
Legislative Auditor

There shall be a legislative auditor responsible solely to the legislature. He shall serve as a fiscal advisor to it and shall perform the duties and functions provided by law related to auditing fiscal records of the state, its agencies, and political subdivisions. He shall be elected by the concurrence of a majority of the elected members of each house and may be removed by the concurrence of two-thirds of the elected members of each house.

Auditors appointed by the legislature had achieved a popular status of serving a watchdog function over state agencies and over local governments. This section constitutionalized the position, although the auditor's duties are to be provided by law. The auditor's position is unique in that removal requires a two-thirds vote of the members of each house.

SECTION 12
Prohibited Local and Special Laws

(A) Prohibitions. Except as a otherwise provided in this constitution, the legislature shall not pass a local or special law:

(1) For the holding and conducting of elections, or fixing or changing the place of voting.
(2) Changing the names of persons; authorizing the adoption or legitimation of children or the emancipation of minors; affecting the estates of minors or persons under disabilities; granting divorces; changing the law of descent or succession; giving effect to informal or invalid wills or deeds or to any illegal disposition of property.
(3) Concerning any civil or criminal actions, including changing the venue in civil or criminal cases, or regulating the practice or jurisdiction of any court, or

changing the rules of evidence in any judicial proceeding or inquiry before courts, or providing or changing methods for the collection of debts or the enforcement of judgments, or prescribing the effects of judicial sales.

(4) Authorizing the laying out, opening, closing, altering, or maintaining of roads, highways, streets, or alleys; relating to ferries and bridges, or incorporating bridge or ferry companies, except for the erection of bridges crossing streams which form boundaries between this and any other state; authorizing the constructing of street passenger railroads in any incorporated town or city.

(5) Exempting property from taxation; extending the time for the assessment or collection of taxes; relieving an assessor or collector of taxes from the performance of his official duties or of his sureties from liability; remitting fines, penalties, and forfeitures; refunding moneys legally paid into the treasury.

(6) Regulating labor, trade, manufacturing, or agriculture; fixing the rate of interest.

(7) Creating private corporations, or amending, renewing, extending, or explaining the charters thereof; granting to any private corporation, association, or individual any special or exclusive right, privilege, or immunity.

(8) Regulating the management of parish or city public schools, the building or repairing of parish or city schoolhouses, and the raising of money for such purposes.

(9) Legalizing the unauthorized or invalid acts of any officer, employee, or agent of the state, its agencies, or political subdivisions.

(10) Defining any crime.

(B) Additional Prohibition. The legislature shall not indirectly enact special or local laws by the partial repeal or suspension of a general law.

SECTION 13
Local or Special Laws; Notice of Intent; Publication

No local or special law shall be enacted unless notice of the intent to introduce a bill to enact such a law has been published on two separate days, without cost to the state, in the official journal of the locality where the matter to be affected is situated. The last day of publication shall be at least thirty days prior to introduction of the bill. The notice shall state the substance of the contemplated law, and every such bill shall recite that notice has been given.

The 1974 Constitution contains the state's first equal protection clause in Article I, section 3, an important innovation that requires uniform application of legislation. In addition, this section also continues the more traditional means of requiring uniformity: limitations on local and special laws. Section 12 prohibits absolutely ten categories of such laws, and section 13 establishes a special presession advertisement procedure for local and special laws that are permitted.

The result of these provisions is a complex analysis under which any statutory classification must first meet the requirements of the equal protection clause. If those are met, the inquiry must then focus on whether the statute is a local or special law. If it is either, it is prohibited if it is the type of law mentioned in section 12. If it is not, the procedural requirements of section 13 must be met.

Section 12(B) also requires that the same rules apply to acts that began as general bills but became local or special laws by amendment or by partial repeal or suspension.

An important innovation in section 12 was the new prohibition against local or special laws "defining any crime." The provision originated in a floor amendment proposed by the delegate appointed to represent wildlife and conservation interests who sought to end the existence of state laws that defined the crime of trespass differently in specified parishes, a special concern of hunters. *State v. LaBauve* (1978) and *State v. Slay* (1979) have been true to the prohibition, invalidating laws regulating the size of fish nets that were not uniformly applicable throughout the state.

In other respects, section 12 is a continuation of the predecessor provision, a lengthy catalog of subjects on which there can be no local or special laws. An attempt was made to adopt the simple formula of the Model State Constitution, which prohibits local or special laws "when a general law is or can be made applicable," but it failed. The long list of limitations came primarily from the 1879 Constitution, which had set a new high for statutory detail and had added fifteen new sections of forbidden local and special laws. Most were reactions to legislation adopted during the Reconstruction government.

Several related provisions in the local government article also come into play. Article VI, section 3 specifically allows the legislature to "classify parishes or municipalities according to population or any other reasonable basis related to the purpose of the classification. Legislation may be limited in its effect to any of such class or classes." Delegates to the 1973 convention almost made it a fetish to eliminate the "Orleans excepted" references of the 1921 Constitution. However, since classifications based on population size are permitted, in practice the state's largest city can in fact be treated differently. Article VI, section 44 also defines "general law," at least when used in that article, as "a law of statewide concern enacted by the legislature which is uniformly applicable to all persons or to all political subdivisions in the state or which is uniformly applicable to all persons or to all political subdivisions within the same class."

Courts have been less than clear in defining local and special laws. Often the terms are used as though they were one concept. However, the constitution does make a distinction between the two. Local laws do not apply uniformly throughout the state, with the exceptions based on geography or location. Special laws do not apply uniformly, with the exceptions based on some other basis.

Court decisions have implemented the prohibition against local laws: a reapportionment statute that applied to only one school board (*Caddo Parish School*

Board v. Board of Elections Supervisors, 1980); a statute that prohibited the banks in nine parishes from opening on Saturdays while allowing banks in other parishes to remain open (*State Through State Banking Department v. Acadiana Bank and Trust Co.,* 1978); a law reorganizing the Audubon Park Commission and requiring the city of New Orleans to appropriate funds to the commission (*City of New Orleans v. Treen,* 1983); and a general statute limiting the debt of school boards to 25 percent of assessed valuation that was amended to allow the parishes of DeSoto, Red River, Sabine and part of Calcasieu to issue debt up to 35 percent (*Concerned Business, and Property Owners v. DeSoto Parish School Board,* 1988). A law prohibiting excavation of the bed and banks of the Comite River in East Baton Rouge Parish was a local law needing advertisement (*State v. Stirgus,* 1983).

It is more difficult to reconcile the special law prohibition with the equal protection guarantee. Both rules use the same concepts of prohibiting statutes that except some groups based on a classification other than geographic location.

Both involve an inquiry into the reasonableness of the classification. Indeed, it is more difficult to relate section 13's advertisment procedure to local laws than to special laws. Advertisement of local laws in specified parishes or cities is feasible. However, if a law is special, it must advertised throughout the state, a seeming anomaly. In any event, recent cases have not been as willing to characterize a law as special when it does not violate the equal protection clause. The court held that a statute treating some medical malpractice victims differently from other victims of other torts was not a special law (*Everett v. Goldman,* 1978).

SECTION 14
Style of Laws; Enacting Clause

The style of a law enacted by the legislature shall be, "Be it enacted by the Legislature of Louisiana." It shall be unnecessary to repeat the enacting clause after the first section of an act.

This section continues a rule of the prior constitution that has been rigidly applied. Failure to use the stated form in a bill renders the statute invalid (*First National Bank of Commerce v. Eaves,* 1973).

SECTION 15
Passage of Bills

(A) Introduction; Title; Single Object; Public Meetings. The legislature shall enact no law except by a bill introduced during that session, and propose no constitutional amendment except by a joint resolution introduced during that session, which shall be processed as a bill. Every bill, except the general appropriation bill and bills for the enactment, rearrangement, codification, or revision of a system of laws, shall be confined to one object. Every bill shall contain a brief title indicative of its object. Action on any matter intended to have the effect of law shall be taken only in open, public meeting.

(B) No General Reference. A bill enacting, amending, or reviving a law shall set forth completely the provisions of the law enacted, amended, or revived. No system or code of laws shall be adopted by general reference to it.

(C) Germane Amendments. No bill shall be amended in either house to make a change not germane to the bill as introduced.

(D) Three Readings. Each bill shall be read at least by title on three separate days in each house. No bill shall be considered for final passage unless a committee has held a public hearing and reported on the bill.

(E) Rejected Bills; Reconsideration. No bill rejected by either house may again be introduced or considered during the same session by the house which rejected it without the consent of a majority of the members to that house.

(F) Concurrence in Amendments. No amendment to a bill by one house shall be concurred in by the other, and no conference committee report shall be concurred in by either house except by the same vote required for final passage of the bill. The vote thereon shall be by record vote.

(G) Majority Vote; Record Vote. No bill shall become law without the favorable vote of at least a majority of the members elected to each house.

Final passage of a bill shall be by record vote. In either house, a record vote shall be taken on any matter upon the request of one-fifth of the elected members.

This section continues the Louisiana penchant for detail in regulating the legislature's internal procedures. In so doing, it establishes the rationale for continued court examination of the legislative process and continuation of the practice of holding statutes unconstitutional if the procedures are not followed.

The 1974 document may suggest more flexibility in the requirement that a bill have a title indicative of its object; added was the reference in paragraph A to a "brief title." The court, however, in *Orleans Parish School Board v. City of New Orleans* (1982), found inadequate the language in a title "to provide relative to quarters for courts and officers in the parish of Orleans and to provide further with respect thereto" when the substance was adding a new requirement that the expenses of tax assessors would be borne by the tax recipient bodies. The title was inadequate to give notice to the legislators and to the public of the scope of the legislation.

Louisiana courts do not honor the "enrolled bill rule" under which the final enrolled bill is conclusively presumed to have been validly adopted. Rather the courts will examine the journals of either house to determine whether the procedural requirements have been met. The journals are given a presumption of correctness. As to other matters, recitations in a bill that the required advertisement of local and special laws has been made are not conclusive and do not preclude the courts otherwise determining if the requirements were met (*State v. Stirgus*, 1983). When faced with a discrepancy between the bill as enrolled and as promulgated by the secretary of state, the court ruled that the enrolled version prevailed (*State v. St. Romain*, 1974).

SECTION 16
Appropriations

(A) Specific Appropriation for One Year. Except as otherwise provided by this constitution, no money shall be withdrawn from the state treasury except through specific appropriation, and no appropriation shall be made under the heading of contingencies or for longer than one year.
(B) Origin in House of Representatives. All bills for raising revenue or appropriating money shall originate in the House of Representatives, but the Senate may propose or concur in amendments, as in other bills.
(C) General Appropriation Bill; Limitations. The general appropriation bill shall be itemized and shall contain only appropriations for the ordinary operating expenses of government, public charities, pensions, and the public debt or interest thereon.
(D) Specific Purpose and Amount. All other bills for appropriating money shall be for a specific purpose and amount.
(E) Extraordinary Session. Except for expenses of the legislature, a bill appropriating money in an extraordinary session convened after final adjournment of the regular session in the last year of the term of office of a governor shall require the favorable vote of three-fourths of the elected members of each house.

The 1974 Constitution, which reduced the governor's powers in several areas, did not reduce the line item veto power, discussed in the commentary following Article IV, section 5(G).

Article VI, section 10 requires the state to have a balanced budget, stating that appropriations by the legislature shall not exceed anticipated state revenues. The constitution, however, has no mechanism for an authoritative determination of anticipated state revenues, so the balanced budget provision is more of a political control than a definitive legal control over the budget process.

SECTION 17
Signing of Bills; Delivery to Governor

(A) Signing; Delivery. A bill passed by both houses shall be signed by the presiding officers and delivered to the governor within three days after passage.

(B) Resolutions. No joint, concurrent, or other resolution shall require the signature or other action of the governor to become effective.

SECTION 18
Gubernatorial Action on Bills; Sign, Failure to Sign, Veto; Veto Session

(A) Gubernatorial Action. If the governor does not approve a bill, he may veto it. A bill, except a joint resolution, shall become law if the governor signs it or if he fails to sign or veto it within ten days after delivery to him if the legislature is in session on the tenth day after such delivery, or within twenty days after delivery if the tenth day after delivery occurs after the legislature is adjourned.
(B) Veto Message. If the governor vetos a bill, he shall return it to the legislature, with his veto message, within twelve days after delivery to him if the legislature is in session. If the governor returns or vetoes a bill after the legislature adjourns, he shall return it, with his veto message, as provided by law.
(C) Veto Session.

(1) A bill vetoed and returned and subsequently approved by two-thirds of the elected members of each house shall become law. The legislature shall meet in veto session in the state capital at noon on the fortieth day following final adjournment of the most recent session, to consider all bills vetoed by the governor. If the fortieth day falls on Sunday, the session shall convene at noon on the succeeding Monday. No veto session shall exceed five calendar days, and any veto session may be finally adjourned prior to the end of the fifth day upon the vote of two-thirds of the elected members of each house.

(2) No veto session shall be held if a majority of the elected members of either house declare in writing that a veto session is unnecessary. The declaration must be received by the presiding officer of the respective houses at least five days prior to the day on which the veto session is to convene. [Amended by Louisiana Acts 1989, No. 842]

SECTION 19
Effective Date of Laws

All laws shall take effect on the sixtieth day after final adjournment of the session in which they were enacted, and shall be published prior thereto in the official journal of the state as provided by law. However, any bill may specify an earlier or later effective date.

It is not unusual for the legislature to take advantage of the last sentence of section 19 and provide that a law shall become effective upon signature of the governor. *Jones v. State* (1976) approved of the practice, finding that the section does not make the effectiveness of the legislation depend on publication in the official journal. In *Jones*, a statute effective June 30, 1976, provided that qualifying for a new judgeship would be from July 2 to July 5, 1976.

SECTION 20
Suspension of Laws

Only the legislature may suspend a law, and then only by the same vote and, except for gubernatorial veto and time limitations for introduction, according to the same procedures and formalities required for enactment of that law. After the effective date of this constitution, every resolution suspending a law shall fix the period of suspension, which shall not extend beyond the sixtieth day after final adjournment of the next regular session.

Article IV

Executive Branch

SECTION 1
Composition; Number of Departments; Reorganization

(A) Composition. The executive branch shall consist of the governor, lieutenant governor, secretary of state, attorney general, treasurer, commissioner of agriculture, commissioner of insurance, superintendent of education, commissioner of elections, and all other executive offices, agencies, and instrumentalities of the state.
(B) Number of Departments. Except for the offices of governor and lieutenant governor, all offices, agencies, and other instrumentalities of the executive branch and their functions, powers, duties, and responsibilities shall be allocated according to function within not more than twenty departments. The powers, functions, and duties allocated by this constitution to any executive office or commission shall not be affected or diminished by the allocation provided herein except as authorized by Section 20 of this Article.
(C) Reorganization. Reallocation of the functions, powers, and duties of all departments, offices, agencies, and other instrumentalities of the executive branch, except those functions, powers, duties, and responsibilities allocated by this constitution, shall be as provided by law.

The state administrative structure had grown in an unplanned manner under the 1921 Constitution. Officers, boards, agencies, commissions, and various other public entities were formed—some in the constitution, some in the statutes, and some by executive orderwithout clear relationships and control. The Constitutional Convention of 1973's response to the problem was section 2(B): to require organization of these agencies into no more than twenty executive departments. Reorganization was accomplished by legislation adopted in 1975 and 1976,[11] and establishment of new departments has been accompanied by the merging of existing ones to maintain the number at twenty.

SECTION 2
Qualifications

To be eligible for any statewide elective office, a person, by the date of his qualification as a candidate, shall have attained the age of twenty-five years, be an elector, and have been a citizen of the United States and of this state for at least the preceding five years. In addition, the attorney general shall have been admitted to the practice of law in the state for at least the five years preceding his election. During his tenure in office, a statewide elected official shall hold no other public office except by virtue of his elected office.

The Committee on the Executive Branch was consistent in requiring that the qualifications for office be met at the time of qualification as a candidate. The special qualifications for the attorney general, however, were proposed by the Committee on the Judiciary, which provided that the requirements be met as of the time of "election."

Although members of the legislature may serve at age 18, statewide officials must be 21 years old.

SECTION 3
Election; Term

(A) Election. Except as provided in Section 20 of this Article, the governor, lieutenant governor, secretary of state, attorney general, treasurer, commissioner of agriculture, commissioner of insurance, superintendent of education, and commissioner of elections each shall be elected for a term of four years by the electors of the state at the time and place of voting for members of the legislature. The term of each such official shall begin at noon on the second Monday in January next following the election.

(B) Limitation on Governor. A person who has served as governor for more than one and one-half terms in two consecutive terms shall not be elected governor for the succeeding term.

---

[11] Acts 1975, No. 720; Acts 1976, No. 513.

(C) Additional Limitation. Except as provided by this constitution, no official shall be elected statewide.

(D) Notwithstanding any other provision of this constitution or of law to the contrary, statewide elected officials and members of the legislature elected in 1987 shall hold office from and after the second Monday in March, 1988. These statewide elected officials and any successor elected to the unexpired term of any of them shall serve for terms which shall expire at noon on January 13, 1992. These members of the legislature and any successor elected to the unexpired term of any of them shall serve for terms which shall expire at ten o'clock a.m. on January 13, 1992. Thereafter, statewide elected officials and members of the legislature shall be elected for terms of four years. For purposes of retirement, the statewide elected officials and members of the legislature elected in 1987 shall be deemed to be elected for a four-year term.

Under the prior constitution, officials took office on the second Monday in May. The 1973 convention advanced this date to the second Monday in March to shorten the lame duck period of an outgoing official. A 1986 amendment to section 3(A) advanced the beginning of the terms once again, to the second Monday in January. The section continues the prohibition of a governor's serving more than two consecutive terms.

SECTION 4
Compensation

Except as otherwise provided by this constitution, the compensation of each statewide elected official shall be provided by law.

Gone from the constitution are the many provisions setting the salary of various officials. Courts had construed these figures to be minimum salaries in any event, and inflation had made them meaningless. This section requires salaries be set by legislation, and Article X, section 23 prohibits reduction of the compensation of an elected official during his or her term.

SECTION 5
Governor; Powers and Duties

(A) Executive Authority. The governor shall be the chief executive officer of the state. He shall faithfully support the constitution and laws of the state and of the United States and shall see that the laws are faithfully executed.

(B) Legislative Reports and Recommendations. The governor shall, at the beginning of each regular session, and may, at other times, make reports and recommendations and give information to the legislature concerning the affairs of state, including its complete financial condition.

(C) Departmental Reports and Information. When requested by the governor, a department head shall provide him with reports and information, in writing or otherwise, on any subject relating to the department, except matters concerning investigations of the governor's office.

(D) Operating and Capital Budget. The governor shall submit to the legislature an operating budget and a capital budget, as provided by Article VII, Section 11 of this constitution.

(E) Pardon, Commutation, Reprieve, and Remission; Board of Pardons.

(1) The governor may grant reprieves to persons convicted of offenses against the state and, upon recommendation of the Board of Pardons, may commute sentences, pardon those convicted of offenses against the state, and remit fines and forfeitures imposed for such offenses. However, a first offender never previously convicted of a felony shall be pardoned automatically upon completion of his sentence, without a recommendation of the Board of Pardons and without action by the governor.

(2) The Board of Pardons shall consist of five electors appointed by the governor, subject to confirmation by the Senate. Each member of the board shall serve a term concurrent with that of the governor appointing him.

(F) Receipt of Bills from the Legislature. The date and hour when a bill finally passed by the legislature is delivered to the governor shall be endorsed thereon.

(G) Item Veto.

(1) Except as otherwise provided by this constitution, the governor may veto any line item in an appropriation bill. Any item vetoed shall be void unless the veto is overridden as prescribed for the passage of a bill over a veto.

(2) The governor shall veto line items or use means provided in the bill so that total appropriations for the year shall not exceed anticipated revenues for that year.

(H) Appointments.

(1) The governor shall appoint, subject to confirmation by the Senate, the head of each department in the executive branch whose election or appointment is not provided by this constitution and the members of each board and commission in the executive branch whose election or appointment is not provided by this constitution or by law.

(2) Should the legislature be in regular session, the governor shall submit for confirmation by the Senate the name of an appointee within forty-eight hours after the appointment is made. Failure of the Senate to confirm the appointment, prior to the end of the session, shall constitute rejection.

(3) If the legislature is not in regular session, the governor may make interim appointments, which shall expire at the end of the next regular session, unless submitted to and confirmed by the Senate during that session.

(4) A person not confirmed by the Senate shall not be appointed to the same office during any recess of the legislature.

(I) Removal Power. The governor may remove from office a person he appoints, except a person appointed for a term fixed by this constitution or by law.
(J) Commander-in-Chief. The governor shall be commander-in-chief of the armed forces of the state, except when they are called into service of the federal government. He may call out these forces to preserve law and order, to suppress insurrection, to repel invasion, or in other times of emergency.
(K) Other Powers and Duties. The governor shall have other powers and perform other duties authorized by this constitution or provided by law.

Pardons. Although the text of section 5(E) makes no distinction between the effects of a gubernatorial pardon and the effect of an automatic pardon granted to first offenders, the supreme court has done so. In *State v. Adams* (1978), the court allowed a first conviction that was pardoned automatically to be considered in applying the enhanced punishment provisions of the multiple offender statute. On the other hand, if a pardon by the governor has been issued, the offense apparently would not have been considered in enhancing punishment under the rule of *State v. Childers* (1941). The court's reasoning was that a regular pardon is supported by pardon board consideration of the circumstances involving the offender, whereas the automatic pardon does not involve such study of one's possible innocence or rehabilitation. The automatic pardon provision was new to the 1974 Constitution, and *State v. Harvey* (1976) did not apply it to convictions and sentences imposed before the effective date of the new document, January 1, 1975.

Under the prior constitution, and under this section as well, the governor's powers to commute or pardon are not subject to legislative control. The legislature may provide for imprisonment without parole or probation, but it cannot impose imprisonment without pardon or commutation of sentence.

Veto. The 1974 Constitution, which reduced the governor's powers in a number of ways, did not abolish the power to "veto any line item in an appropriation bill." Indeed, the governor is required by section 5(F)(2) to use the line item veto to balance the budget. This power is a corollary to the requirement that a bill have but one object, the latter rule protecting the governor's veto power by prohibiting unrelated riders and the related logrolling in bills. The appropriations bill is an explicit exception, provided in Article III, section 15(A), to the single object requirement.

Exercise of this power poses little problem with most monetary items in appropriations bill. Difficulty has arisen when the appropriations bill contains provisions that do something other than specify the agency to receive the funds, the amount, and the use of the funds. Over the years, the legislature has used many such provisions, attaching conditions like those that were at issue in *Henry v. Edwards* (1977). In that case, the governor approved $495,000 for salary payments to assistant district attorneys but vetoed the language immediately below, which stated the recipients "shall be prohibited from electioneering and campaigning in any precinct." The court allowed the governor to veto the condition but not the appropriation. The majority's view was to consider such substantive items as separate items subject to the veto. Another view would consider them inappropriate matter for an appropriations bill and thus in violation of the single object rule. Under either view, those provisions do not apply when the governor vetoes them. If they are not vetoed, under the latter view, they could be contested and invalidated for failure to comply with the single object requirements.

SECTION 6
Lieutenant Governor; Powers and Duties

The lieutenant governor shall serve ex officio as a member of each committee, board, and commission on which the governor serves. He shall exercise the powers delegated to him by the governor and shall have other powers and perform other duties in the executive branch authorized by this constitution or provided by law.

Under the prior constitution, the lieutenant governor was the presiding officer of the senate. That position was removed from the lieutenant governor as part of an effort to increase the independence of the legislature. The senate now elects its own presiding officer. The lieutenant governor's position has become one of little power, dependent on legislation for assignment of authority.

SECTION 7
Secretary of State; Powers and Duties

There shall be a Department of State. The secretary of state shall head the department and shall be the chief election officer of the state. He shall prepare and certify the ballots for all elections, promulgate all election returns, and administer the election laws, except those relating to voter registration and custody of voting machines. He shall administer the state corporation and trademark laws; serve as keeper of the Great Seal of the State of Louisiana and attest therewith all official laws, documents, proclamations, and commissions; administer and preserve the official archives of the state; promulgate and publish all laws enacted by the legislature and retain the originals thereof; and countersign and keep an official registry of all commissions. He may administer oaths, and shall have other powers and perform other duties authorized by this constitution or provided by law.

The secretary of state is primarily the keeper and promulgator of state documents. Although the secretary is denominated the state's chief election officer, section 12 establishes a commissioner of elections who administers laws governing voter registration and custody of voting machines.

SECTION 8
Attorney General; Powers and Duties

There shall be a Department of Justice, headed by the attorney general, who shall be the chief legal officer of the state. The attorney general shall be elected for a term of four years at the state general election. The assistant attorneys general shall be appointed by the attorney general to serve at his pleasure.

As necessary for the assertion or protection of any right or interest of the state, the attorney general shall have authority (1) to institute, prosecute, or intervene in any civil action or proceeding; (2) upon the written request of a district attorney, to advise and assist in the prosecution of any criminal case; and (3) for cause, when authorized by the court which would have original jurisdiction and subject to judicial review, (a) to institute, prosecute, or intervene in any criminal action or proceeding, or (b) to supersede any attorney representing the state in any civil or criminal action.

The attorney general shall exercise other powers and perform other duties authorized by this constitution or by law.

The Louisiana attorney general has much less power than those in most other states. Elected district attorneys attached to the district courts prosecute criminal cases; Article V, section 26 gives them "charge of every criminal prosecution by the state" in the appropriate judicial district. The attorney general can institute a criminal proceeding or oust a district attorney only for cause and after court approval. The relationship between the state's chief legal officer and the local district attorneys under the 1921 Constitution was not clear and was debated at length during the convention. The Committee on the Executive Branch and the Committee on the Judiciary proposed conflicting articles, the former granting the state officer more power. The latter proposal won, a typical response being that some delegates "seem to assume that a statewide elected official will be inherently more virtuous than a locally elected official. I challenge that assumption."[12]

The text relates the cause requirement to a right or interest of the state not being satisfactorily represented or asserted by a district attorney. In *In re Superseding the District Attorney of the 25th Judicial District* (1981), the supreme court allowed the attorney general to supersede a district attorney who dismissed a grand jury when he learned that it had voted to indict him for theft. In *In re Superseding the District Attorney of the 19th Judicial District* (1989), the cause consisted of alleged personal misconduct in failing to investigate properly crimes committed by the district attorney and his staff. That district attorney subsequently resigned and pleaded guilty to a charge of false accounting.

---

[12] Lee Hargrave, "The Judiciary Article of the Louisiana Constitution of 1974," *Louisiana Law Review* 37 (1977):833.

The cause requirement comes into play when a dispute arises between a district attorney and the attorney general over institution or prosecution of a suit; the judge then becomes the umpire between the two officials. Court authorization is not necessary when a district attorney requests that the attorney general conduct a prosecution.

The attorney general has more authority in civil matters. In *State ex rel. Guste v. Audubon Park Commission* (1975), the court recognized that his power to institute litigation to protect the state's interests included suing to enjoin a city agency from enlarging a zoo located on state property. The constitutional grant to intervene, however, does not free the attorney general from procedural rules of the Code of Civil Procedure. The court in *In re BASF Corporation, Chemical Division* (1988) held the attorney general could not intervene at the appellate level to contest the penalty assessed by the Department of Environmental Quality against a chemical company.

SECTION 9
Treasurer; Powers and Duties

There shall be a Department of the Treasury. The treasurer shall head the department and shall be responsible for the custody, investment, and disbursement of the public funds of the state, except as otherwise provided by this constitution. He shall report annually to the governor and to the legislature at least one month before each regular session on the financial condition of the state, and shall have other powers and perform other duties authorized by this constitution or provided by law.

SECTION 10
Commissioner of Agriculture; Powers and Duties

There shall be a Department of Agriculture. The commissioner of agriculture shall head the department and shall exercise all functions of the state relating to the promotion, protection, and advancement of agriculture, except research and educational functions expressly allocated by this constitution or by law to other state agencies. The department shall exercise such functions and the commissioner shall have other powers and perform other duties authorized by this constitution or provided by law.

SECTION 11
Commissioner of Insurance; Powers and Duties

There shall be a Department of Insurance, headed by the commissioner of insurance. The department shall exercise such functions and the commissioner shall have powers and perform duties authorized by this constitution or provided by law.

SECTION 12
Commissioner of Elections; Powers and Duties

There shall be a Department of Elections and Registration. The commissioner of elections shall head the department and shall administer the laws relating to custody of voting machines and voter registration. He shall have other powers and perform other duties authorized by this constitution or provided by law.

SECTION 13
First Assistants; Appointment

Each statewide elected official except the governor and lieutenant governor shall appoint a first assistant, subject to public confirmation by the Senate, and may remove him at his pleasure. The official shall submit the appointment to the Senate in the manner and subject to the procedures and limitations applicable to appointments submitted by the governor. The first assistant shall possess the qualifications required for election to the office.

The treasurer, commissioner of agriculture, commissioner of insurance, and commissioner of elections are elected statewide officials. The constitution, though guaranteeing the existence of these positions, does not provide in detail for their duties. The scope of their authority is primarily a legislative matter, and the last three positions can be made appointive under the provisions of section 20.

SECTION 14
Vacancy in Office of Governor

When a vacancy occurs in the office of governor, the order of succession shall be (1) the elected lieutenant governor, (2) the elected secretary of state, (3) the elected attorney general, (4) the elected treasurer, (5) the presiding officer of the Senate, (6) the presiding officer of the House of Representatives, and then (7) as provided by law. The successor shall serve the remainder of the term for which the governor was elected.

SECTION 15
Vacancy in Office of Lieutenant Governor

Should a vacancy occur in the office of lieutenant governor, the governor shall nominate a lieutenant governor, who shall take office upon confirmation by a majority vote of the elected members of each house of the legislature.

SECTION 16
Vacancies in Other Statewide Elective Offices

A vacancy in a statewide elective office other than that of governor or lieutenant governor shall be filled by the first assistant. If the unexpired term exceeds one year, the office shall be filled by election at the next regularly scheduled congressional or statewide election, and the first assistant shall serve only until the person then elected takes office.

SECTION 17
Declaration of Inability by Statewide Elected Officials

When a statewide elected official transmits to the presiding officers of the Senate and House of Representatives a written declaration of his inability to discharge the powers and duties of his office, and until he transmits to them a written declaration to the contrary, the person who would succeed to the office when a vacancy occurs shall assume the powers and duties of the office as acting official.

SECTION 18
Determination of Inability of Statewide Elected Official

(A) Declaration and Counter-Declaration. When a majority of the statewide elected officials determine that any other such official is unable to discharge the powers and duties of his office, they shall transmit a written declaration to this effect to the presiding officer of each house and to the official, and shall file a copy of the declaration in the office of the secretary of state. Thereafter, the constitutional successor shall assume the office as acting official unless, within forty-eight hours after the declaration is filed in the office of the secretary of state, the elected official files in that office and transmits to the presiding officer of each house his written counter-declaration of his ability to exercise the powers and perform the duties of his office.

(B) Determination by the Legislature. The legislature shall convene at noon on the third calendar day after the filing of any counter-declaration, which may be filed by the official at any time. Should two-thirds of the elected members of each house fail to adopt a resolution within seventy-two hours declaring probable justification for the determination that inability exists, the official shall continue in or resume office.

(C) Assumption of Office by Constitutional Successor. If two-thirds of the elected members of each house adopt a resolution declaring that probable justification exists for the declaration of inability, the constitutional successor shall assume the powers and duties of the office and a copy of the resolution shall be transmitted forthwith to the supreme court.

(D) Determination by Supreme Court. By preference and with priority over all other matters, the supreme court shall determine the issue of inability after due notice and hearing, by a majority vote of members elected to the court, under such rules as it may adopt.
(E) Reconsideration by Supreme Court. A judgment of the supreme court affirming inability may be reconsidered by the court, after due notice and hearing, either upon its own motion or upon the application of the official. Upon proper showing and by majority vote of its elected members, the court may determine that no inability then exists, whereupon the official shall immediately resume the powers and duties of his office.

SECTION 19
Temporary Absences

When the governor is temporarily absent from the state, the lieutenant governor shall act as governor. When any other statewide elected official is temporarily absent from the state, the appointed first assistant shall act in his absence.

The reference to absence from the state is to be read in the light of past cases, which suggested in 1874 that the governor's short vacation in neighboring Mississippi was not an absence, since he could return in a few hours (*State ex rel. Warmoth v. Graham*). In 1877, however, an absence included the governor's being in New York for four or five weeks (*State ex rel. Attorney General and Thomas Carey v. Barrow*). With modern communications available, the scope of the *Graham* rule will expand and the scope of the *Barrow* case will no doubt narrow.

SECTION 20
Appointment of Officials; Merger, Consolidation of Offices and Departments

After the first election of state officials following the effective date of this constitution, the legislature may provide, by law enacted by two-thirds of the elected members of each house, for appointment, in lieu of election, of the commissioner of agriculture, the commissioner of insurance, the superintendent of education, the commissioner of elections, or any of them. In that event, the legislature shall prescribe qualifications and method of appointment and by similar vote, may provide by law for the merger or consolidation of any such office, its department, and functions with any other office or department in the executive branch. No action of the legislature pursuant hereto shall reduce the term or compensation of any incumbent elected official. By law enacted by two-thirds of the elected members of each house, the legislature may reestablish any such office as elective and, in that event, shall prescribe qualifications.

The legislature has used its power under this section to provide for appointment of the superintendent of education by the Board of Elementary and Secondary Education.

SECTION 21
Public Service Commission

(A) Composition; Term; Domicile. There shall be a Public Service Commission in the executive branch. It shall consist of five members, who shall be elected for overlapping terms of six years at the time fixed for congressional elections from single member districts established by law. Each commissioner serving on the effective date of this constitution shall be the commissioner for the new district in which he resides and shall complete the term for which he was elected. The commission annually shall elect one member as chairman. It shall be domiciled at the state capital, but may meet, conduct investigations, and render orders elsewhere in this state.
(B) Powers and Duties. The commission shall regulate all common carriers and public utilities and have such other regulatory authority as provided by law. It shall adopt and enforce reasonable rules, regulations, and procedures necessary for the discharge of its duties, and shall have other powers and perform other duties as provided by law.
(C) Limitation. The commission shall have no power to regulate any common carrier or public utility owned, operated, or regulated on the effective date of this constitution by the governing authority of one or more political subdivisions, except by the approval of a majority of the electors voting in an election held for that purpose; however, a political subdivision may reinvest itself with such regulatory power in the manner in which it was surrendered. This Paragraph shall not apply to safety regulations pertaining to the operation of such utilities.
(D) Applications, Petitions, and Schedules; Protective Bond and Security.

(1) Within twenty days after a common carrier or public utility files a proposed rate schedule which would result in a change in rates, it shall give notice thereof by publication in the official state journal and in the official journal of each parish within the geographical area in which the schedule would become applicable.
(2) Within twelve months after the effective filing date, the commission shall render a full decision on each application, petition, and proposed rate schedule.
(3) After the effective filing date of any proposed schedule by a public utility which would result in a rate increase, the commission may permit the proposed schedule to be put into effect, in whole or in part, pending its decision on the application for rate increase and subject to protective bond or security approved by the commission. If no decision is rendered on the application within twelve months after such filing date, the proposed increase may be put into effect, but only if and as provided by law and subject to protective bond or security requirements, until final action by a court of last resort.

(4) If a proposed increase which has been put into effect is finally disallowed, in whole or in part, the utility shall make full refund, with legal interest thereon, within the time and in the manner prescribed by law.

(E) Appeals. Appeal may be taken in the manner provided by law by any aggrieved party or intervenor to the district court of the domicile of the commission. A right of direct appeal from any judgment of the district court shall be allowed to the supreme court. These rights of appeal shall extend to any action by the commission, including but not limited to action taken by the commission or by a public utility under the provisions of Subparagraph (3) of Paragraph (D) of this Section.

The 1974 Constitution enlarged the Public Service Commission from three to five members. It has the constitutional power to regulate "all common carriers and public utilities." Construing that language of section 21(B), the supreme court in *Cajun Electric Power Cooperative v. Louisiana Public Service Commission* (1989) held that rural electrification cooperatives were subject to the commission's jurisdiction despite legislation excluding them from that control.

The power granted in paragraph B to adopt and enforce reasonable rules was construed to be free of control by the legislature in *Louisiana Consumers League v. Louisiana Public Service Commission* (1977), a plurality of the supreme court holding that the Administrative Procedure Act did not apply to the commission. Nonetheless, the commission's rules are subject to review by the courts as to reasonableness.

Article V

Judicial Branch

Article V made few basic changes in the court system that existed in 1973. In some respects, this was unfortunate, for many reforms were desirable, including a truly integrated court system. Indeed, significant changes were needed by 1980, when amendments were adopted to give the courts of appeal jurisdiction in criminal cases.

The constitution established the structure of the court system and did not follow the federal pattern or the Model State Constitution, which allows legislative authority great flexibility in organizing and changing the system. The article that emerged from the constitutional convention was nonetheless an improvement over the previous constitution because it omitted much detail and gave the legislature more flexibility to change the system in a number of desirable ways.

SECTION 1
Judicial Power

The judicial power is vested in a supreme court, courts of appeal, district courts, and other courts authorized by this Article.

This section prevents the legislature from divesting the three named courts of their judicial power. It also limits the legislature in another way; judicial power can be vested only in courts "authorized by this Article." *Bordelon v. Louisiana*

Department of Corrections (1981) allows assignment of some court-related functions to magistrates and special masters not mentioned in this article "as long as the judges retain the responsibility for making ultimate decisions in the case."

Experts recommended a uniform three-tiered judicial system under which each district court would hear all cases arising within its territorial jurisdiction. Thepolitical risks of dismantling the existing specialized courts and courts of limited jurisdiction were so high that neither the Judiciary Committee nor the 1973 convention was willing to impose it. The compromise that emerged continues the existing courts of specialized and limited jurisdiction but restricts the establishment of similar ones in the future. The "other courts authorized by this Article" include the "family, juvenile, parish, city, and magistrate courts existing on the effective date of this constitution" mentioned in section 15. Section 20 adds "mayors' courts and justice of the peace courts existing on the effective date of this constitution." In New Orleans, section 32 applies, continuing "the city, municipal, traffic, and juvenile courts."

Although the constitution does allow much legislative flexibility in abolishing or merging these lower courts and allows their continuation until legislative action, no such new courts can be established by the legislature. The policy the committee recommended, and the convention accepted, was to allow the legislature to move to a uniform three-tiered or four-tiered court system.

SECTION 2
Habeas Corpus, Needful Writs, Orders and Process; Contempt

> A judge may issue writs of habeas corpus and all other needful writs, orders, and process in aid of the jurisdiction of his court. Exercise of this authority by a judge of the supreme court or of a court of appeal is subject to review by the whole court. The power to punish for contempt of court shall be limited by law.

The separation of powers doctrine adopted in Article II recognizes the existence of some inherent powers in the judiciary. These powers associated with the essence of the judicial function vest not in the supreme court alone but in all courts. Such would be the case without the constitution's saying more. This section, however, goes further and states the principle in specific language. The power extends even to city courts; the court in *City of Baton Rouge v. Ross* (1978) held that the city court had jurisdiction over a writ of habeas corpus alleging that a conviction obtained in that court was illegal.

Section 2 also continues the provision requiring that the power to punish for contempt be limited by law. That provision too reflects the view that the contempt power is inherent and could not be limited but for this authorization and mandate to do so. Considering the relationship of this section to the inherent powers concept, there is a basis for the chair of the judiciary committee's telling the convention that any legislative limitation of the contempt power be "reasonable."[13]

SECTION 3
Supreme Court; Composition; Judgments; Terms

The supreme court shall be composed of a chief justice and six associate justices, four of whom must concur to render judgment. The term of a supreme court justice shall be ten years.

The constitution continues the existence of the one supreme court of the state composed of seven justices. Although it does not require full court participation to decide a case, that is the likely effect since it does require that four judges must concur to render judgment. The prior constitution allowed the court to sit in divisions composed of three judges, but that provision was not continued. In an important political battle, the constitution reduced the term of a justice from fourteen to ten years.

SECTION 4
Supreme Court; Districts

The state shall be divided into at least six supreme court districts, and at least one judge shall be elected from each. The districts and the number of judges assigned to each on the effective date of this constitution are retained, subject to change by law enacted by two-thirds of the elected members of the legislature.

Section 4 allows the legislature to provide for single-member supreme court districts. Until such action, the existing six districts are maintained, five districts electing one judge each and the populous First District, composed of New Orleans and the surrounding parishes, electing two members to the court. The constitution does not enumerate the geographic area of each district as the prior constitution did, but any change in the composition of the existing districts requires a law enacted by a two-thirds vote of the elected membership of each house. The convention did not reapportion the districts according to population, nor did it require the legislature to do so.

Under the Judiciary Committee proposal, a provision like that of the prior constitution establishing staggered terms for supreme court judges was unnecessary since staggering would occur automatically as existing terms expired. Under that proposal, with its fourteen-year terms for supreme court judges, one seat on the court would be vacated every two years. Since the convention reduced

---

[13] VI Records, Aug. 15, 1973.

the judges' terms to ten years, however, and made no other provision for staggering terms, the stability resulting from having one judge elected every second year will no longer exist.

SECTION 5
Supreme Court; Jurisdiction; Rule-Making Power; Assignment of Judges

(A) Supervisory Jurisdiction; Rule-Making Power; Assignment of Judges. The supreme court has general supervisory jurisdiction over all the courts. It may establish procedural and administrative rules not in conflict with the law and may assign a sitting or retired judge to any court. The supreme court shall have sole authority to provide for by rule for appointments of attorneys as temporary or ad hoc judges of city, municipal, parish, juvenile, or family courts.
(B) Original Jurisdiction. The supreme court has exclusive original jurisdiction of disciplinary proceedings against a member of the bar.
(C) Scope of Review. Except as otherwise provided by this constitution, the jurisdiction of the supreme court in civil cases extends to both law and facts. In criminal matters, its appellate jurisdiction extends only to questions of law.
(D) Appellate Jurisdiction. In addition to other appeals provided by this constitution, a case shall be appealable to the supreme court if (1) a law or ordinance has been declared unconstitutional or (2) the defendant has been convicted of a capital offense and a penalty of death has been imposed.
(E) Additional Jurisdiction until July 1, 1982. In addition to the provisions of Section 5(D) and not withstanding the provisions of Section 5(D), or Sections 10(A)(3) and 10(C), the supreme court shall have exclusive appellate jurisdiction to decide criminal appeals where the defendant has been convicted of a felony or a fine exceeding five hundred dollars or imprisonment exceeding six months actually has been imposed, but only when an order of appeal has been entered prior to July 1, 1982 and shall have exclusive supervisory jurisdiction of all criminal writ applications relating to convictions and sentences imposed prior to July 1, 1982.
(F) Appellate Jurisdiction; Civil Cases; Extent. Subject to the provisions in Paragraph (C), the supreme court has appellate jurisdiction over all issues involved in a civil action properly before it. [The additional language in 5A and 5E comes from amendments—Acts 1987, No. 945 and Acts 1980, No. 843. The first was effective December 23, 1987, and the second was effective July 1, 1982.]

Supervisory Jurisdiction. Although the demands of localism are accommodated in the constitution by provisions making it difficult for the legislature to change the structure of the district courts, the necessity of centralized control over the operations of the lower courts is also accommodated. The constitution increases the power of the supreme court to exercise administrative control over the entire judicial system. Two groups of provisions in the constitution establish this power.

In Article II the constitution continues the division of governmental power into separate legislative, executive, and judicial branches and provides that no one branch shall exercise powers belonging to the others. Continuation of these provisions supports the existence of some inherent powers in the courts that the legislature and the executive cannot abridge. As the highest court, the supreme court is the final arbiter of the exercise of those inherent judicial powers. Although their extent is not defined, they include powers of administration, judicial review, control of officers of the court, and the contempt power.

Inherent powers also include power over officers of the court, among them attorneys. This had traditionally included control over admission to the bar and has been extended, in *Leenerts Farms v. Rogers* (1982), to prohibiting excessive attorney fees. In *Imbornone v. Early* (1981), it included assigning courtrooms to judges involved in a dispute over the means of handling overcrowded conditions in a courthouse.

In addition to the inherent powers, section 5(A) grants "general supervisory jurisdiction over all other courts." This is the basis for the supreme court's discretionary jurisdiction to review decisions of lower courts, as well as its administrative control over those courts.

The section provides the supreme court with a third type of power: it "may establish procedural and administrative rules not in conflict with law and may assign a sitting or retired judge to any court." In *State v. Petterway* (1981), the power to assign judges was held to include assignment of three court of appeal judges to sit with four members of the supreme court to hear criminal cases. *Babineawc v. Judiciary Commission* (1976) upheld a provision in the Canons of Judicial Ethics prohibiting judges from serving on the boards of directors of financial institutions. The canons were promulgated by the supreme court under its rule-making authority.

The last sentence of paragraph A was added by amendment in 1987 to allow temporary appointments of attorneys to the fourth-tier courts and courts of specialized jurisdiction. It was adopted to overcome the otherwise applicable requirement of section 22 that all judges be elected.

Original Jurisdiction. Under section 5(B) the court has exclusive original jurisdiction over disclipinary proceedings against attorneys. In addition, a number of provisions outside the judiciary article also provide for supreme court original jurisdiction of specific disputes. Under Article III, section 6, if the legislature fails to reapportion itself, "the supreme court, upon petition of any elector, shall re-apportion the representation in each house." In a dispute over the inability of a state official to serve, Article IV, section 17 provides that the supreme court shall determine the issue of inability to serve "by preference and with priority over all other matters." Section 25 of this article establishes the powers of the supreme court to discipline judges upon the recommendations of a judiciary commission.

Scope of Review. Section 5(C) continues Louisiana's unique appellate review of facts in civil cases. An attempt to abolish this broad scope of review, which derives from European procedure, was defeated by a vote of 18–96. The same appellate power is also continued for the courts of appeal. This review has traditionally encompassed facts determined by a judge or by a jury. Indeed, the constitution establishes no right to a jury trial in civil cases, except for the limited provision of Article I, section 4 in expropriations.

Review of facts includes changing the amount of awards for damages awarded in lower courts and in determining the relative fault of persons involved in tort litigation.

Review of facts can promote judicial efficiency. In *Giarratano v. Krewe of Argus, Inc.* (1984), for example, the court found the lower court erred in excluding the question of assumption of the risk from the jury. Rather than remanding for another jury to decide, the appellate court examined the appellate record and made its own determination of the extent of the risk that spectators assume at Mardi Gras parades. Appellate courts do, however, give deference to lower court factual findings and do not reverse unless they are "manifestly erroneous." Appeals from juvenile courts are considered civil matters, and *State in the Interest of Batiste* (1979) holds the court can review facts as well as law in such matters.

In criminal cases, review is limited to matters of law, as in the rest of the United States. It is recognized, however, that absence of adequate evidence to prove guilt is a question of law that can be reviewed. Indeed, by the U. S. Supreme Court decision in *Jackson v. Virginia* (1979), the state is required to make such a review. Article I, section 20 requires the courts to review criminal sentences to determine their excessiveness, in effect making such an inquiry a matter of law.

Appellate Jurisdiction. Sections (A) and (D) distinguish between the court's supervisory or discretionary jurisdiction and its appellate jurisdiction in which a party has a right to have the court hear a case. Paragraph D narrowed the scope of the appellate jurisdiction. When the constitution grants specific jurisdiction to the supreme court, the legislature is, of course, prohibited from depriving the court of that jurisdiction. It is less clear, however, whether the legislature by law can add to the supreme court's appellate jurisdiction. In *State v. James* (1976), the court indicated by a 4–3 vote that the legislature could not do so. It held unconstitutional a statute granting the state a right of appeal from a judgment sustaining a motion to quash an indictment. In *State v. Ijaz* (1983), only one judge dissented from a holding that the state could not appeal from a lower court grant of a defendant's motion in arrest of judgment. In such cases, however, the court may issue writs of review at its discretion.

The 1974 Constitution did not relieve the court of hearing appeals in cases where ordinances had been declared unconstitutional or from hearing appeals of right in most criminal cases. By 1980, the court's work load in handling criminal appeals was overwhelming, and the amendment to paragraph D was adopted to restrict the criminal appellate jurisdiction to cases in which the death penalty was imposed. Jurisdiction over other criminal appeals was transferred to the courts of appeal, as provided in section 10.

SECTION 6
Supreme Court; Chief Justice

The judge oldest in point of service on the supreme court shall be chief justice. He is the chief administrative officer of the judicial system of the state, subject to the rules adopted by the court.

The chief justice is denominated the administrator of the judicial system of the state, and not just the administrator of the supreme court. That power is another indication of the 1973 convention's aim of establishing a strong central authority to administer the entire court system. The acts of the chief justice in this regard are subject to being exercised according to rules adopted by the entire supreme court.

During the 1973 convention, the Judiciary Committee struggled with the method of selecting the chief justice. Many members were concerned that the existing seniority system had resulted in the unstable situation of having three chief justices in a ten-month period. Initially the committee opted for election of the chief justice by the members of the court, but Justice Frank W. Summers appeared before the committee and strongly urged retaining the seniority system to avoid infighting in the court and to minimize political influences on decision making. The committee reversed its position and adopted a modified seniority system under which the senior judge would become chief justice if below the age of 65 at the time a vacancy occurred. Ultimately the convention adopted an amendment deleting the 65-year limitation and continued the existing straight seniority system.

SECTION 7
Supreme Court; Personnel

The supreme court may select a judicial administrator, its clerks, and other personnel and prescribe their rules.

SECTION 8
Courts of Appeal; Circuits; Panels; Judgments; Terms

(A) Circuits; Panels.The state shall be divided into at least four circuits, with one court of appeal in each. Each court shall sit in panels of at least three judges selected according to rules adopted by the court.
(B) Judgments. A majority of the judges sitting in a case must concur to render a judgment. However in civil matters only, when a judgment of a district court is to be modified or reversed and one judge dissents, the case shall be reargued before a panel of at least five judges prior to rendition of judgment, and a majority must concur to render judgment.
(C) Terms. The term of a court of appeal judge shall be ten years.

By requiring the state to be divided into at least four circuits, with one court of appeal in each, this section prevents the establishment of one statewide court of appeal. It also allows the legislature to establish additional courts and circuits within courts as the caseload requires. The new document deletes much of the detail of the prior constitution; it does not state the domicile of the appellate courts, does not require them to sit at a designated domicile, and does not provide the length of the sessions of those courts. Such matters are left to legislation and rules of court.

The constitution establishes no procedural limitations on the manner in which the supreme court exercises its power to review facts in civil cases. However, when the convention later considered the courts of appeal, further attempts were made to abolish review of facts by those courts. Those amendments were defeated, but a compromise was adopted to limit the manner in which the courts of appeal exercise this power. The language of that amendment, however, went further than governing review of facts and required, in section (B), a special reargument whenever a district court judgment is to be modified or reversed and one judge dissents. In such reversals or modifications when one judge dissents, the case is reargued before a panel of at least five judges prior to rendition of judgment. The 1980 amendment made clear that the reargument is not required in criminal cases.

Under the prior constitution, the term of a court of appeal judge was twelve years; the 1974 Constitution reduced that to ten years, the same as for justices of the supreme court.

SECTION 9
Courts of Appeal; Circuits and Districts

Each circuit shall be divided into at least three districts, and at least one judge shall be elected from each. The circuits and districts and number of judges as elected in each circuit on the effective date of this constitution are retained, subject to change by law enacted by two-thirds of the elected members of each house of the legislature.

SECTION 10
Courts of Appeal; Jurisdiction

(A) Jurisdiction. Except as otherwise provided by this constitution, a court of appeal has appellate jurisdiction of (1) all civil matters, (2) all matters appealed from family and juvenile courts, and (3) all criminal cases triable by a jury, except as provided in Section 5, Paragraph (D)(2) of this article. It has supervisory jurisdiction over cases which arise in its circuit.

(B) Scope of Review. Except as limited to questions of law by this constitution, or as provided by law in the review of administrative agency determinations, appellate jurisdiction of a court of appeal extends to law and facts. In criminal cases, its appellate jurisdiction extends only to questions of law.

(C) Other Criminal Matters. In criminal cases not provided for in Paragraph (D)(2) or Paragraph (E) of Section 5, a defendant has a right of appeal or review, as provided by law.

The 1974 Constitution gave the courts of appeal jurisdiction only in civil cases. A 1980 amendment added paragraph A(3) to give them jurisdiction of appeals of criminal cases triable by a jury in which the possible penalty is greater than $500 or six months' imprisonment.

The constitution does not explicitly provide for the means of appellate review of convictions of minor offenses—those for which the possible punishment is less than $500 or six months' imprisonment. Originally section 5(E) simply stated that in such cases, a defendant has a right of appeal or review, as provided by law. The 1980 amendment transferred that provision to section 10(C). Providing some type of review of misdemeanor convictions in which no right of appeal was granted did cause difficulty. The Judiciary Committee's first draft proposal made no provision for review of such cases. That failure caused some concern about inadequate protection of individual rights and a later draft added, "In other criminal cases, an accused shall have a right of appeal or review as provided by law or by rule of the supreme court not inconsistent therewith." This was changed by floor amendment to delete the power of the supreme court to provide for such review by rule, thus requiring that the appeal or review mechanism be provided by law.

The limited nature of the right of appeal or review in these minor criminal cases prompted further action when the convention was considering the bill of rights. Additional protection for the individual in such cases is provided in Article I, section 19: "No person shall be subjected to imprisonment or forfeiture of rights or property without the right of judicial review based upon a complete record of all evidence upon which the judgment is based."

The commentary following section 5(C) contains a general discussion of the power to review facts. It is somewhat anomalous that the legislature is granted the power to limit review of facts by courts of appeal but not by the supreme court in the same class of cases. An attempt to eliminate the anomaly by deleting the legislative authority with respect to the courts of appeal was defeated.

SECTION 11
Courts of Appeal; Certification

A court of appeal may certify any question of law before it to the supreme court, and the supreme court then may give its binding instruction or decide the case upon the record.

SECTION 12
Courts of Appeal; Chief Judge

The judge oldest in point of service on each court shall be chief judge of that court and shall administer the court subject to the rules adopted by it.

Concern with efficient court administration did not end with the supreme court. Section 12 was a new provision providing that the senior judge of each court of appeal shall be chief judge of that court. The prior law did not contain that statement of administrative duties, and the convention defeated by a vote of 12–99 an amendment that sought to delete the reference to the administrative role of the chief judge.

SECTION 13
Courts of Appeal; Personnel

Each court of appeal may select its clerk and other personnel and prescribe their duties.

SECTION 14
District Courts; Judicial Districts

The state shall be divided into judicial districts, each composed of at least one parish and served by at least one district judge.

The whole state must be divided into judicial districts, each composed of at least one parish and served by at least one district judge. Although the convention did omit the detailed listing of the area of each district, it made changes in those districts more difficult. Under section 15(B), the legislature may not make the changes without approval in a referendum in each affected district and parish.

By its silence on the subject, the constitution allows the legislature to exercise its discretion in devising a system for electing district judges. It is free to continue the existing system of having candidates compete in divisions with the winner in each division being elected or to change the process.

The number of judges attached to each district court is not specified in the constitution, though the document continues the existing number of judges in each district, subject to change by law enacted by two-thirds vote of the elected membership of each house of the legislature.

SECTION 15
Courts; Retention; Jurisdiction; Judicial District Changes; Terms

(A) Court Retention; Trial Courts of Limited Jurisdiction. The district, family, juvenile, parish, city, municipal, and magistrate courts existing on the effective date of this constitution are retained. Subject to the limitation in Sections 16 and 21 of this Article, the legislature by law may abolish or merge trial courts of limited or specialized jurisdiction. The legislature by law may establish trial courts of limited jurisdiction with parishwide territorial jurisdiction and subject matter jurisdiction which shall be uniform throughout the state. The office of city marshal is continued until the city court he serves is abolished.

(B) Judicial Districts. The judicial districts existing on the effective date of this constitution are retained. Subject to the limitation in Section 21 of this Article, the legislature by law may establish, divide, or merge judicial districts with the approval in a referendum in each district and parish affected.

(C) Term. The term of a district, parish, or city court judge shall be six years.

(D) Number of Judges. The legislature may change the number of judges in any judicial district by law enacted by two-thirds of the elected members of each house.

The only new courts of limited jurisdiction that can be established are those that the constitution authorizes in section 15(A)—those with parishwide territorial jurisdiction and subject matter jurisdiction uniform throughout the state.

SECTION 16
District Courts; Jurisdiction

(A) Original Jurisdiction. Except as otherwise authorized in this constitution, a district court shall have original jurisdiction of all civil and criminal matters. It shall have exclusive original jurisdiction of felony cases and of cases involving title to immovable property; the right to office and other public positions; civil or political rights; probate or succession matters; the state, a political corporation, or political subdivisions, or a succession, as a defendant; and the appointment of receivers or liquidators for corporations or partnerships.

(B) Appellate Jurisdiction. A district court shall have appellate jurisdiction as provided by law.

The district courts continue to be the basic courts of original jurisdiction, with power to hear "all civil and criminal matters." It is a broad grant of jurisdiction consistent with the committee purpose of allowing the legislature to convert the judicial system to a three-tiered one in which no courts of original jurisdiction other than the district courts would exist.

The constitution itself lists the types of cases in which the district courts have exclusive original jurisdiction. This approach makes it clear that such cases cannot be included by law in the jurisdiction of courts of limited or specialized original jurisdiction. Matters not within this listing are not exclusive to the district courts; the legislature can grant courts of limited or specialized jurisdiction concurrent jurisdiction over those matters.

SECTION 17
District Courts; Chief Judge

Each district court shall elect from its members a chief judge who shall exercise, for a term designated by the court, the administrative functions prescribed by rule of court.

Concern for administration on the district court level is shown in the new requirement that each district court elect a chief judge to exercise administrative functions. The position is a new one in the constitution, one that did not involve existing expectations of reaching that office, as was the case with the chief justice and chief judge of a court of appeal. Thus, it was easier for the 1973 convention to accept the Judiciary Committee's recommendation that the position be filled by election.

SECTION 18
Juvenile and Family Courts; Jurisdiction

Notwithstanding any contrary provision of Section 16 of this Article, juvenile and family courts shall have jurisdiction as provided by law.

SECTION 19
Special Juvenile Procedures

The determination of guilt or innocence, the detention, and the custody of a person who is alleged to have committed a crime prior to his seventeenth birthday shall be pursuant to special juvenile procedures which shall be provided by law. However, the legislature may (1) by a two-thirds vote of the elected members of each house provide that special juvenile procedures shall not apply to juveniles arrested for having committed first or second degree murder, manslaughter, aggravated rape, armed robbery, aggravated burglary or aggravated kidnapping, and (2) by two-thirds vote of the elected members of each house lower the maximum ages of persons to whom juvenile procedures shall apply, and (3) by two-thirds vote of the elected members of each house establish a procedure by which the court of original jurisdiction may waive special juvenile procedures in order that adult procedures shall apply in individual cases. The legislature, by a majority of the elected members of each house, shall make special provisions for detention and custody of juveniles who are subject to the jurisdiction of the district court pending determination of guilt or innocence.

Sections 18 and 19 were adopted after bitter floor fights during the 1973 convention. Floor amendments were introduced to attempt to preserve the concept of juvenile courts as institutions, but they were defeated, and a requirement of special procedures for juveniles was adopted instead. The approach adopted gives protection to juveniles while not fragmenting the court system. Separate courts would lessen the flexibility of assignment of judges and arrangement of work load that is possible when only one district court hears all types of cases.

The concept that the constitution adopts prevents new specialized courts but does not prevent district courts or parish courts from being organized into specialized divisions. If the desirability of specialization by judges is recognized, this can be accommodated by having such judges assigned primarily to specialized divisions. These judges would still be available for assignment and rotation to other divisions of the court depending on the work load in the different divisions.

SECTION 20
Mayors' Courts; Justice of the Peace Courts

Mayors' courts and justice of the peace courts existing on the effective date of this constitution are continued, subject to change by law.

SECTION 21
Judges; Decrease in Terms and Compensation Prohibited

The term of office, retirement benefits, and compensation of a judge shall not be decreased during the term for which he is elected.

SECTION 22
Judges; Election; Vacancy

(A) Election. Except as otherwise provided in this Section, all judges shall be elected. Election shall be at the regular congressional election.
(B) Vacancy. A newly-created judgeship or a vacancy in the office of a judge shall be filled by special election called by the governor and held within twelve months after the day on which the vacancy occurs or the judgeship is established, except when the vacancy occurs in the last twelve months of an existing term. Until the vacancy is filled, the supreme court shall appoint a person meeting the qualifications for the office, other than domicile, to serve at its pleasure. The appointee shall be ineligible as a candidate at the election to fill the vacancy or the newly created judicial office. No person serving as an appointed judge, other than a retired judge, shall be eligible for retirement benefits provided for the elected judiciary.
(C) End of Term. A judge serving on the effective date of this constitution shall serve through December thirty-first of the last year of his term or, if the last year of his term

is not in the year of a regular congressional election, then through December thirty-first of the following year. The election for the next term shall be held in the year in which the term expires, as provided above.

Section 22(A) requires that all judges be elected, making exception only for the temporary filling of vacancies by appointment. The judicial elections continue to be held at the time of the regular congressional elections, separating the judicial contests from the races for the bulk of local and state offices. Another exception to the election requirement resulted from a 1987 amendment to section 5(A) allowing the supreme court to appoint attorneys as temporary judges of courts of limited jurisdiction.

During the 1973 convention, the Judiciary Committee heard a great deal of testimony from proponents of merit selection of judges and was aware of the close vote favoring merit selection in a poll of members of the Louisiana Bar Association that disclosed strong sentiment for merit selection in Orleans Parish. However, of the 34 judicial districts from which responses were received, only 4 favored merit selection. On the other side, Chief Justice Joe W. Sanders and former Chief Justice John B. Fournet, among others, advocated election of judges, Sanders telling the committee that the Missouri plan (appointment from a list of nominees) "in my opinion, does not eliminate politics in judicial selection but narrows it to a small group."

Although the committee spent much time hearing testimony on the issue, the result in favor of election was a foregone conclusion. The basic populist orientation of the convention tended toward a greater voice for the people and a resistance to gubernatorial or small-group power. A convention that resisted reducing the number of statewide elected officials and was intent on shortening the terms of appellate judges was not likely to abolish election of judges. A floor amendment that did not require but simply authorized the legislature to adopt a merit selection plan was overwhelmingly defeated by a vote of 26–87.

The convention strengthened the institution of an elected judiciary in its provisions for filling vacancies and newly created judgeships. Although Louisiana has traditionally provided for election of judges, a substantial number of judges first reached the bench by gubernatorial appointment to fill a vacancy or a new judgeship. With an incumbent's advantage, the appointee was likely to be elected in the ensuing election, if opposed at all. One delegate estimated that 60 percent of the sitting judges were initially appointed by the governor.[14] The new constitution terminated the prior practice.

Under section 22(B), a newly created judgeship or a vacancy is filled by appointment by the supreme court until a special election is held. The appointee, who need not be a judge, must meet the qualifications of the office other than domicile and serves at the court's pleasure. Not only is the governor's power of

[14] R. Harmon Drew, VI Records: Convention Transcripts, Aug. 18, 1973.

appointment ended, but to abolish the advantage the appointee might have in an election to fill the vacancy, it is provided that the appointee is ineligible as a candidate at the election to fill the vacancy or the newly created judgeship.

Little opposition developed to the committee's proposal to remove the power of the governor to make these appointments, and the delegates who were allies of Governor Edwin W. Edwards made no strong effort to oppose the change. The attempt to continue the old system was sponsored by black delegates who saw it as a mechanism to obtain more black judges. They argued that minority group members would be unlikely to be elected as judges but that some blacks could and would be appointed by governors to vacant or new judgeships.

The purpose of section 22(C) was to remove an anomaly under the prior law under which the term of a court of appeal judge would end in an odd-numbered year but the election for the subsequent term would be held at the congressional election of the preceding year. This could lead to a defeated judge's continuing to serve for more than a year past defeat.

SECTION 23
Judges; Retirement

(A) Retirement System. Within two years after the effective date of this constitution, the legislature shall provide for a retirement system for judges which shall apply to judges taking office after the effective date of the law enacting the system and in which a judge in office at that time may elect to become a member, with credit for all prior years of judicial service and without contribution therefor. The retirement benefits, and judicial service rights of a judge in office or retired on the effective date of this constitution shall not be diminished, nor shall the benefits to which a surviving spouse is entitled be reduced.
(B) Mandatory Retirement. Except as otherwise provided in this Section, a judge shall not remain in office beyond his seventieth birthday.

The prior constitution contained a detailed retirement system for judges, one that required no contribution by them but lacked many benefits common to most modern pension systems. In the 1973 convention, the committee proposed a new system that required contribution and established more liberal benefits. Strong opposition to the proposal developed, led by the chairman of the convention and the governor. The crucial vote on an amendment to delete the detailed plan was 58–57. The section that was adopted instead simply mandates the legislature to enact a new retirement system for judges that must grant credit for prior service without contribution.

Section 23 also establishes mandatory retirement for judges at age 70, a reduction from a mandatory retirement age of 75 under the prior law. The supreme court has authority under section 5, however, to assign a retired judge to any court.

The mandatory retirement age of 70 applies only to judges who assumed office after January 1, 1975, the effective date of the 1974 Constitution. Judges already in office are protected by Section 23(A), which provides that their "judicial service rights . . . shall not be diminished." Some judges could continue in office under some circumstances to age 80 under a provision of the prior constitution, which provided that some judges could serve to that age if necessary for them to serve twenty years, when their retirement benefits would have vested.The supreme court, in *In re Levy* (1983), involuntarily retired a judge who reached the age of 80 and refused to step down.

SECTION 24
Judges; Qualifications

A judge of the supreme court, a court of appeal, district court, family court, a parish court, or court having sole juvenile jurisdiction shall have been admitted to the practice of law in this state for at least five years prior to his election, and shall have been domiciled in the respective district, circuit, or parish for the two years preceding election. He shall not practice law.

Section 24 establishes uniform qualifications for judges of the main components of the judicial system and prevents them from practicing law. The section does not apply to city court judges, who were deliberately omitted from the listing. Although a number of committee members thought it desirable that city court judges be full time and not engage in law practice, such a provision might have had a drastic effect on the smaller city courts. It is also the expectation that city courts will be phased out and either incorporated into district courts or changed into parish courts.

SECTION 25
Judiciary Commission

(A) Composition. The judiciary commission shall consist of

(1) one court of appeal judge and two district court judges selected by the supreme court;

(2) two attorneys admitted to the practice of law for at least ten years and one attorney admitted to the practice of law for at least three years but not more than ten years, selected by the Conference of Court of Appeal Judges or its successor. They shall not be judges, active or retired, or public officials, other than notaries public; and

(3) three citizens, not lawyers, judges active or retired, or public officials, selected by the Louisiana District Judges' Association or its successor.

(B) Term; Vacancy. A member of the commission shall serve a four-year term and shall be ineligible to succeed himself. His term shall end upon the occurrence of any event which would have made him ineligible for appointment.

When a vacancy occurs, a successor shall be appointed for a four-year term by the authority which appointed his predecessor.

(C) Powers. On recommendation of the judiciary commission, the supreme court may censure, suspend with or without salary, remove from office, or retire involuntarily a judge for willful misconduct relating to his official duty, willful and persistent failure to perform his duty, persistent and public conduct prejudicial to the administration of justice that brings the judicial office into disrepute, conduct while in office which would constitute a felony, or conviction of a felony. On recommendation of the judiciary commission, the supreme court may disqualify a judge from exercising any judicial function, without loss of salary, during pendency of proceedings in the supreme court. On recommendation of the judiciary commission, the supreme court may retire involuntarily a judge for disability that seriously interferes with the performance of his duties and that is or is likely to become permanent. The supreme court shall make rules implementing this Section and providing for confidentiality and privilege of commission proceedings.

(D) Other Disciplinary Action. Action against a judge under this Section shall not preclude disciplinary action against him concerning his license to practice law.

A judge is subject to impeachment under Article X, section 24, based on "commission or conviction, during his term of office, of a felony or for malfeasance or gross misconduct while in such office." Judges, however, are excepted from removal by suit under Article X, section 25 or by recall elections under Article X, section 26. The alternate means for disciplining judges is provided in this section: discipline by the supreme court on recommendation of a judiciary commission.

The 1973 convention accepted the committee proposal to enlarge the existing judiciary commission from seven to nine members and to provide more citizen and lawyer representation. Judges constituted four of the seven members of the old commission; under the new panel, judges account for three of the nine members, along with three attorneys and three nonlawyers.

Continued as grounds for discipline are "willful misconduct relating to his official duty" and "persistent failure to perform his duty." The prior ground, "conviction, while in office, of a felony," is expanded to encompass "conduct while in office which would constitute a felony," as well as "conviction of a felony" regardless of the time the conviction or the conduct occurred. The convention adopted a new ground for discipline based on less serious infractions: "persistent and public conduct prejudicial to the administration of justice that brings the judicial office into disrepute."

Section 25 is more flexible than its predecessor in that it expands the range of disciplinary sanctions. It continues the prior sanctions of removal from office and involuntary retirement but adds provisions for censure and suspension from performance of duties with or without salary. Another innovation allows disqualification of a judge from exercising any judicial function, without loss of salary, during the pendency of proceedings in the supreme court. The supreme court exercised in that power to suspend a judge while charges were pending in *In re Whitaker* (1984).

New in the section is provision for situations in which a judge, though committing no act of misconduct, suffers from some "disability that seriously interferes with the performance of his duties and that is or is likely to become permanent." In such a case, the judge may be retired involuntarily.

SECTION 26
District Attorneys

(A) Election; Qualifications; Assistants. In each judicial district a district attorney shall be elected for a term of six years. He shall have been admitted to the practice of law in the state for at least five years prior to his election and shall have resided in the district for the two years preceding election. A district attorney may select assistants as authorized by law, and other personnel.
(B) Powers. Except as otherwise provided by this constitution, a district attorney, or his designated assistant, shall have charge of every criminal prosecution by the state in his district, be the representative of the state before the grand jury in his district, and be the legal advisor to the grand jury. He shall perform other duties provided by law.
(C) Prohibition. No district attorney or assistant district attorney shall appear, plead, or in any other way defend or assist in defending any criminal prosecution or charge. A violation of this Paragraph shall be cause for removal.

The district attorney is a constitutional officer, one elected in each judicial district for a term of six years. The qualifications for the office parallel those of judges: admitted to the practice of law for five years preceding election and residence in the district for two years. The Judiciary Committee did not specify the powers and duties of the office (the prior constitution had not either). The 1983 convention, on the other hand, did adopt an amendment stating the powers and duties of the office, borrowing language of the Code of Criminal Procedure.

The introductory exception clause in paragraph B was included to make it clear that the attorney general, after he supersedes a district attorney as provided in Article IV, section 8, will have charge of criminal prosecutions.

The provision adopted in the 1973 convention gave the district attorney charge of "every criminal prosecution in his district." An amendment changed the phrase to read instead, "prosecution by the state in his district," to make clear he or she would not have charge of prosecutions by municipalities and other subdivisions of the state. The provision does not require that the district attorney prosecute all cases involving state law. Others, including city prosecutors, can be allowed to do so, so long as the district attorney retains control of the course of the prosecution.

Paragraph C does not prevent a district attorney from practicing law and handling civil matters. An amendment to prohibit all law practice by district attorneys failed, though the debate makes it clear that the legislature can impose that restriction in the future.

SECTION 27
Sheriffs

In each parish a sheriff shall be elected for a term of four years. He shall be the chief law enforcement officer in the parish, except as otherwise provided by this constitution, and shall execute court orders and process. He shall be the collector of state and parish ad valorem taxes and such other taxes and license fees as provided by law. This section shall not apply to Orleans Parish.

As officials elected to serve in a parish, sheriffs might well have been assigned to the Committee on Local and Parochial Government; however, since the 1921 Constitution included sheriffs in Article VII on the judiciary and the Judiciary Committee was allotted jurisdiction of all of that article by convention rules, provisions relating to sheriffs were drafted by that committee. Consideration by the Judiciary Committee was not opposed by the politically powerful sheriffs, who had two of their number represented on that committee.

Section 27, which provides for one sheriff in each parish and states the duties, does not by its terms apply to Orleans Parish. There the existing civil and criminal sheriffs (without law enforcement and tax collecting duties) are continued by section 32.

The new language making the sheriff responsible for enforcement of court orders and process was proposed by the committee and raised little controversy. As adopted, the unqualified provision makes the sheriff's obligation extend to executing the orders and process of any court. This relationship to the district courts and the appellate courts is clear. However, the sheriff's role in executing orders of courts below the district court level is less clear. Article V, section 15 continues the office of city marshal until a city court he serves is abolished. Continuing the marshal, who serves to enforce orders and process of city courts, contemplates no doubt his having duties somewhat similar to those under existing law, including serving process and executing orders.

New is the provision naming the sheriff the chief law enforcement officer in the parish. The contours of this power are vague, but neither the committee debates nor the 1973 convention debates suggest that the sheriff will be the exclusive law enforcement agent. During its deliberations, the committee had before it the existing statutory provisions dealing with activities of the state police in municipalities, and there was no apparent sentiment to restrict the state police further or to abolish municipal law enforcement agencies.

SECTION 28
Clerks of Court

(A) Powers and Duties. In each parish a clerk of the district court shall be elected for a term of four years. He shall be ex officio notary public and parish recorder of conveyances, mortgages, and other acts, and shall have other duties and powers as provided by law. The clerk may appoint deputies with duties and powers as provided by law and, with the approval of the district judges, he may appoint minute clerks with duties and powers provided by law.
(B) Office Hours. The legislature shall establish uniform statewide office hours for clerks of the district courts.

The clerk of the district court is continued as a constitutional officer. Section 28 also indicates that a clerk in each parish functions as recorder of conveyances, mortgages, and other acts. Article 32, however, keeps separate clerks for the civil and criminal courts in New Orleans, as well as a separate register of conveyances and recorder of mortgages.

New is the requirement that mandates the legislature to establish uniform statewide office hours for clerks of the district court. The 1973 convention adopted the provision in response to complaints by lawyers about lack of uniformity. The Clerk of Court Association endorsed this provision, and the convention rejected an amendment to delete the requirement.

SECTION 29
Coroners

In each parish a coroner shall be elected for a term of four years. He shall be a licensed physician and possess the other qualifications and perform the duties provided by law. The requirement that he be a licensed physician shall be inapplicable in any parish in which no physician will accept the office.

The coroner remains a constitutional officer to be elected in each parish for a four-year term. The constitution, however, no longer states duties for the office; they are simply those provided by law. Deleted were the provisions of the 1921 Constitution making the coroner the successor upon a vacancy in the office of sheriff. To allow the legislature more flexibility in providing for expert determination of forensic medicine problems that could arise in relation to court operations, the committee also proposed to delete the requirement that the coroner be a licensed physician. The convention, however, at the urging of a physician-delegate, reinstated the provision of the 1921 document that the coroner must be a licensed physician if one is willing to serve.

SECTION 30
Vacancies

When a vacancy occurs in the following offices, the duties of the office, until it is filled by election as provided by law, shall be assumed by the persons herein designated: (1) sheriff, by the chief criminal deputy; (2) district attorney, by the first assistant district attorney; (3) clerk of a district court, by the chief deputy; (4) coroner, by the chief deputy. If there is no such person to assume the duties when the vacancy occurs, the governing authority or authorities of the parish or parishes concerned shall appoint a qualified person to assume the duties of office until filled by election.

The governor's power to fill vacancies in the offices of sheriff, district attorney, clerk, and coroner ended with adoption of this section. It provides that until the vacancies are filled by election as provided by law, the duties of those offices shall be assumed by the chief assistant.

SECTION 31
Reduction of Salaries and Benefits Prohibited

The salary and retirement benefits of an attorney general, district attorney, sheriff, coroner, or clerk of the district court shall not be diminished duringhis term of office.

SECTION 32
Orleans Parish Courts; Officials

Except for provisions relating to terms of office as provided elsewhere in this Article, and notwithstanding any other contrary provision of this constitution, the following courts and officers in Orleans Parish are continued, subject to change by law: the civil and criminal district courts; the city, municipal, traffic, and juvenile courts; the clerks of the civil and criminal district courts; the civil and criminal sheriffs; the constables and the clerks of the first and second city courts; the register of conveyances; and the recorder of mortgages.

Section 16 provides the jurisdiction of all the district courts, making no exception for Orleans Parish, where separate criminal and civil district courts have long existed. This section, however, does continue the existence of the separate criminal and civil district courts until merged by law. In effect, the Orleans district is being served by one district court that is by constitutional provision continued as separate civil and criminal divisions until merged by an act of the legislature.

Organization of the Orleans courts was the issue that occupied the most time in the Judiciary Committee and provoked the most controversy during the 1973 convention. To placate the Orleans interests, the committee did not urge merger and in fact proposed making merger quite difficult by requiring approval of the legislature and a referendum in Orleans Parish. The convention would not give such strong protection to the status quo. It rejected the committee proposal, first in favor of requiring a two-thirds vote to change the existing Orleans courts and then in favor of permitting change simply by law, meaning the normal legislative majority vote. The legislature's power in this regard was upheld in *State v. Francois* (1983), in which the criminal court was required to take jurisdiction of the "civil" commitment under the mental health laws of a person acquitted of a crime because of insanity.

The convention's action reflected dissatisfaction with the nonuniform structure of Orleans courts. That dissatisfaction was also reflected in the reduction of the term of Orleans district judges from twelve to six years, thus giving them the same terms as the district judges serving the rest of the state. Other than section 32, the constitution does not contain provisions unique to the Orleans district courts. This approach is quite different from the 1921 Constitution, which contained several sections devoted to establishing detailed rules for the Orleans courts that were often different from those applicable to the rest of the state.

SECTION 33
Jurors

(A) Qualifications. A citizen of the state who has reached the age of majority is eligible to serve as a juror within the parish in which he is domiciled. The legislature may provide additional qualifications.
(B) Exemptions. The supreme court shall provide by rule for exemption of jurors.

The constitution deletes the previous requirement that a woman would not be considered for jury service unless she filed with the clerk of court a declaration of her desire to be called.

The Judiciary Committee had proposed to give the supreme court power to determine "qualifications and exemption of jurors. " The 1973 convention instead established the minimum requirements in the constitution and provided that the legislature could enact additional qualifications. However, the convention did concur in removing from the legislature and placing in the supreme court the power to provide for exemptions from jury service. Ambroise H. Landry, a member of the committee and a clerk of court experienced with jury selection, pointed out to the convention that existing legislative exemptions excluded from jury service large numbers of the best-qualified people. It was thought that the supreme court would be less sensitive to interest group pressure for exemptions and that it would provide for fewer of them. The court has done so in Rule 25. An exemption is personal and must be claimed. When jury commissioners removed from the venire the names of persons who had not claimed an exemption, the jury was not properly selected, and a conviction was overturned (*State v. Procell*, 1976).

SECTION 34
Grand Jury

(A) Grand Jury. There shall be a grand jury or grand juries in each parish, whose qualifications, duties, and responsibilities shall be provided by law. The secrecy of the proceedings, including the identity of witnesses, shall be provided by law.
(B) Right to Counsel. The legislature may establish by law terms and conditions under which a witness may have the right to advice of counsel while testifying before the grand jury.

Section 34 does not continue the detail of the predecessor provision regulating the number of jurors required, the number required to indict, the term of the grand jury, and the times for empanelment. Article I, section 15 specifies the cases in which indictment is required (crimes punishable by death or by life imprisonment).

Early in the 1973 convention, a floor amendment was adopted to provide a right to counsel to all persons testifying before a grand jury. Opposition to the provision developed, particularly from district attorneys, and because the convention was coming to an end, the self-enforcing provision was deleted and replaced with the mild legislative mandate of section 34(B).

Article VI

Local Government

Louisiana traditionally followed Dillon's Rule under which local governments were creatures of the state with limited powers; they exercised only the authority the legislature granted them. Over the years, constitutional provisions and amendments granted New Orleans and some other cities home rule charters that gave them broader powers free of legislative control. Continuing in that trend toward greater local government autonomy, the Committee on Local Government in the 1973 Constitutional Convention sought to reverse Dillon's Rule so that local governments could do anything not prohibited by the state government. The provisions that were finally adopted, however, are not simple. After a number of political compromises were adopted, the constitution established four categories of local government units, with varying powers:

1. Section 4 allows units with home rule charters under prior constitutions to continue to operate under those charters. They have the rights afforded by both the 1921 and 1974 constitutions.
2. Section 5 authorizes the adoption of new home rule charters that grant any power not denied by general law.
3. Section 7 allows local government units without home rule charters, upon a vote of the people allowing it, to exercise any power not denied by general law.
4. Units without home rule charters that have not taken advantage of section 7 are subject to their legislative charters and greater legislative control.

PART I. GENERAL PROVISIONS

SECTION 1
Parishes

(A) Parishes and Boundaries Ratified. Parishes and their boundaries as established on the effective date of this constitution are recognized and ratified.
(B) Creation; Dissolution; Merger; Boundaries. The legislature by law may establish and organize new parishes, dissolve and merge parishes, and change parish boundaries if approved by two-thirds of the electors in each parish affected voting thereon at an election held for that purpose.
(C) Change of Parish Seat. The governing authority of a parish may call an election on the question of changing the parish seat. The parish seat shall be changed if approved by two-thirds of the electors voting thereon.
(D) Adjustment of Assets and Liabilities. When a parish is enlarged or established from contiguous territory, it shall be entitled to a just proportion of the property and assets and shall be liable for a just proportion of the existing debts and liabilities of the parish or parishes from which the territory is taken.

The basic local governmental entity is the parish, Louisiana's equivalent of counties in most other states. Change in the territory of any of the state's 64 parishes is quite difficult: a two-thirds majority of the voters in each parish affected is required, in addition to legislative action. Change in the designation of the parish seat is also difficult: a two-thirds vote of the voters in the parish.

SECTION 2
Municipalities

The legislature shall provide by general law for the incorporation, consolidation, merger, and government of municipalities. No local or special law shall create a municipal corporation or amend, modify, or repeal a municipal charter. However, a special legislative charter existing on the effective date of this constitution may be amended, modified, or repealed by local or special law.

Although this section does provide for substantial state control over cities as a general proposition, New Orleans and the larger cities in the state are governed by home rule charters and are protected in sections 4 and 5.

SECTION 3
Classification

The legislature may classify parishes or municipalities according to population or on any other reasonable basis related to the purpose of the classification. Legislation may be limited in its effect to any of such class or classes.

Louisiana statutes for generations provided general rules that excepted New Orleans. Special rules for the state's largest city are hardly done away with in the 1974 Constitution, but the 1973 convention made a deliberate effort to avoid the usual formula. Section 3, however, by making it clear that legislation may classify cities or parishes according to population, continues to allow the practice of treating New Orleans differently, as well as allowing other classifications based on population.

SECTION 4
Existing Home Rule Charters and Plans of Government

Every home rule charter or plan of government existing or adopted when this constitution is adopted shall remain in effect and may be amended, modified, or repealed as provided therein. Except as inconsistent with this constitution, each local governmental subdivision which has adopted such a home rule charter or plan of government shall retain the powers, functions, and duties in effect when this constitution is adopted. If its charter permits, each of them also shall have the right to powers and functions granted to other local governmental subdivisions.

SECTION 5
Home Rule Charter

(A) Authority to Adopt; Commission. Subject to and not inconsistent with this constitution, any local governmental subdivision may draft, adopt, or amend a home rule charter in accordance with this Section. The governing authority of a local governmental subdivision may appoint a commission to prepare and propose a charter or an alternate charter, or it may call an election to elect such a commission.

(B) Petition to Elect Commission. The governing authority shall call an election to elect such a commission when presented with a petition signed by not less than ten percent of the electors or ten thousand electors, whichever is fewer, who live within the boundaries of the affected subdivision, as certified by the registrar of voters.

(C) Adoption; Amendment; Repeal. A home rule charter shall be adopted, amended, or repealed when approved by a majority of the electors voting thereon at an election held for that purpose.

(D) Adoption by Two or More Local Governmental Subdivisions. Two or more local governmental subdivisions within the boundaries of one parish may adopt a home rule charter under this Section if approved by a majority of the electors in each affected local governmental subdivision voting thereon in an election held for that purpose. The legislature shall provide by lawthe method of appointment or election of a commission to prepare and propose a charter consistent with Paragraph (A) of this Section and the method by which the electors may petition for an election consistent with Paragraph (B) of this Section. However, at least one member of the commission shall be elected or appointed from each affected local governmental subdivision.

(E) Structure and Organization; Powers; Functions. A home rule charter adopted under this Section shall provide the structure and organization, powers, and functions of the government of the local governmental subdivision, which may include the exercise of any power and performance of any function necessary, requisite, or proper for the management of its affairs, not denied by general law or inconsistent with this constitution.

(F) Additional Powers and Functions. Except as prohibited by its charter, a local governmental subdivision adopting a home rule charter under this Section shall have the additional powers and functions granted to local governmental subdivisions by other provisions of this constitution.

(G) Parish Officials and School Boards Not Affected. No home rule charter or plan of government shall contain any provision affecting a school board or the offices of district attorney, sheriff, assessor, clerk of a district court, or coroner, which is inconsistent with this constitution or law.

SECTION 6

Home Rule Charter or Plan of Government; Action by Legislature Prohibited

The legislature shall enact no law the effect of which changes or affects the structure and organization or the particular distribution and redistribution of the powers and functions of any local governmental subdivision which operates under a home rule charter.

The power of the legislature to set minimum pay levels for local government employees has been a continuing problem. Under the prior constitution, the supreme court ruled that legislation affecting the "structure and organization" of a local government unit operating under a home rule charter was unconstitutional. *LaFleur v. City of Baton Rouge* (1960) and *Letellier v. Parish of Jefferson* (1969) reasoned that salary of employees was a matter of structure and organization that the legislature could not control. Delegate Gordon Kean, a member of the Committee on Local and Parochial Government, suggested that the same rule applies under the 1974 Constitution, section 6 explicitly providing protection for the "structure and organization" of home rule charter units in exactly the same terms *LaFleur* and *Letellier* used.[15]

---

[15] R. Gordon Kean, "Local Government and Home Rule," *Loyola Law Review* 21 (1975):63, 70.

The supreme court, however, has relied on the exception of Article VI, section 14 to allow the state legislature to require increased salaries to be paid to fire-fighters and police. That exception would not extend to other categories of employees. *New Orleans Firefighters Association v. Civil Service Commission* (1982) required the New Orleans Civil Service Commission to follow a state statute governing the means for computing overtime pay of firefighters. The court of appeal in *Ruby v. City of Shreveport* (1983) also applied a state statute governing overtime pay for city police officers, again relying on the exception of section 14. In *Spillman v. City of Baton Rouge* (1983), another court of appeal applied the state statute on firefighters' wages to the city of Baton Rouge. Although the Jefferson Parish home rule charter established a civil service system for fire-fighters and police, *West v. Allen* (1980) held that the constitutional provisions in Article X, section 16 (establishing a system of fire and police civil service applicable to parishes) were paramount and superseded the local provisions.

In other matters, the supreme court has recognized local powers. The court in *Francis v. Morial* (1984) faced the problem of governance of an airport owned by the city of New Orleans but located in the suburban city of Kenner. The New Orleans home rule charter established an aviation board appointed by its mayor and council. State legislation sought to change the composition of the governing board to provide wider representation of and appointment by neighboring local government entities. The court found that the legislation was a violation of the protections of this section and that "the act does not constitute a reasonable exercise of police power under Article VI, Section 9(B) so as to qualify as an exception to the prohibition against state interference with home rule discretion. "

SECTION 7
Powers Of Other Local Governmental Subdivisions

(A) Powers and Functions. Subject to and not inconsistent with this constitution, the governing authority of a local governmental subdivision which has no home rule charter or plan of government may exercise any power and perform any function necessary, requisite, or proper for the management of its affairs, not denied by its charter or by general law, if a majority of the electors voting in an election held for that purpose vote in favor of the proposition that the governing authority may exercise such general powers. Otherwise, the local governmental subdivision shall have the powers authorized by this constitution or by law.

(B) Parish Officials and School Boards Not Affected. Nothing in this Section shall affect the powers and functions of a school board or the offices of district attorney, sheriff, assessor, clerk of a district court, or coroner.

This section gives the voters of a local governmental subdivision the option to give its government wider authority free of legislative control. That expansion of power, however, is not automatic. A parish in which the voters had not opted under section 7(A) to allow its police jury to exercise any power not denied by state law could not enact an ordinance to prohibit hazardous waste disposal in the parish. Language in *Rollins Environmental Services of Louisiana Inc. v. Iberville Parish Police Jury* (1979) suggests, however, that the result would be otherwise if the option to exercise the broader powers were taken by the voters.

SECTION 8
Home Rule Parish; Incorporation of Cities, Towns, and Villages

No parish plan of government or home rule charter shall prohibit the incorporation of a city, town, or village as provided by general law.

This section limits the ability of home rule charters to require a single parish governing entity. The state legislature continues to exercise the power to allow incorporation of subunits within a parish even if a home rule charter provides otherwise.

SECTION 9
Limitations of Local Governmental Subdivisions

(A) Limitations. No local governmental subdivision shall (1) define and provide for the punishment of a felony; or (2) except as provided by law, enact an ordinance governing private or civil relationships.
(B) Police Power Not Abridged. Notwithstanding any provision of this Article, the police power of the state shall never be abridged.

The limitation on enacting felonies was subject to two constructions: no punishment at hard labor or no punishment at all for conduct that the state defines as a felony. The supreme court in *State v. Foy* (1981) opted for the first view, the option less intrusive on local government, and permitted a prosecution for burglary under a city ordinance. Once that was done, the state, under double jeopardy principles, could not later try the defendants for the more serious offense of burglary under state law. The legislature responded in 1983 with Louisiana Revised Statute 14:143, which provides that local governments cannot "enact an ordinance defining as an offense conduct that is defined and punishable as a felony under state law."

The court of appeal in *Javers v. Council of the City of New Orleans* (1977) reasoned that the city's attempt at rent control, which would involve the regulation of provisions in lease contracts, was a prohibited ordinance governing private or civil relationships.

The statement in paragraph B that the state's police power shall never be abridged operates as a limitation on local governments in that provisions in home rule charters must give way to the state laws if the latter are an exercise of the state's police power. That term is not precisely defined, giving the courts some flexibility in adjusting the relationship between the state and its local government subdivisions. The supreme court in *City of New Orleans v. State* (1978) held that the city could not use its zoning power to prohibit the state from housing prisoners on state property within the city.

The court of appeal in *Yoes v. St. Charles Parish Council* (1981) went so far as to suggest that selection of an official parish journal was a matter within the state's police power and that state laws governing selection of a journal applied to a home rule parish. Similarly, in *Boh Bros. Construction Co. v. City of New Orleans* (1986), a state law limiting political subdivisions from withholding more than 5 percent of the contract price on public works projects was within the ambit of paragraph B; the city's ordinance providing for 10 percent withholding had to give way to the state law.

SECTION 10
Codification of Ordinances

Within two years after the effective date of this constitution, the governing authority of each political subdivision shall have a code prepared containing all of its general ordinances. When the code is prepared, the governing authority shall make copies available for public distribution. All general ordinances adopted after the approval of the code shall be amendments or additions to the code.

Section 10 resulted from a delegate proposal designed to make local laws more accessible: "to put that law into a form that people can get their hands on and read so that they will know what law they are subject to."[16] Although the issue of the proper means of enforcement of this section has not been raised before the courts, some commentators have suggested that nullity of noncodified ordinances might be a possibility, under an analogy to the principles of promulgation. On the other hand, an opinion of the attorney general (76–800) suggests that nullity is not an appropriate solution. Court orders to comply with the law (mandamus) would, of course, be available since a nondiscretionary duty is involved.

SECTION 11
Local Officials

The electors of each local governmental subdivision shall have the exclusive right to elect their governing authority. Nothing herein shall be construed to prohibit the election of the members from single-member districts.

---

[16] VII Records of the 1973 Louisiana Constitutional Convention: Convention Transcripts, Sept. 27, 1973, 1465.

The right of citizens to elect their local governing authority is a continuation of prior law. The second sentence was adopted in the 1973 convention at the urging of a black delegate to make clear that multimember districts were not to be required by the constitution and that single-member districts, usually preferred by black candidates, would be permitted.

SECTION 12
Local Officials; Compensation

The compensation or method of fixing the compensation of an elected official of any local governmental subdivision which operates under a home rule harter or plan of government, as provided in Section 4 and 5 of this Article, shall be provided in its charter. The compensation or method of fixing the compensation of an elected official of any other local governmental subdivision shall be provided by law. Compensation of a local official shall not be reduced during the term for which he is elected.

The protection against reduction in salary continues the 1952 constitutional amendment that added Article XIV, section 40 to the 1921 Constitution. It parallels similar protections granted to state officials (Art. X, sec. 23; Art. V, sec. 21, 31).

SECTION 13
Vacancies

(A) Vacancy; Appointment. Except as otherwise provided by this constitution, a vacancy in any local office filled by election wholly within the boundaries of a local governmental subdivision or a school district shall be filled by appointment by the particular governing authority of the local governmental subdivision or school district in which the vacancy occurs, until it is filled by election as provided by law.
(B) Exception. This Section shall apply to each local governmental subdivision unless otherwise provided by its home rule charter or plan of government.

The primary impact of this section was to decrease the power of the governor, who under prior constitutional provisions had substantial appointment powers to fill local vacancies. Under section 13, such vacancies are filled by the local governing subdivisions until an election can be held. The local governing authority of a city, according to the court of appeal in *Hammontree v. Patterson* (1978), consists of the mayor and the city council. If all members of the council are recalled, section 13 cannot be applied, for there is no legally constituted unicipal governing authority to make the appointment to the vacant council seats.

In such a case, the court applied Article 10, section 27, which allows the governor to make appointments not otherwise provided for.

SECTION 14
Increasing Financial Burden of Political Subdivisions

No law requiring increased expenditures for wages, hours, working conditions, pension and retirement benefits, vacation, or sick leave benefits of political subdivision employees, except a law providing for civil service, minimum wages, working conditions, and retirement benefits for firemen and municipal policemen, shall become effective until approved by ordinance enacted by the governing authority of the affected political subdivision or until the legislature appropriates funds for the purpose to the affected political subdivision and only to the extent and amount that such funds are provided. This Section shall not apply to a school board.

The major impact of this section is the hard-fought exception that allows the state to regulate the wages and working conditions of firefighters and police employed by local governmental units. The exception has been construed broadly and is applicable to home rule units, as discussed in the commentary to section 6.

SECTION 15
Local Governmental Subdivisions; Control over Agencies

The governing authority of a local governmental subdivision shall have general power over any agency heretofore or hereafter created by it, including, without limitation, the power to abolish the agency and require prior approval of any charge or tax levied or bond issued by the agency.

The section continues a 1966 amendment designed to reinforce the powers of local governments and to decrease the powers of the state government. That amendment added Article XIV, section 46 to the 1921 Constitution. Its continuation complements the newer provisions of section 16, which establish similar powers of merger and consolidation of entities that were not created by the local governing authority; however, in the latter case, a vote by the people is also required.

SECTION 16
Special Districts and Local Public Agencies

(A) Consolidation. A local governmental subdivision may consolidate and merge into itself any special district or local public agency, except a school district, situated

and having jurisdiction entirely within the boundaries of the local governmental subdivision. Upon the consolidation and merger, the local governmental subdivision shall succeed to and be vested with all of the rights, revenues, resources, jurisdiction, authority, and powers of the special district or local public agency. A consolidation and merger shall become effective only if approved by a majority of the electors voting thereon in the local governmental subdivision as a whole and by a majority of the electors voting thereon in the affected special district. A local public agency shall be consolidated and merged only if approved by a majority of the electors voting thereon in an election held for that purpose in the local governmental subdivision in which the agency is located.
(B) Assumption of Debt. If the special district or local public agency which is consolidated and merged has outstanding indebtedness, the authority provided by this Section shall not be exercised unless provision is made for the assumption of the indebtedness by the governing authority of the local governmental subdivision involved.

SECTION 17
Land Use; Zoning; Historic Preservation

Subject to uniform procedures established by law, a local governmental subdivision may (1) adopt regulations for land use, zoning, and historic preservation, which authority is declared to be a public purpose; (2) create commissions and districts to implement those regulations; (3) review decisions of any such commission; and (4) adopt standards for use, construction, demolition, and modification of areas and structures. Existing constitutional authority for historic preservation commissions is retained.

Under the prior constitution, amendments were adopted to establish special powers over use of property in New Orleans's French Quarter to preserve the historic character of the area. The last sentence of the section continues the authority for the Vieux Carré Commission, which exercised those powers. The first part of the section allows other such entities to be established without the need for constitutional amendments.

SECTION 18
Industrial Areas

(A) Authorization. The legislature by law may authorize parishes to create and define industrial areas within their boundaries in accordance with procedures and subject to regulations which it determines. An industrial area shall not be a political subdivision of the state.

(B) Access by Public Road; Police Protection. When an industrial area is so created, provision shall be made for access by public road to each entrance to the premises of every plant in the area, which is provided for use by employees of the company, or for use by employees of independent contractors working on the premises, or for delivery of materials or supplies, other than by rail or water transportation, to the premises. Police protection provided by any plant in an industrial area shall be confined to the premises of that plant.

Industrial inducement through establishment of areas with special regulation is permitted. The unusual provisions of paragraph B were added at the urging of labor union representatives who wanted to ensure public areas within the districts where picketing would be allowed. The last sentence, was an attempt to prevent private police from interfering with picketing in public areas.

SECTION 19
Special Districts; Creation

Subject to and not inconsistent with this constitution, the legislature by general law or by local or special law may create or authorize the creation of special districts, boards, agencies, commissions, and authorities of every type, define their powers, and grant to the special districts, boards, agencies, commissions, and authorities so created such rights, powers, and authorities at it deems proper, including, but not limited to, the power of taxation and the power to incur debt and issue bonds.

The power of the legislature to create special districts is broad. The supreme court ruled in *Board of Directors of Louisiana Recovery District v. All Taxpayers* (1988) that the legislature "has plenary power to create any type of special district and to vest it with powers as it deems proper." It can "create a district of statewide geographical dimension and to grant it the powers to tax and to issue bonds for any public purpose." The court so held although the district would be taxing and issuing bonds in a manner that the legislature and governor could not because of the constitutional limitations of Article VII, section 6.

SECTION 20
Intergovernmental Cooperation

Except as otherwise provided by law, a political subdivision may exercise and perform any authorized power and function, including financing, jointly or in cooperation with one or more political subdivisions, either within or without the state, or with the United States or its agencies.

Absent a state law limiting that power, local governments can engage in joint ventures with each other and, more important, the federal government. Promoting the securing of federal aid was the primary motive for this new provision.

SECTION 21
Assistance to Local Industry

(A) Authorization. In order to (1) induce and encourage the location of or addition to industrial enterprises therein which would have economic impact upon the area and thereby the state, (2) provide for the establishment and furnishing of such industrial plant, or (3) provide movable or immovable property, or both, for pollution control facilities, the legislature by law may authorize, subject to restrictions it may impose, any political subdivision, deep-water port commission, or deep-water port, harbor, and terminal district to

(a) issue bonds, subject to approval by the State Bond Commission or its successor, and use the funds derived from the sale of the bonds to acquire and improve industrial plant sites and other property necessary to the purposes thereof;

(b) acquire, through purchase, donation, exchange, and (subject to Article I, Section 4) expropriation, and improve industrial plant buildings and industrial plant equipment, machinery, furnishings, and appurtenances; and

(c) sell, lease, lease-purchase, or demolish all or any part of the foregoing.

(B) Property Expropriated; Sale to Aliens Prohibited. No property expropriated under the authority of this Section shall ever, directly or indirectly, be sold or donated to any foreign power, any alien, or any corporation in which the majority of the stock is controlled by any foreign power, alien corporation, or alien.

(C) Exception. This Section shall not apply to a school board.

Probably unnecessary, section 21 nonetheless makes clear that use of governmental funds or property for industrial inducement purposes is a proper public purpose not otherwise prohibited by the constitution. The prior constitution's drastic limitation on alien landownership, (Art. XIX, sec. 21) is continued in part by the limitation that property expropriated under this section cannot be transferred to aliens.

SECTION 22
Procedure for Certain Special Elections

When an election is required in a political subdivision under the provisions of this constitution which require submission to the electors of a proposition or question, the election shall be called, conducted, and the returns thereof canvassed, in accordance with the procedures established by the law then in effect pertaining to elections for incurring bonded indebtedness and special taxes relative to local finance, or as may be otherwise provided by law.

Several types of local elections are required in the constitution; this section seeks to achieve uniformity in the conduct of elections by requiring the rules for bond elections to be applied in these elections unless the legislature might provide otherwise.

SECTION 23
Acquisition of Property

Subject to and not inconsistent with this constitution and subject to restrictions provided by general law, political subdivisions may acquire property for any public purpose by purchase, donation, expropriation, exchange, or otherwise.

Local governments have the authority to acquire property without special legislative authorization, although laws may be adopted to limit this power.

SECTION 24
Servitudes of Way; Acquisition by Prescription

The public, represented by local governmental subdivisions, may acquire servitudes of way by prescription in the manner prescribed by law.

This authorization was seen as perhaps necessary to the continuation of legislation (Louisiana Revised Statutes 48:491) that allows local governments to acquire a right of public use over any private roads they have maintained for three years.

SECTION 25
Courts not Affected

Notwithstanding any provision of this Article, courts and their officers may be established or affected only as provided in Article V of this constitution.

Although Article VI would not seem to establish any local governmental power over the courts, this section was adopted at the suggestion of the chair of the Committee on the Judiciary to make clear that courts are governed solely by Article V.

PART II. FINANCE

The ad valorem tax on immovable property remains the basic local government tax source. The 1974 Constitution allows parishes a 4 mill tax (sec. 26) and the municipalities a 7 mill tax (sec. 27) without a vote of the people. Upon voter approval, ad valorem taxes beyond those amounts are allowed. Greater flexibility is thus provided and the amount of tax so allowed is not restricted, unlike the provisions of the prior constitution. Occupational license taxes are allowed (sec. 28) but are limited in amount absent state approval. Sales taxes up to 3 percent are reserved to local government (sec. 29). General obligation bonds require approval of a majority of electors voting on the proposition (sec. 33).

SECTION 26
Parish Ad Valorem Tax

(A) Parish Tax for General Purposes; Millage Limits; Increase. The governing authority of a parish may levy annually an ad valorem tax for general purposes not to exceed four mills on the dollar of assessed valuation. However, in Orleans Parish the limitation shall be seven mills, and in Jackson Parish the limitation shall be five mills. Millage rates may be increased in any parish when approved by a majority of the electors voting thereon in an election held for that purpose.
(B) Millage Increase Not for General Purposes. When the millage increase is for other than general purposes, the proposition shall state the specific purpose or purposes for which the tax is to be levied and the length of time the tax is to remain in effect. All proceeds of the tax shall be used solely for the purpose or purposes set forth in the proposition.
(C) Parish Tax in Municipality. The amount of the parish tax for general purposes which any parish, except Orleans Parish, may levy, without a vote of the electors, on property located wholly within any municipality which has a population exceeding one thousand inhabitants according to the last federal decennial census, or other census authorized by law, and which provides and maintains a system of street paving, shall not exceed one-half the tax levy for general purposes.
(D) Withdrawal from Parish Taxing Authority. This Section shall not affect the withdrawal of property in a municipality from parish taxing authority, in whole or in part, by a provision of the legislative charter of a municipality in effect on the effective date of this constitution.

SECTION 27
Municipal Ad Valorem Tax

(A) Municipal Tax for General Purposes; Millage Limits; Increase. The governing authority of a municipality may levy annually an ad valorem tax for general

purposes not to exceed seven mills on the dollar of assessed valuation. However, if a municipality, by its charter or by law, is exempt from payment of parish taxes or, under legislative or constitutional authority, maintains its own public schools, it may levy an annual tax not to exceed ten mills on the dollar of assessed valuation. Millage rates may be increased in any municipality when approved by a majority of the electors voting thereon in an election held for that purpose.
(B) Millage Increase Not for General Purposes. When the millage increase is for other than general purposes, the proposition shall state the specific purpose or purposes for which the tax is to be levied and the length of time the tax is to remain in effect. All proceeds of the tax shall be used solely for the purpose or purposes set forth in the proposition.
(C) Exception. This Section shall not apply to the city of New Orleans.

SECTION 28
Local Governmental Subdivisions; Occupational License Tax

The governing authority of a local governmental subdivision may impose an occupational license tax not greater than that imposed by the state. Those who pay a municipal occupational license tax shall be exempt from a parish occupational license tax in the amount of the municipal tax. The governing authority of a local governmental subdivision may impose an occupational license tax greater than that imposed by the state when authorized by law enacted by the favorable vote of two-thirds of the elected members of each house of the legislature.

SECTION 29
Local Governmental Subdivisions and School Boards; Sales Tax

(A) Sales Tax Authorized. Except as otherwise authorized in a home rule charter as provided for in Section 4 of this Article, the governing authority of any local governmental subdivision or school board may levy and collect a tax upon the sale at retail, the use, the lease or rental, the consumption, and the storage for use or consumption, of tangible personal property and on sales of services as denned by law, if approved by a majority of the electors voting thereon in an election held for that purpose. The rate thereof, when combined with the rate of all other sales and use taxes, exclusive of state sales and use taxes, levied and collected within any local governmental subdivision, shall not exceed three percent.
(B) Additional Sales Tax Authorized. However, the legislature, by general or by local or special law, may authorize the imposition of additional sales and use taxes by local governmental subdivisions or school boards, if approved by a majority of the electors voting thereon in an election held for that purpose.

(C) Bonds; Security. Nothing in this Section shall affect any sales or use tax authorized or imposed on the effective date of this constitution or affect or impair the security of any bonds payable from the proceeds of the tax.
(D) Exemptions; Protection of Bonds. Except when bonds secured thereby have been authorized, the legislature by law may uniformly exempt or exclude any goods, tangible personal property, or services from sales or use taxes levied by local governmental subdivisions, school boards, and the state.

SECTION 30
Political Subdivisions; Taxing Power

A political subdivision may exercise the power of taxation, subject to limitations elsewhere provided by this constitution, under authority granted by the legislature for parish, municipal, and other local purposes, strictly public in their nature. This Section shall not affect similar grants to political subdivisions under self-operative sections of this constitution.

SECTION 31
Taxes; Ratification

Any tax validly being levied by a political subdivision under prior legislative or constitutional authority on the effective date of this constitution is ratified.

SECTION 32
Special Taxes; Authorization

For the purpose of acquiring, constructing, improving, maintaining, or operating any work of public improvement, a political subdivision may levy special taxes when authorized by a majority of the electors in the political subdivision who vote thereon in an election held for that purpose.

SECTION 33
Political Subdivision; General Obligation Bonds

(A) Authorization. Subject to approval by the State Bond Commission or its successor, general obligation bonds may be issued only after authorization by a majority of the electors voting on the proposition at an election in the political subdivision issuing the bonds. Bonds to refund outstanding indebtedness at the same or at a lower effective rate of interest, even though payable solely from ad valorem taxes, need not be authorized at an election if the indebtedness refunded is paid or canceled at the time of the delivery of the refunding bonds, or if money, or securities made eligible for such purpose by law, are deposited in escrow in an adequate amount, with interest, to be utilized solely to retire the refunded indebtedness or bonds and to pay interest thereon and redemption premiums, if any, to the time of retirement.

(B) Full Faith and Credit. The full faith and credit of a political subdivision is hereby pledged to the payment of general obligation bonds issued by it under this constitution or the statute or proceedings pursuant to which they are issued. The governing authority of the issuing political subdivision shall levy and collect or cause to be levied and collected on all taxable property in the political subdivision ad valorem taxes sufficient to pay principal and interest and redemption premiums, if any, on such bonds as they mature.

SECTION 34
Limitation on Bonded Indebtedness

The legislature by law shall fix the limitation on bonded indebtedness payable solely from ad valorem taxes levied by political subdivisions.

SECTION 35
Contesting Political Subdivision Bonds

(A) Contesting Election; Time Limit. For sixty days after promulgation of the result of an election held to incur or assume debt, issue bonds, or levy a tax, any person in interest may contest the legality of the election, the bond issue provided for, or the tax authorized, for any cause. After that time no one shall have any cause or right of action to contest the regularity, formality, or legality of the election, tax provisions, or bond authorization, for any cause whatsoever. If the validity of any election, tax, debt assumption, or bond issue authorized or provided for is not raised within the sixty days, the authority to incur or assume debt, levy the tax, or issue the bonds, the legality thereof, and the taxes and other revenues necessary to pay the same shall be conclusively presumed to be valid, and no court shall have authority to inquire into such matters.

(B) Contesting Ordinance or Resolution; Time Limit. Every ordinance or resolution authorizing the issuance of bonds or other debt obligation by a political subdivision shall be published at least once in the official journal of the political subdivision or, if there is none, in a newspaper having general circulation therein. For thirty days after the date of publication any person in interest may contest the legality of the ordinance or resolution and of any provision therein made for the security and payment of the bonds. After that time, no one shall have any cause of action to test the regularity, formality, legality, or effectiveness of the ordinance or resolution, and provisions thereof for any cause whatever. Thereafter, it shall be conclusively presumed that every legal requirement for the issuance of the bonds or other debt obligation, including all things pertaining to the election, if any, at which the bonds or other debt obligation were authorized, has been complied with. No court shall have authority to inquire into any of these matters after the thirty days.

SECTION 36
Local Improvement Assessments

(A) Authorization. The legislature shall provide by general law or by local or special law the procedures by which a political subdivision may levy and collect local or special assessments on real property for the purpose of acquiring, constructing, or improving works of public improvement.
(B) Certificates of Indebtedness; Security. Certificates of indebtedness may be issued to cover the cost of any such public improvement. They shall be secured by the pledge of the local or special assessments levied therefor and may be further secured by the pledge of the full faith and credit of the political subdivision.
(C) Exception. This Section shall not apply to a school board.

SECTION 37
Revenue-Producing Property

(A) Authorization. The legislature by law may authorize political subdivisions to issue bonds or other debt obligations to construct, acquire, extend, or improve any revenue-producing public utility or work of public improvement. The bonds or other debt obligations may be secured by mortgage on the lands, buildings, machinery, and equipment or by the pledge of the income and revenues of the public utility or work of public improvement. They shall not be a charge upon the other income and revenues of the political subdivision.
(B) Exception. This Section shall not apply to a school board.

PART III. LEVEE DISTRICTS

Flooding on Louisiana's waterways, especially the Mississippi River, has long been a problem. Flood control efforts moved from small to large levees, and from individual responsibility of riparian landowners to governmental programs, both state and federal. In this process, the state's agencies dealing with flood control also grew and became more complex, moving from a central state agency to decentralized local and regional bodies. Typically, persons with interests in the operation of these bodies and with the validity of the bonds they issued, sought constitutional protection for them. Constitutional amendments that provided elaborate details of governance for the districts were adopted, and additional districts were established with little state control. As the structure became more complex, a movement began to make these bodies more responsive to state control. By the time the constitutional convention was held, several amendments toward that end had been adopted, and the convention continued that trend. Section 38 does continue the existing levee districts, but adds flexibility in the state's power to merge and reorganize them.

SECTION 38
Levee Districts

(A) Retention; Reorganization; Consolidation. Levee districts as organized and constituted on January 1, 1974 shall continue to exist, except that

(1) The legislature may provide by law for the consolidation, division, or reorganization of existing levee districts or may create new levee districts. However, the members of the board of commissioners of a district heretofore or hereafter created shall be appointed or elected from among residents of the district, as provided by law.

(2) A levee district whose flood control responsibilities are limited to and which is situated entirely within one parish may be consolidated and merged into such parish under the terms and conditions and in the manner provided in Section 16 of this Article.

(B) Obligation of Contract Affirmed. No action taken under this Section shall impair the obligation of outstanding bonded indebtedness or of any other contract of a levee district.

SECTION 39
Levee District Taxes

(A) District Tax; Millage Limit. For the purpose of constructing and maintaining levees, levee drainage, flood protection, hurricane flood protection, and for all other purposes incidental thereto, the governing authority of a levee district may levy annually a tax not to exceed five mills, except the Board of Levee Commissioners of the Orleans Levee District which may levy annually a tax not to exceed two and one-half mills, on the dollar of the assessed valuation of all taxable property situated within the alluvial portions of the district subject to overflow.

(B) Millage Increase. If the necessity to raise additional funds arises in any levee district for any purpose set forth in Paragraph (A), or for any other purpose related to its authorized powers and functions as specified by law, the tax may be increased.

However, the necessity and the rate of the increase shall be submitted to the electors of the district, and the tax increase shall take effect only if approved by a majority of the electors voting thereon in an election held for that purpose.

SECTION 40
Bond Issues

(A) Authorization. Subject to approval by the State Bond Commission or its successor, the governing authority of a levee district may fund the proceeds of its taxes or other revenues into bonds or other evidences of indebtedness. Proceeds thus derived shall be used for the purposes mentioned in Part III of this Article or for the funding or payment of any outstanding indebtedness.
(B) Sale. Bonds issued under the authority of Paragraph (A) shall be sold as provided by law concerning the issuance of bonds by levee districts.

SECTION 41
Cooperation with Federal Government

The governing authority of any levee district may cooperate with the federal government in constructing and maintaining levees in this state, under terms and conditions provided by the federal authorities and accepted by the governing authority.

SECTION 42
Compensation for Property used or Destroyed; Tax

(A) Compensation. Notwithstanding any contrary provision of this constitution, lands and improvements thereon hereafter actually used or destroyed for levees or levee drainage purposes shall be paid for as provided by law. However, nothing contained in this Paragraph with respect to compensation for lands and improvements shall apply to batture or to property the control of which is vested in the state or any political subdivision for the purpose of commerce. If the district has no other funds or resources from which the payment can be made, it shall levy on all taxable property within the district a tax sufficient to pay for property used or destroyed to be used solely in the district where collected.
(B) Appropriation. Nothing in this Section shall prevent the appropriation of such property before payment.

PART IV. PORT COMMISSIONS AND DISTRICTS

The prior constitution established and regulated in detail a number of port commissions, following the pattern established with the Port of New Orleans.

Section 43 continues the existing powers of those bodies, adding some legislative flexibility to change them by two-thirds vote.

SECTION 43
Port Commissions and Districts

All deep-water port commissions and all deep-water port, harbor, and terminal districts as organized and constituted on January 1, 1974, including their powers and functions, structure and organization, and territorial jurisdiction, are ratified and confirmed and shall continue to exist, except that

(1) The legislature by law may grant additional powers and functions to any such commission or district and may create new port commissions or port, harbor, and terminal districts.

(2) Only by law enacted by the favorable vote of two-thirds of the elected members of each house, may the legislature consolidate or abolish any such commission or district or diminish, reduce, or withdraw from any such commission or district any of its powers and functions and affect the structure and organization, distribution, and redistribution of the powers and functions of any such commission or district, including additions to or reductions of its territorial jurisdiction.

(3) The legislature shall enact laws with respect to the membership of the commissions provided in this Section. Once the law with respect to membership is enacted, it may be changed only by law enacted by the favorable vote of two-thirds of the elected members of each house.

PART V. DEFINITIONS

SECTION 44
Terms Defined

Section 44. As used in this Article:

(1) "Local governmental subdivision" means any parish or municipality.

(2) "Political subdivision" means a parish, municipality, and any other unit of local government, including a school board and a special district, authorized by law to perform governmental functions.

(3) "Municipality" means an incorporated city, town, or village.

(4) "Governing authority" means the body which exercises the legislative functions of the political subdivision.

(5) "General law" means a law of statewide concern enacted by the legislature which is uniformly applicable to all persons or to all political subdivisions in the state or which is uniformly applicable to all persons or to all political subdivisions within the same class.

(6) "General obligation bonds" means those bonds, the principal and interest of which are secured by and payable from ad valorem taxes levied without limitation as to rate or amount.
(7) "Deep-water port commissions" and "deep-water port, harbor, and terminal districts" mean those commissions or districts within whose territorial jurisdiction exist facilities capable of accommodating vessels of at least twenty-five feet of draft and of engaging in foreign commerce.

Article VII

Revenue and Finance

Delegate David Conroy, though acknowledging that the Model State Constitution contains no mention of taxes, wrote that the 1973 convention "never seriously suggested that such an approach was desirable for the State of Louisiana. To the contrary, history and the mood of the people demanded restraints."[17] The restraints included requirement of a two-thirds vote to levy or increase taxes, income tax rates and homestead exemptions from property tax fixed in the constitution, and a three dollar automobile license tax. This constitutional detail and resulting lack of flexibility has prompted numerous amendments and proposed amendments. Seventeen amendments were proposed before 1989; eight were adopted.

In 1989 Louisiana faced a serious fiscal crisis prompted by declining oil and gas revenues. Article VII was also seen by some, particularly business interests, as impeding economic growth. Governor Charles E. Roemer III, himself a delegate to the 1973 convention, proposed a comprehensive revision of the entire article, which was accomplished partly by Conroy. The voters, however, were not willing to make the changes and defeated the proposed constitutional amendments by a large majority in April 1989. More modest piecemeal reform was attempted again in fall 1989, and some of the proposals were adopted.

[17] David Conroy, "Louisiana Constitution of 1974: Taxation," *Loyola Law Review* 21 (1975):97.

PART I. GENERAL PROVISIONS

SECTION 1
Power to Tax; Public Purpose

Except as otherwise provided by this constitution, the power of taxation shall be vested in the legislature, shall never be surrendered, suspended, or contracted away, and shall be exercised for public purposes only.

By vesting the power to tax in the legislature, the constitution removes that power from other governmental entities, which thus need constitutional or statutory authorization to impose taxes. These other bodies, however, may collect fees. Also, imposition of taxes requires a two-thirds vote of each house of the legislature, and imposition of fees does not. The distinction between taxes and fees, though vague, is thus an important one that predictably has spawned a number of cases.

Audubon Insurance Co. v. Bernard (1983) classified as a tax an assessment charged to insurance companies for support of firefighter retirement systems; the court found its primary object was raising revenue. On the other hand, "fees to persons receiving grants or benefits not shared by other members of society" would not be considered taxes. The court of appeal in *D'Amico v. Rapides Parish Coliseum Authority* (1986) considered as a fee a twenty-five cent surcharge on all tickets for events held at a publicly owned coliseum. The revenue produced was to be used to provide security and related services for the events.

SECTION 2
Power to Tax; Limitation

The levy of a new tax, an increase in an existing tax, or a repeal of an existing tax exemption shall require the enactment of a law by two-thirds of the elected members of each house of the legislature.

Section 2 enlarged the scope of a 1955 amendment to the 1921 Constitution by making it clear that the two-thirds vote requirement applies to repeal of existing tax exemptions. The related provisions of Article III, section 2 also limit the levying of taxes. A holdover from the prior practice of limiting alternate sessions of the legislature to fiscal matters, the section provides, "No measure levying a new tax of increasing an existing tax shall be introduced or enacted during a regular session held in an odd-numbered year."

SECTION 3
Collection of Taxes

The legislature shall prohibit the issuance of process to restrain the collection of any tax. It shall provide a complete and adequate remedy for the prompt recovery of an illegal tax paid by a taxpayer.

The mandate of this section and a similar provision of the 1921 Constitution is carried out by Louisiana Revised Statutes 47:1575, 1576, and 2110. Injunctions against the collection of taxes are prohibited, but taxes can be paid under protest. When paid under protest, the payments are normally segregated and held pending the outcome of the suit contesting the validity of the tax.

SECTION 4
Income Tax; Severance Tax; Political Subdivisions

(A) Income Tax. Equal and uniform taxes may be levied on net incomes, and these taxes may be graduated according to the amount of net income. However, the individual joint income tax schedule of rates shall never exceed the rates set forth in Title 47, Section 32 of the Louisiana Revised Statutes on January 1, 1974. Federal income taxes paid shall be allowed as a deductible item in computing state income taxes for the same period.

(B) Severance Tax. Taxes may be levied on natural resources severed from the soil or water, to be paid proportionately by the owners thereof at the time of severance. Natural resources may be classified for the purpose of taxation. Such taxes may be predicated upon either the quantity or value of the products at the time and place of severance. No further or additional tax or license shall be levied or imposed upon oil, gas, or sulphur leases or rights. No additional value shall be added to the assessment of land by reason of the presence of oil, gas, or sulphur therein or their production therefrom. However, sulphur in place shall be assessed for ad valorem taxation to the person, firm, or corporation having the right to mine or produce the same in the parish where located, at no more than twice the total assessed value of the physical property subject to taxation, excluding the assessed value of sulphur above ground, as is used in sulphur operations in such parish. Likewise, the severance tax shall be the only tax on timber; however, standing timber shall be liable equally with the land on which it stands for ad valorem taxes levied on the land.

(C) Severance Tax; Political Subdivision. A political subdivision of the state shall not levy a severance tax, income tax, or tax on motor fuel.

(D) Severance Tax Allocation. One-third of the sulphur severance tax, but not to exceed one hundred thousand dollars; one-fifth of the severance tax on all natural resources, other than sulphur or timber, but not to exceed five hundred thousand dollars; and three-fourths of the timber severance tax shall be remitted to the governing authority of the parish in which severance or production occurs.

(E) Royalties Allocation. One-tenth of the royalties from mineral leases on state-owned land, lake and river beds and other water bottoms belonging to the state or the title to which is in the public for mineral development shall be remitted to the governing authority of the parish in which severance or production occurs. A parish governing authority may fund these royalties into general obligation bonds of the parish in accordance with law. The provisions of this Paragraph shall not apply to properties comprising the Russell Sage Wildlife and Game Refuge.

Although the Committee on Revenue, Finance and Taxation recommended more flexibility in the income tax, delegates retained the constitutional limits on income taxation of individuals (at 2 percent and 4 percent). In doing so, they incorporated by reference the income tax statutes existing on January 1, 1974. They also went further and constitutionalized the deduction for federal income tax paid.

Paragraph C prohibits local governments from imposing an income tax. In spite of this provision, the city of New Orleans attempted to impose an earnings tax, a tax of 1.5 percent on gross earnings that applied to persons who worked but did not live in the city. The city argued it was not an income tax because it applied only to gross earnings, as distinguished from the traditional income tax premised upon a different structure. The supreme court in *City of New Orleans v. Scramuzza* (1987) disagreed, reasoning the prohibition would extend to any tax on earnings.

The severance tax provisions were continuations of the prior articles with little change. Severance taxes on oil and gas production, long a mainstay of the state budget, are reserved to the state, with local authorities sharing in the proceeds from those taxes under paragraph D. Paragraph E provides for sharing one-tenth of the royalties from mineral production on state-owned lands with the local government in which production occurs.

SECTION 5
Motor Vehicle License Tax

The legislature shall impose an annual license tax of not more than one dollar per each one thousand dollars of actual value on automobiles for private use based on the actual value of the vehicle, as provided by law. However, the annual license tax shall not be less than ten dollars per automobile for private use. On other motor vehicles, the legislature shall impose an annual license tax based upon carrying capacity, horsepower, value, weight, or any of these. After satisfying pledges respecting that portion of the revenues attributable to the tax rates in effect at the time of such pledges for the payment of obligations for bonds or other evidences of indebtedness and upon the creation of a Transportation Trust Fund within this constitution, the revenues from the license tax on automobiles for private use shall be deposited therein. In the event no such trust fund is established in this constitution, the revenues shall be used exclusively and solely as provided by law for the construction, maintenance, and safety of the federal and state system of roads and bridges, for the parish and municipal road systems, for the operations of the office of state police, Department of Public Safety and Corrections or its successor, and for the payment of any obligation for bonds issued or indebtedness incurred in connection with any of the foregoing, which bonds may be issued as revenue bonds under Article VII, Section 6(C) of this constitution, subject to existing pledges only as to that portion of the tax collections attributable to the rates in effect at the time of such pledges for the payment of any obligations for bonds or other evidences of indebtedness outstanding on the effective date of this Section. No parish or municipality may impose a license fee on motor vehicles.

The 1973 convention maintained the automobile license tax at three dollars per year, a political placebo that was in the prior constitution. A constitutional amendment to raise the fee to twenty-five dollars was defeated in 1986. In 1989, however, voters approved an increase tied to committing the funds collected to highway-related expenditures. The amount of the tax remains fixed in the constitution.

The last sentence prohibits local governments from imposing "a license fee on motor vehicles." This prohibition was construed to allow the city of New Orleans to "tax" all city residents who owned automobiles. The supreme court in *Acorn v. City of New Orleans* (1981) reasoned that the annual charge was not related to use of or a right to use the roads and was thus not a fee but instead a tax for raising revenue.

SECTION 6
State Debt; Full Faith and Credit Obligations

(A) Authorization. Unless otherwise authorized by this constitution, the state shall have no power, directly or indirectly, or through any state board, agency, commission, or otherwise, to incur debt or issue bonds except by law enacted by two-thirds of the elected members of each house of the legislature. The debt may be incurred or the bonds issued only if the funds are to be used to repel invasion; suppress insurrection; provide relief from natural catastrophes; refund outstanding indebtedness at the same or a lower effective interest rate; or make capital improvements, but only in accordance with a comprehensive capital budget, which the legislature shall adopt.

(B) Capital Improvements. If the purpose is to make capital improvements, the nature and location and, if more than one project, the amount allocated to each and the order of priority shall be stated in the comprehensive capital budget which the legislature adopts.

(C) Full Faith and Credit. The full faith and credit of the state shall be pledged to the repayment of all bonds or other evidences of indebtedness issued by the state directly or through any state board, agency, or commission pursuant to the provisions of Paragraphs (A) and (B) hereof. The full faith and credit of the state is not hereby pledged to the repayment of bonds of a levee district, political subdivision, or local public agency. In addition, any state board, agency, or commission authorized by law to issue bonds, in the manner so authorized and with the approval of the State Bond Commission or its successor, may issue bonds which are payable from fees, rates, rentals, tolls, charges, grants, or other receipts or income derived by or in connection with an undertaking, facility, project, or any combination thereof, without a pledge of the full faith and credit of the state. Such revenue bonds may, but are not required to, be issued in accordance with the provisions of Paragraphs (A) and (B) hereof. If issued other than as provided in Paragraphs (A) and (B), such revenue bonds shall not carry the pledge of the full faith and credit of the state and the issuance of the bonds shall not constitute the incurring of state debt under this constitution. The rights granted to deep-water port commissions or deep-water port, harbor, and terminal districts under this constitution shall not be impaired by this Section.

(D) Referendum. The legislature, by law enacted by two-thirds of the elected members of each house, may propose a statewide public referendum to authorize incurrence of debt for any purpose for which the legislature is not herein authorized to incur debt.

(E) Exception. Nothing in this Section shall apply to any levee district, political subdivision, or local public agency unless the full faith and credit of the state is pledged to the payment of the bonds of the levee district, political subdivision, or local public agency.

Section 6 was designed to limit the state's ability to incur debt or issue bonds, imposing a two-thirds vote requirement on their issuance. It also attempted to limit the uses of bond proceeds, primarily to capital improvements. Despite these provisions, the supreme court has given the legislature considerable latitude in issuing bonds. In *State Bond Commission v. All Taxpayers* (Bond Commission I, 1987), the court allowed the issuance of revenue anticipation notes payable in the same fiscal year as issued. The court reasoned such notes are not debt in the sense of section 6 and do not carry the full faith and credit of the state. The court relied on a technical definition of the term *debt* rather than on the records of the 1973 convention. The notes approved in the case did not solve the state's cash flow crisis, and when funds were not available to pay them all, the legislature issued additional notes that would not necessarily be paid from funds received during the same fiscal year but from revenues "which will accrue and be credited" in that same fiscal year. The supreme court in 1988 validated such notes in *State Bond Commission v. All Taxpayers* (Bond Commission II).

Although paragraph A limits the state "directly or indirectly, or though any state board, agency, commission, or otherwise, to incur debt or issue bonds," the court allowed the state to establish a special district under Article VI, section 30 with the power to issue bonds and to impose a sales tax. The court upheld the district in *Board of Directors of Louisiana Recovery District v. All Taxpayers* (1988), although the boundaries of the district were identical with those of the state and the tax was applied statewide.

Paragraph C attempts to make the state's bonds more creditworthy by requiring that the state's full faith and credit be pledged to the state's general obligation bonds issued under the authority of paragraph A. It is clear, however, that the state's faith and credit is not pledged to pay the bonds of local governments and levee districts. It is also clear that the state can issue revenue bonds that do not carry the state's full faith and credit but are payable out of a specified stream of revenue.

SECTION 7
State Debt; Interim Emergency Board

(A) Composition. The Interim Emergency Board is created. It shall be composed of the governor, lieutenant governor, state treasurer, presiding officer of each house of the legislature, chairman of the Senate Finance Committee, and chairman of the House Appropriations Committee, or their designees.
(B) Powers. Between sessions of the legislature, when the board by majority vote determines that an emergency exists, it may appropriate from the state general fund or borrow on the full faith and credit of the state an amount to meet the emergency. The appropriation may be made or the indebtedness incurred only for a purpose for which the legislature may appropriate funds and then only after the board obtains, as provided by law, the written consent of two-thirds of the elected members of each house of the legislature. For the purposes of this Paragraph, an emergency is an event or occurrence not reasonably anticipated by the legislature.
(C) Limits. The aggregate of indebtedness outstanding at any one time and the amount appropriated from the state general fund for the current fiscal year under the authority of this Section shall not exceed one-tenth of one percent of total state revenue receipts for the previous fiscal year.
(D) Allocation. An amount sufficient to pay indebtedness incurred during the preceding fiscal year under the authority of this Section is allocated, as a first priority, each year from the state general fund.

This section continues a similar provision of the 1921 Constitution designed to provide a fund for emergencies, defined rather broadly as "an event or occurrence not reasonably anticipated by the legislature." Under the prior provision, the fund available was $1 million. Now the amount is a percentage (one-tenth of 1 percent) of the previous year's revenues. Written approval, by mail ballot, of two-thirds of the members of each house is required for the allocations.

SECTION 8
State Bond Commission

(A) Creation. The State Bond Commission is created. Its membership and authority shall be determined by law.
(B) Approval of Bonds. No bonds or other obligations shall be issued or sold by the state, directly or through any stated board, agency, or commission, or by any political subdivision of the state, unless prior written approval of the bond commission is obtained.
(C) Contesting State Bonds. Bonds, notes, certificates, or other evidences of indebtedness of the state (hereafter referred to as "bonds") shall not be invalid because of any irregularity or defect in the proceedings or in the issuance and sale thereof and shall be incontestable in the hands of a bona fide purchaser or holder. The issuing agency, after authorizing the issuance of bonds by resolution, shall publish once in the official journal of the state, as provided by law, a notice of intention to issue the bonds. The notice shall include a description of the bonds and the security therefor. Within thirty days after the publication, any person in interest may contest the legality of the resolution, any provision of the bonds to be issued pursuant to it, the provisions securing the bonds, and the validity of all other provisions and proceedings relating to the authorization and issuance of the bonds. If no action or proceeding is instituted within the thirty days, no person may contest the validity of the bonds, the provisions of the resolution pursuant to which the bonds were issued, the security of the bonds, or the validity of any other provisions or proceedings relating to their authorization and issuance, and the bonds shall be presumed conclusively to be legal. Thereafter no court shall have authority to inquire into such matters.

Although the membership of the bond commission and the full statement of its powers are left to the legislature, paragraph B requires that no state bonds be issued without approval of the commission. This limitation was designed to centralize the issuance of state bonds as one means of improving their credit rating.

Paragraph C establishes one of the strongest and shortest preemptive periods in Louisiana law. If action is not instituted within 30 days of a notice of intent to sell bonds, no one may contest the validity of those bonds. They "shall be presumed conclusively to be legal. Thereafter, no court shall have authority to inquire into such matters."

SECTION 9
State Funds

(A) Deposit in State Treasury. All money received by the state or by any state board, agency, or commission shall be deposited immediately upon receipt in the state treasury, except that received:

(1) as a result of grants or donations or other forms of assistance when the terms and conditions thereof or of agreements pertaining thereto require otherwise;

(2) by trade or professional associations;

(3) by the employment security administration fund or its successor;

(4) by retirement system funds;

(5) by state agencies operating under authority of this constitution preponderantly from fees and charges for the shipment of goods in international maritime trade and commerce; and

(6) by a state board, agency, or commission, but pledged by it in connection with the issuance of revenue bonds as provided in Paragraph (C) of Section 6 of this Article, other than any surplus as may be defined in the law authorizing such revenue bonds.

(B) Bond Security and Redemption Fund. Subject to contractual obligations existing on the effective date of this constitution, all state money deposited in the state treasury shall be credited to a special fund designated as the Bond Security and Redemption Fund, except money received as the result of grants or donations or other forms of assistance when the terms and conditions thereof or of agreements pertaining thereto require otherwise. In each fiscal year an amount is allocated from the bond security and redemption fund sufficient to pay all obligations which are secured by the full faith and credit of the state and which become due and payable within the current fiscal year, including principal, interest, premiums, sinking or reserve fund, and other requirements. Thereafter, except as otherwise provided by law, money remaining in the fund shall be credited to the state general fund.

(C) Exception. Nothing in this Section shall apply to a levee district or political subdivision unless the full faith and credit of the state is pledged to the payment of the bonds of the levee district or political subdivision.

The purpose of this new provision was to centralize management of state funds. Although there is no state treasury as such, most funds received by any state agency must be deposited in state bank accounts under the control of the state treasurer. The state is thus better able to command more interest on state deposits or other more favorable terms from banks. Prior practice had allowed use of state deposits as a means of providing patronage benefits to some financial institutions.

Paragraph B is an automatic constitutional appropriation of funds to pay the amounts due on the state's general obligation bonds. No legislative appropriation is necessary. Revenues are not credited to the general fund until the amount due on the bonds is covered.

SECTION 10
Expenditure of State Funds

(A) Appropriations. Except as otherwise provided by this constitution, money shall be drawn from the state treasury only pursuant to an appropriation made in accordance with law.
(B) Balanced Budget. Total appropriations by the legislature for any fiscal year shall not exceed anticipated state revenues for that fiscal year.
(C) Publication. The legislature shall have published a regular statement of receipts and expenditures of all state money at intervals of not more than one year.
(D) Public Purpose. No appropriation shall be made except for a public purpose.

Paragraph A provides that state money cannot be expended without a legislative appropriation. This section prevails over constitutional mandates that the legislature shall appropriate funds for various purposes. The supreme court in *Louisiana Association of Educators v. Edwards* (1988) recognized that such mandates to appropriate are not enforceable by court order.

Although paragraph B appears to require a balanced budget, the constitution does not specify how anticipated state revenues are to be determined, thus providing some discretion to the legislature in making revenue projections.

SECTION 10-A
Wildlife and Fisheries; Conservation Fund

(A) Conservation Fund. Effective July 1, 1988, there shall be established in the state treasury, as a special fund, the Louisiana Wildlife and Fisheries Conservation Fund, hereinafter referred to as the Conservation Fund. Out of the funds remaining in the Bond Security and Redemption Fund after a sufficient amount is allocated from that fund to pay all obligations secured by the full faith and credit of the state which become due and payable within any fiscal year as required by Article VII, Section 9(B) of this constitution, the treasurer shall pay into the Conservation Fund all of the following, except as provided in Article VII, Section 9(A), and except for the amount provided in R.S. 56:10(B)(1)(a) as that provision existed on the effective date of this Section:

(1) All revenue from the types and classes of fees, licenses, permits, royalties, or other revenue paid into the Conservation Fund as provided by law on the effective

date of this Section. Such revenue shall be deposited in the Conservation Fund even if the names of such fees, licenses, permits, or other revenues are changed.

Any increase in the amount charged for such fees, licenses, permits, royalties, and other revenue, or any new fee, license, permit, royalty, or other revenue, enacted by the legislature after the effective date of this Section, shall be irrevocably dedicated and deposited in the Conservation Fund unless the legislature enacts a law specifically appropriating or dedicating such revenue to another fund or purpose.

(2) The balance remaining on June 30, 1988 in the Conservation Fund established pursuant to R.S. 56:10.

(3) All funds or revenues which may be donated expressly to the Conservation Fund.

(B) The monies in the Conservation Fund shall be appropriated by the legislature to the Department of Wildlife and Fisheries, or its successor, and shall be used solely for the programs and purposes of conservation, protection, preservation, management, and replenishment of the state's natural resources and wildlife, including use for land acquisition or for federal matching fund programs which promote such purposes, and for the operation and administration of the Department and the Wildlife and Fisheries Commission, or their successors.

(C) All unexpended and unencumbered monies in the Conservation Fund at the end of the fiscal year shall remain in the fund. The monies in the fund shall be invested by the treasurer in the manner provided by law. All interest earned on monies invested by the treasurer shall be deposited in the fund. The treasurer shall prepare and submit to the department on a quarterly basis a printed report showing the amount of money contained in the fund from all sources.

The 1973 convention removed most of the constitutional dedications that had accumulated by amendments to the 1921 Constitution. Under those amendments, funds were dedicated or appropriated (they had to be spent for the purposes specified) in the constitution, thus depriving the legislature of flexibility in rearranging spending priorities.

The constitutional dedications are slowly returning in response to perceived needs and to guarantee to voters that the funds will be spent as promised. This section, adopted in 1987, dedicates revenues obtained from hunting and fishing fees and licenses to conservation purposes.

SECTION 10.1
Quality Trust Fund; Education

(A) Louisiana Education Quality Trust Fund.

(1) Effective January 1, 1987, there shall be established in the state treasury as a special permanent trust fund the Louisiana Education Quality Trust Fund,

hereinafter referred to as the "Permanent Trust Fund." After allocation of money to the Bond Security and Redemption Fund as provided in Article VII, Section 9(B) of this constitution, and notwithstanding Article XIV, Section 10 of this constitution, the treasurer shall deposit in and credit to the Permanent Trust Fund all money which is received after the first one hundred million dollars from the federal government under Section 1337(g) of Title 43 of the United States Code which is attributable to mineral production activity or leasing activity on the Outer Continental Shelf which has been held in escrow pending a settlement between the United States and the state of Louisiana; twenty-five percent of the recurring revenues received under Section 1337(g) of Title 43 of the United States Code which are attributable to mineral production activity or leasing activity on the Outer Continental Shelf; and twenty-five percent of the earnings on investment of monies in the Permanent Trust Fund. No appropriation shall be made from the Permanent Trust Fund. If any such money has been received prior to the effective date of this Section, the treasurer shall transfer from the state general fund to the Permanent Trust Fund on the effective date of this Section an amount of money which shall make the Permanent Trust Fund balance equal to the amount of such money previously received, except for the first one hundred million dollars. After six hundred million dollars has been credited to the Permanent Trust Fund, the sum of fifty million dollars shall be credited to the Coastal Environment Protection Trust Fund, as established in [Louisiana Revised Statutes] R.S. 30:313, from those monies received from the federal government under Section 1337(g) of Title 43 of the United States Code which is attributable to mineral production activity or leasing activity on the Outer Continental Shelf and which has been held in escrow pending a settlement between the United States and the state of Louisiana; all funds in excess of seven hundred fifty million dollars shall be credited to the Permanent Trust Fund.

(2) After allocation of money to the Bond Security and Redemption Fund as provided in Article VII, Section 9(B) of the constitution, and notwithstanding Article XIV, Section 10 of the constitution, seventy-five percent of the recurring revenues received under Section 1337(g) of Title 43 of the United States Code which are attributable to mineral production activity or leasing activity, and seventy-five percent of the earnings on investment of the Permanent Trust Fund shall be deposited and credited to a special fund which is hereby created in the state treasury and which shall be known as the Louisiana Quality Education Support Fund, hereinafter referred to as the "Support Fund".

(3) All recurring revenues and interest earnings shall be credited to the respective funds as provided in Subparagraphs (1) and (2) above until the balance in the Permanent Trust Fund equals two billion dollars. After the Permanent Trust Fund reaches a balance of two billion dollars, all interest earnings on the Permanent Trust Fund shall be credited to the Support Fund and all recurring revenues shall be credited to the State General Fund.

(B) Investment. The money credited to the Permanent Trust Fund pursuant to Paragraph (A) of this Section shall be permanently credited to the Permanent Trust Fund and shall be invested by the treasurer. The amounts in the Support Fund shall be available for appropriation and then only as provided in this Paragraphs (C) and (D) of this Section.

(C) Reports; Allocation.

(1) The State Board of Elementary and Secondary Education and the Board of Regents shall annually submit to the legislature and the governor not less than sixty days prior to the beginning of each regular session of the legislature a proposed program and budget for the expenditure of the monies in the Support Fund. Proposals for such expenditures shall be designed to improve the quality of education.

(2) The legislature shall appropriate from the Support Fund only for educational purposes provided in Paragraph (D) of this Section and shall appropriate fifty percent of the available funds for higher educational purposes and fifty percent for elementary and secondary and vocational-technical educational purposes.

(3) The legislature shall appropriate the total amount intended for higher educational purposes to the Board of Regents and the total amount intended for elementary, secondary and vocational-technical educational purposes to the State Board of Elementary and Secondary Education which boards shall allocate the monies so appropriated to the programs as previously approved by the legislature.

(4) The monies appropriated by the legislature and disbursed from the Support Fund shall not displace, replace, or supplant appropriations from the general fund for the purposes of implementing the Minimum Foundation Program or displace, replace, or supplant funding for higher education or vocational-technical education. For higher education, this Paragraph shall mean that no appropriation for any fiscal year from the Support Fund shall be made for any higher education purpose for which a general fund appropriation was made in the previous year unless the total appropriations for that fiscal year from the state general fund for higher education exceed general fund appropriations for higher education for the previous year. This Paragraph shall in no way limit general fund appropriations in excess of the minimum amounts herein established.

(D) Disbursement; higher education, elementary and secondary education, and vocational-technical education.

(1) The treasurer shall disburse not more than fifty percent of the monies in the Support Fund as that money is appropriated by the legislature and allocated by the Board of Regents for any or all of the following higher educational purposes to enhance economic development:

(a) The carefully defined research efforts of public and private universities in Louisiana.

(b) The endowment of chairs for eminent scholars.

(c) The enhancement of the quality of academic, research or agricultural departments or units within a university. These funds shall not be used for athletic purposes or programs.

(d) The recruitment of superior graduate students.

(2) The treasurer shall disburse not more than fifty percent of the monies in the Support Fund as that money is appropriated by the legislature and allocated by the State Board of Elementary and Secondary Education for any or all of the following elementary, secondary, or vocational-technical educational purposes:

(a) To provide compensation to city or parish school board or postsecondary vocational-technical professional instructional employees.

(b) To insure an adequate supply of superior textbooks, library books, equipment, and other instructional materials.

(c) To fund exemplary programs in elementary, secondary, or vocational-technical schools designed to improve elementary, secondary, or vocational-technical student academic achievement or vocational-technical skill.

(d) To fund carefully defined research efforts, including pilot programs, designed to improve elementary and secondary student academic achievement.

(e) To fund school remediation programs and preschool programs.

(f) To fund the teaching of foreign languages in elementary and secondary schools.

(g) To fund an adequate supply of teachers by providing scholarships or stipends to prospective teachers in academic or vocational-technical areas where there is a critical teacher shortage.

Adopted in 1986, section 10.1 was designed to dedicate the windfall received by the state in settlement of the dispute with the federal government over offshore oil and gas revenues. It is a further reflection of distrust in the legislature's ability to use state funds wisely. The section establishes a permanent trust fund of several hundred million dollars, the income from which must be allocated to the educational expenditures provided in section 10.1(D): 50 percent to higher education and 50 percent to elementary, secondary, and vocational-technical education.

SECTION 10.2

Wetlands Conservation and Restoration Fund

(A) Effective July 1, 1990, there shall be established in the state treasury the Wetlands Conservation and Restoration Fund to provide a dedicated, recurring source of revenues for the development and implementation of a program to conserve and restore Louisiana's vegetated wetlands. Of revenues received in each fiscal year by the state as a result of the production of or exploration for minerals, hereinafter referred to as mineral revenues from severance taxes, royalty payments, bonus payments, or rentals, and excluding such revenues received by the state as a result of grants or donations when the terms or conditions thereof require otherwise, the treasurer shall make the following allocations:

(1) To the Bond Security and Redemption Fund as provided in Article VII, Section 9(B) of this constitution.

(2) To the political subdivisions of the state as provided in Article VII, Sections 4(D) and (E) of this constitution.

(3) As provided by the requirements of Article VII, Sections 10-A and 10.1 of this constitution.

(B)(1) After making the allocations provided for in Paragraph (A), the treasurer shall then deposit in and credit to the Wetlands Conservation and Restoration Fund any amount of mineral revenues that may be necessary to insure that a total of five million dollars is deposited into such fund for the fiscal year from this source; provided that the balance of the fund which consists of mineral revenues from severance taxes, royalty payments, bonus payments, or rentals shall not exceed forty million dollars.

(2) After making the allocations and deposits provided for in Paragraphs (A) and (B)(1) of this Section, the treasurer shall deposit in and credit to the Wetlands Conservation and Restoration Fund as follows:

(a) Ten million dollars of the mineral revenues in excess of six hundred million dollars which remain after the allocations provided for in Paragraph (A) are made by the treasurer.

(b) Ten million dollars of the mineral revenues in excess of six hundred fifty million dollars which remain after the allocations provided in Paragraph (A) are made by the treasurer.

However, the balance of the fund which consists of mineral revenues from severance taxes, royalty payments, bonus payments, or rentals shall not exceed forty million dollars.

(C) The money in the fund shall be invested as provided by law and any earnings realized on investment money in the fund shall be deposited in and credited to the fund. Money from other sources, such as donations, appropriations, or dedications, may be deposited in and credited to the fund; however, the balance of the fund which consists of mineral revenues from severance taxes, royalty payments, bonus payments, or rentals shall not exceed forty million dollars. Any unexpended money remaining in the fund at the end of the fiscal year shall be retained in the fund.

(D) The money in the fund may be appropriated for purposes consistent with the Wetlands Conservation and Restoration Plan developed by the Wetlands Conservation and Restoration Authority, or its successor.

No appropriation shall be made from the fund inconsistent with the purposes of the plan.

Section 10.2, adopted by a 1989 constitutional amendment, dedicates part of the state's mineral revenues to use in restoring the state's wetlands, which have been eroding seriously. It is another example of the increasing trend of constitutional dedications adopted by amendments.

SECTION 11
Budgets

(A) Operating Budget. The governor shall submit to the legislature, at a time fixed by law, a budget estimate for the next fiscal year setting forth all proposed state expenditures and anticipated state revenues. He shall cause to be submitted a general appropriation bill for proposed ordinary operating expenditures and, if necessary, a bill or bills to raise additional revenues.
(B) Capital Budget. The governor shall submit to the legislature, at each regular session, a proposed five-year capital outlay program and request implementation of the first year of the program. Capital outlay projects approved by the legislature shall be made a part of the comprehensive state capital budget, which shall be adopted by the legislature.

Although section 10(B) requires that the budget adopted by the legislature must be balanced, section 11 does not specify that the governor's budget recommendations must be balanced.

SECTION 12
Reports and Records

Reports and records of the collection, expenditure, investment, and use of state money and those relating to state obligations shall be matters of public record, except returns of taxpayers and matters pertaining the those returns.

The state's financial records, other than tax returns filed by taxpayers, are determined public records and thus available for inspection by the public. No provision is made for limiting this right by law, as is the case in the more general provisions of Article XII, section 3 applicable to other public documents.

SECTION 13
Investment of State Funds

All money in the custody of the state treasurer which is available for investment shall be invested as provided by law.

Before 1973, legislation was adopted requiring investment of the state's idle funds instead of depositing them in noninterest-bearing accounts. Section 13 is a hortatory provision reflecting these reforms, but the legislature still has the power to determine which funds must be invested and how they are to be invested.

SECTION 14
Donation, Loan, or Pledge of Public Credit

(A) Prohibited Uses. Except as otherwise provided by this constitution, the funds, credit, property, or things of value of the state or of any political subdivision shall not be loaned, pledged, or donated to or for any person, association, or corporation, public or private. Neither the state nor a political subdivision shall subscribe to or purchase the stock of a corporation or association or for any private enterprise.
(B) Authorized Uses. Nothing in this Section shall prevent (1) the use of public funds for programs of social welfare for the aid and support of the needy; (2) contributions of public funds to pension and insurance programs for the benefit of public employees; (3) the pledge of public funds, credit, property, or things of value for public purposes with respect to the issuance of bonds or other evidences of indebtedness to meet public obligations as provided by law; or (4) the return of property, including mineral rights, to a former owner from whom the property had previously been expropriated, or purchased under threat of expropriation, when the legislature by law declares that the public and necessary purpose which originally supported the expropriation has ceased to exist and orders the return of the property to the former owner under such terms and conditions as specified by the legislature.
(C) Cooperative Endeavors. For a public purpose, the state and its political subdivisions or political corporations may engage in cooperative endeavors with each other, with the United States or its agencies, or with any public or private association, corporation, or individual.
(D) Prior Obligations. Funds, credit, property, or things of value of the state or of a political subdivision heretofore loaned, pledged, dedicated, or granted by prior state law or authorized to be loaned, pledged, dedicated, or granted by the prior laws and constitution of this state shall so remain for the full term as provided by the prior laws and constitution and for the full term as provided by any contract, unless the authorization is revoked by law enacted by two-thirds of the elected members of each house of the legislature prior to the vesting of any contractual rights pursuant to this Section.

Provisions in the 1868 Constitution allowing the state to invest in corporations constructing internal improvements, especially railroads, led to substantial corruption. The response in subsequent constitutions was to limit the power of the state to use its funds or credit for the benefit of private development. Section 14(A) continues those limitations, although the growing list of authorized "public purposes" allowed by paragraph B is typical of developments in other states. The supreme court in *Arnold v. Board of Levee Commissioners* (1978), for example, permitted the lease of government property to a private foundation for the construction of a library and museum named after a former congressman. Although the lease was for a nominal one dollar per year, the foundation was obliged to construct a building that would become the board's property at the termination of the lease.

When the state teachers and employee retirement systems sought to invest in common stock, the attorney general rendered an opinion that such purchases were prohibited by this section. The court of appeal in *Louisiana State Employees' Retirement System v. State* (1983) held otherwise, ruling that the retirement systems were not governed by the section.

Paragraph B was amended in 1983 to add item 4. The amendment allowed the state to return to private landowners land (and valuable mineral interests) that had been expropriated or purchased for the Bohemia Spillway, a flood project that had served its purpose and was no longer needed. The supreme court in *Board of Commissioners v. Department of Natural Resources* (1986) allowed the transfer, rejecting an argument that the provision deprived the levee board of property without compensation.

SECTION 15
Release of Obligations to State, Parish, or Municipality

The legislature shall have no power to release, extinguish, or authorize the releasing or extinguishing of any indebtedness, liability, or obligation of a corporation or individual to the state, a parish, or a municipality. However, the legislature, by law, may establish a system under which claims by the state or a political subdivision may be compromised, and may provide for the release of heirs to confiscated property from taxes due thereon at the date of its reversion to them.

An anticorruption provision similar to section 14, this section is a continuation of a provision going back to Article 157 of the 1879 Constitution. Although it prohibits canceling of debts due the state, it allows the state to settle disputed claims against private persons.

SECTION 16
Taxes; Prescription

Taxes, except real property taxes, and licenses shall prescribe in three years after the thirty-first day of December in the year in which they are due, but prescription may be interrupted or suspended as provided by law.

Normally the state is not subject to loss of rights through liberative prescription (statutes of limitation). This section makes it clear that claims for taxes, except real property taxes, are subject to a specified three-year liberative prescription.

Additionally, legislation can provide for suspension and interruption of those periods, that is, provided that the running of the period will cease for stated reasons.

SECTION 17
Legislation to Obtain Federal Aid

The legislature may enact laws to enable the state, its agencies, boards, commissions, and political subdivisions and their agencies to comply with federal laws and regulations in order to secure federal participation in funding capital improvement projects.

A continuation of a provision of the 1921 Constitution, this section authorizes legislation required to comply with conditions federal law imposes on recipients of grants for capital improvement projects.

PART II. PROPERTY TAXATION

SECTION 18
Ad Valorem Taxes

(A) Assessments. Property subject to ad valorem taxation shall be listed on the assessment rolls at its assessed valuation, which, except as provided in Paragraph (C), shall be a percentage of its fair market value. The percentage of fair market value shall be uniform throughout the state upon the same class of property.
(B) Classification. The classifications of property subject to ad valorem taxation and the percentage of fair market value applicable to each classification for the purpose of determining assessed valuation are as follows:

Classifications	*Percentages*
1. Land	10%
2. Improvements for residential purposes	10%
3. Electric cooperative properties, excluding land	15%
4. Public service properties, excluding land	25%
5. Other property	15%

The legislature may enact laws defining electric cooperative properties and public service properties.
(C) Use Value. Bona fide agricultural, horticultural, marsh, and timber lands, as defined by general law, shall be assessed for tax purposes at ten percent of use value rather than fair market value. The legislature may provide by law similarly for buildings of historic architectural importance.

(D) Valuation. Each assessor shall determine the fair market value of all property subject to taxation within his respective parish or district except public service properties, which shall be valued at fair market value by the Louisiana Tax Commission or its successor. Each assessor shall determine the use value of property which is to be so assessed under the provisions of Paragraph (C). Fair market value and use value of property shall be determined in accordance with criteria which shall be established by law and which shall apply uniformly throughout the state.

(E) Review. The correctness of assessments by the assessor shall be subject to review first by the parish governing authority, then by the Louisiana Tax Commission or its successor, and finally by the courts, all in accordance with procedures established by law.

(F) Reappraisal. All property subject to taxation shall be reappraised and valued in accordance with this Section, at intervals of not more than four years. [Amended by Acts 1979, No. 799, approved October 27, 1979, effective November 30, 1979]

In the past, both the state and the local governments imposed property taxes, the state tax depending on property assessments made by locally elected assessors. Unequal application of the state taxes resulted from a lack of uniformity of assessment practices. This section was designed to provide statewide uniformity by requiring assessors, still locally elected officials under section 24, to assess property at the same percentage of value throughout the state. Originally section 18(B) simply provided that land and residential improvements would be assessed at 10 percent of value and that other property would be assessed at 15 percent. A 1979 amendment added the provision for assessment of public service properties at 25 percent and the property of electric cooperatives at 15 percent.

Assessments are subject to review by the local governing authorities and State Tax Commission, as well as by the courts. Reappraisals every four years are required by paragraph F, but the constitution does not provide a mechanism to enforce that obligation. Paragraph C was adopted primarily as a concession to agricultural interests that asserted that high taxes on farmland near growing urban areas were causing farmers to sell their land for development. Assessment of property at use value, based on the economic return of the property as used, is allowed under Louisiana Revised Statutes 47:2301–2309.

SECTION 19

State Property Taxation; Rate Limitation

State taxation on property for all purposes shall not exceed an annual rate of five and three-quarter mills on the dollar of assessed valuation.

The limitation provided in section 19 is on ad valorem property taxation of immovable property (real estate) by the state; it does not apply to local government taxation, which is governed by Article VI. The state has since repealed its tax on immovable property, thus relieving it of equal protection problems because of uneven assessment practices by local assessors.

SECTION 20
Homestead Exemption

(A) Homeowners

(1) The bona fide homestead, consisting of a tract of land or two or more tracts of land with a residence on one tract and a field, pasture, or garden on the other tract or tracts, not exceeding one hundred sixty acres, buildings and appurtenances, whether rural or urban, owned and occupied by any person, shall be exempt from state, parish, and special ad valorem taxes to the extent of seven thousand five hundred dollars of the assessed valuation.

(2) The homestead exemption shall extend to the surviving spouse or minor children of a deceased owner and shall apply when the homestead is occupied as such and title to it is in either husband or wife but not to more than one homestead owned by the husband or wife.

(3) This exemption shall not extend to municipal taxes. However, the exemption shall apply (a) in Orleans Parish, to state, general city, school, levee, and levee district taxes and (b) to any municipal taxes levied for school purposes.

(B) Residential Lessees. Notwithstanding any contrary provision in this constitution, the legislature may provide for tax relief to residential lessees in the form of credits or rebates in order to provide equitable tax relief similar to that granted to homeowners through homestead exemptions.

Section 20 (A) initially protected from property taxation the first $30,000 of value of a homestead, granting a $3,000 exemption in a scheme where residences are assessed at 10 percent of value. A 1980 amendment raised the exemption to $7,500, freeing homes worth $75,000 or less from tax. Subsequent attempts at fiscal reform have sought to reduce that exemption, but they have failed.

SECTION 21
Other Property Exemptions

In addition to the homestead exemption provided for in Section 20 of this Article, the following property and no other shall be exempt from ad valorem taxation:

(A) Public lands; other public property used for public purposes.

(B)(1) Property owned by a nonprofit corporation or association organized and operated exclusively for religious, dedicated places of burial, charitable, health, welfare, fraternal, or educational purposes, no part of the net earnings of which inure to the benefit of any private shareholder or member thereof and which is declared to be exempt from federal or state income tax;

(2) property of a bona fide labor organization representing its members or affiliates in collective bargaining efforts; and

(3) property of an organization such as a lodge or club organized for charitable and fraternal purposes and practicing the same, and property of a nonprofit corporation devoted to promoting trade, travel, and commerce, and also property of a trade, business, industry or professional society or association, if that property is owned by a nonprofit corporation or association organized under the laws of this state for such purposes.

None of the property listed in Paragraph (B) shall be exempt if owned, operated, leased, or used for commercial purposes unrelated to the exempt purposes of the corporation or association.

(C)(1) Cash on hand or deposit;

(2) stocks and bonds, except bank stocks, the tax on which shall be paid by the banking institution;

(3) obligations secured by mortgage on property located in Louisiana and the notes or other evidence thereof;

(4) loans by life insurance companies to policyholders, if secured solely by their policies;

(5) the legal reserve of domestic life insurance companies;

(6) loans by a homestead or building and loan association to its members, if secured solely by stock of the association;

(7) debts due for merchandise or other articles of commerce or for services rendered;

(8) obligations of the state or its political subdivisions;

(9) personal property used in the home or on loan in a public place;

(10) irrevocably dedicated places of burial held by individuals for purposes of burial of themselves or members of their families;

(11) agricultural products while owned by the producer, agricultural machinery and other implements used exclusively for agricultural purposes, animals on the farm, and property belonging to an agricultural fair association;

(12) property used for cultural, Mardi Gras carnival, or civic activities and not operated for profit to the owners;

(13) rights-of-way granted to the State Department of Highways;

(14) boats using gasoline as motor fuel;

(15) commercial vessels used for gathering seafood for human consumption; and

(16) ships and oceangoing tugs, towboats, and barges engaged in international trade and domiciled in Louisiana ports. However, this exemption shall not apply to harbor, wharf, shed, and other port dues or to any vessel operated in the coastal trade of the states of the United States.

(17) Materials, boiler fuels, and energy sources used by public utilities to fuel the generation of electricity.

(D)(1) Raw materials, goods, commodities, and articles imported into this state from outside the states of the United States:

(a) so long as the imports remain on the public property of the port authority or docks of the common carrier where they first entered this state;

(b) so long as the imports (other than minerals and ores of the same kind as any mined or produced in this state and manufactured articles) are held in this state in the original form in bales, sacks, barrels, boxes, cartons, containers, or other original packages, and raw materials held in bulk as all or a part of the new material inventory of manufacturers or processors, solely for manufacturing or processing; or

(c) so long as the imports are held by an importer in any public or private storage in the original form in bales, sacks, barrels, boxes, cartons, containers, or other original packages and agricultural products in bulk.

This exemption shall not apply to these imports when held by a retail merchant as part of his stock-in-trade for sale at retail.

(2) Raw materials, goods, commodities, and other articles being held on the public property of a port authority, on docks of any common carrier, or in a warehouse, grain elevator, dock, wharf, or public storage facility in this state for export to a point outside the states of the United States.

(3) Goods, commodities, and personal property in public or private storage while in transit through this state which are moving in interstate commerce through or over the territory of the state or which are in public or private storage within Louisiana, having been shipped from outside Louisiana for storage in transit to a final destination outside Louisiana, whether such destination was specified when transportation began or afterward. Property described in Paragraph (D), whether or not entitled to exemption, shall be reported to the proper taxing authority on the forms required by law.

(E) Motor vehicles used on the public highways of this state, from state, parish, and special ad valorem taxes. This exemption shall not extend to any general or special tax levied by a municipal governing authority, or by a district created by it, unless the governing authority thereof provides for the exemption by ordinance or resolution.

(F) Notwithstanding any contrary provision of this Section, the State Board of Commerce and Industry or its successor, with the approval of the governor, may enter into contracts for the exemption from ad valorem taxes of a new manufacturing establishment or an addition to an existing manufacturing establishment, on such terms and conditions as the board, with the approval of the governor, deems in the best interest of the state.

The exemption shall be for an initial term of no more than five calendar years, and may be renewed for an additional five years. All property exempted shall be listed on the assessment rolls and submitted to the Louisiana Tax Commission or its successor, but no taxes shall be collected thereon during the period of exemption.

The terms "manufacturing establishment" and "addition" as used herein mean a new plant or establishment or an addition or additions to any existing plant or establishment which engages in the business of working raw materials into wares suitable for use or which gives new shapes, qualities or combinations to matter which already has gone through some artificial process.

(G) Coal or lignite stockpiled in Louisiana for use in Louisiana for industrial or manufacturing purposes or for boiler fuel, gasification, feedstock, or process purposes.

(H) Notwithstanding any contrary provision of this constitution, the State Board of Commerce and Industry or its successor, with the approval of the governor and the local governing authority and in accordance with procedures and conditions provided by law, may enter into contracts granting to a property owner, who proposes the expansion, restoration, improvement, or development of an existing structure or structures in a downtown, historic, or economic development district established by a local governing authority or in accordance with law, the right for five years after completion of the work to pay ad valorem taxes based upon the assessed valuation of the property for the year prior to the commencement of the expansion, restoration, improvement, or development.

The 1973 convention continued prior exemptions and added some. Subsequent amendments have added more. The result is a long and complex list of types of property exempt from ad valorem taxation. The legislature is prohibited, by the terms of the first paragraph of the section, from providing for exemptions, so any additional ones must be obtained by constitutional amendment.

SECTION 22
No Impairment of Existing Taxes or Obligations

This Part shall not be applied in a manner which will (a) invalidate taxes authorized and imposed prior to the effective date of this constitution or (b) impair the obligations, validity, or security of any bonds or other debt obligations authorized prior to the effective date of this constitution.

SECTION 23
Adjustment of Ad Valorem Tax Millages

(A) First Adjustment. Prior to the end of the third year after the effective date of this constitution, the assessors and the Louisiana Tax Commission or its successor shall complete determination of the fair market value or the use value of all property subject to taxation within each parish for use in implementing this Article. Except as provided in this Section, the total amount of ad valorem taxes collected by any taxing authority in the year in which Sections 18 and 20 of this Article are implemented shall not be increased or decreased, because of their provisions, above or below ad valorem taxes collected by that taxing authority in the year preceding implementation. To accomplish this result, it shall be mandatory for each affected taxing authority, in the year in which Sections 18 and 20 of this Article are implemented, to adjust millages upwards or downwards without regard to millage limitations contained in this constitution, and the maximum authorized millages shall be increased or decreased, without further voter approval, in proportion to the amount of the adjustment upward or downward. Thereafter, such millages shall remain in effect unless changed as permitted by this constitution.

(B) Subsequent Adjustments. Except as otherwise permitted in this Section, the total amount of ad valorem taxes collected by any taxing authority in the year in which the reappraisal and valuation provisions of Section 18, Paragraph (F) of this Article are implemented shall not be increased or decreased because of a reappraisal or valuation or increases or decreases in the homestead exemption above or below the total amount of ad valorem taxes collected by that taxing authority in the year preceding implementation of the reappraisal and valuation. To accomplish this result, the provisions of millage adjustments relative to implementation of Section 18 and Section 20 of this Article, as set forth in Paragraph (A) of this Section shall be mandatory. Thereafter, following implementation of each subsequent reappraisal and valuation required by Paragraph (F) of Section 18 of this Article, the millages as fixed in each such implementation shall remain in effect unless changed as permitted by Paragraph (C) of this Section.

(C) Increases Permitted. Nothing herein shall prohibit a taxing authority from collecting, in the year in which Sections 18 and 20 of this Article are implemented or in any subsequent year, a larger dollar amount of ad valorem taxes by (1) levying additional or increased millages as provided by law or (2) placing additional property on the tax rolls. Increases in the millage rate in excess of the rates established as provided by Paragraph (B) above but not in excess of the prior year's maximum authorized millage rate may be levied by two-thirds vote of the total membership of a taxing authority without further voter approval but only after a public hearing held in accordance with the open meetings law.

(D) Application. This Section shall not apply to millages required to be levied for the payment of general obligation bonds. [As amended in 1980]

The adjustment of assessments to conform to the new statewide uniform requirements of section 18 could have resulted in substantial tax increases or substantial tax decreases in various subdivisions of the state. To avoid that impact, this section requires that tax millages be adjusted, upward or downward, so that the total tax burden in the jurisdiction will not be changed by virtue of the adjustments in assessments. The 1980 amendments, adding paragraphs B and C applied the same concept to future readjustments required to be made every four years under the terms of paragraph F.

SECTION 24
Tax Assessors

(A) Election; Term. A tax assessor shall be elected by the electors of each parish, Orleans Parish excepted. His term of office shall be four years. His election, duties, and compensation shall be as provided by law.
(B) Orleans Parish. There shall be seven assessors in New Orleans, who shall compose the Board of Assessors for Orleans Parish. One shall be elected from each municipal district of New Orleans, and each shall be a resident of the district from which he is elected. The assessors shall be elected at the same time as the municipal officers of New Orleans, for terms of four years each. Their duties and compensation shall be as provided by law.
(C) Vacancy. When a vacancy occurs in the office of tax assessor, the duties of the office, until filled by election as provided by law, shall be assumed by the chief deputy assessor, except in Orleans Parish where the Board of Assessors shall appoint an interim assessor.

This section continues the disparate treatment for New Orleans, which has seven assessors, one elected from each of seven districts. One assessor is elected in each of the other parishes.

SECTION 25
Tax Sales

(A) Tax Sales. There shall be no forfeiture of property for nonpayment of taxes. However, at the expiration of the year in which the taxes are due, the collector, without suit, and after giving notice to the delinquent in the manner provided by law, shall advertise for sale the property on which the taxes are due. The advertisement shall be published in the official journal of the parish or municipality, or, if there is no official journal, as provided by law for sheriffs' sales, in the manner provided for judicial sales. On the day of sale, the collector shall sell the portion of the property which the debtor points out. If the debtor does not point out property, the collector shall sell immediately the least quantity of property which any bidder will buy for the amount of the taxes, interest, and costs. The sale shall be without appraisement. A tax deed by a tax collector shall be prima facie evidence that a valid sale was made.
(B) Redemption. The property sold shall be redeemable for three years after the date of recordation of the tax sale, by paying the price given, including costs, five percent penalty thereon, and interest at the rate of one percent per month until redemption.
(C) Annulment. No sale of property for taxes shall be set aside for any cause, except on proof of payment of the taxes prior to the date of the sale, unless the proceeding to annul is instituted within six months after service of notice of sale. A notice of sale shall not be served until the final day for redemption has ended. It must be served

within five years after the date of the recordation of the tax deed if no notice is given. The fact that taxes were paid on a part of the property sold prior to the sale thereof, or that a part of the property was not subject to taxation, shall not be cause for annulling the sale of any part thereof on which the taxes for which it was sold were due and unpaid. No judgment annulling a tax sale shall have effect until the price and all taxes and costs are paid, and until ten percent per annum interest on the amount of the price and taxes paid from date of respective payments are paid to the purchaser; however, this shall not apply to sales annulled because the taxes were paid prior to the date of sale.

(D) Quieting Tax Title. The manner of notice and form of proceeding to quiet tax titles shall be provided by law.

(E) Movables; Tax Sales. When taxes on movables are delinquent, the tax collector shall seize and sell sufficient movable property of the delinquent taxpayer to pay the tax, whether or not the property seized is the property which was assessed. Sale of the property shall be at public auction, without appraisement, after ten days advertisement, published within ten days after date of seizure. It shall be absolute and without redemption. If the tax collector can find no corporeal movables of the delinquent to seize, he may levy on incorporeal rights, by notifying the debtor thereof, or he may proceed by summary rule in the courts to compel the delinquent to deliver for sale property in his possession or under his control.

(F) Postponement of Taxes. The legislature may postpone the payment of taxes, but only in cases of overflow, general conflagration, general crop destruction, or other public calamity, and may provide for the levying, assessing, and collecting of such postponed taxes. In such case, the legislature may authorize the borrowing of money by the state on its faith and credit, by bond issue or otherwise, and may levy taxes, or apply taxes already levied and not appropriated, to secure payment thereof, in order to create a fund from which loans may be made through the Interim Emergency Board to the governing authority of the parish where the calamity occurs. The money loaned shall be applied to and shall not exceed the deficiency in revenue of the parish or a political subdivision therein or of which the parish is a part, caused by postponement of taxes. No loan shall be made to a parish governing authority without the approval of the Interim Emergency Board.

This section continues the complex provisions of prior constitutions that regulated tax sales in detail and established a constitutional right to redeem, within three years, property sold at a tax sale.

PART III. REVENUE SHARING

SECTION 26
Revenue Sharing Fund

(A) Creation of Fund. The Revenue Sharing Fund is created as a special fund in the state treasury.

(B) Annual Allocation. The sum of ninety million dollars is allocated annually from the state general fund to the revenue sharing fund. The legislature may appropriate additional sums to the fund.
(C) Distribution Formula. The revenue sharing fund shall be distributed annually as provided by law solely on the basis of population and number of homesteads in each parish in proportion to population and the number of homesteads throughout the state. Unless otherwise provided by law, population of the last federal decennial census shall be utilized for this purpose. After deductions in each parish for retirement systems and commissions as authorized by law, the remaining funds, to the extent available, shall be distributed by first priority to the tax recipient bodies within the parish, as defined by law, to offset current losses because of homestead exemptions granted in this Article. Any balance remaining in a parish distribution shall be allocated to the municipalities and tax recipient bodies within each parish as provided by law.
(D) Distributing Officer. The funds distributed to each parish as provided in Paragraph (C) shall be distributed in Orleans Parish by the city treasurer of New Orleans and in all other parishes by the parish tax collector. The funds allocated to the Monroe City School Board or its successor shall be distributed to and by the city treasurer of Monroe.
(E) Bonded Debt. A political subdivision, as defined by Article VI of this constitution, may incur debt by issuing negotiable bonds and may pledge for the payment of all or part of the principal and interest of such bonds the proceeds derived or to be derived from that portion of the funds received by it from the revenue sharing fund, to offset current losses caused by homestead exemptions granted by this Article. Unless otherwise provided by law, no moneys allocated within any parish from the balance remaining in its distribution may be pledged to the payment of the principal or interest of any bonds. Bonds issued under this Paragraph shall be issued and sold as provided by law, and shall require approval of the State Bond Commission or its successor prior to issuance and sale.

A 1972 amendment to the 1921 Constitution established a revenue-sharing fund to be distributed to local governments. It contained a self-operative annual appropriation of $80 million to the fund. Local government interests in the 1973 Convention continued the fund in the new constitution, increasing the automatic annual appropriation to $90 million.

SECTION 27
Transportation Trust Fund

(A) Creation of fund. Effective January 1, 1990, there shall be established in the state treasury as a special permanent trust fund the Transportation Trust Fund ("the trust fund") in which shall be deposited the "excess revenues" as defined herein which are a portion of the avails received in each year from all taxes levied on gasoline and motor fuels and on special fuels (said avails being referred to as the "revenues") as provided herein. After satisfying pledges respecting that portion of the revenues attributable to the tax rates in effect at the time of such pledges for the payment of obligations for bonds or other evidences of indebtedness on the effective date of this Section, the treasurer shall allocate such portion of the revenues received in each year as necessary to pay all principal, interest, premium, if any, and other obligations incident to the issuance, security, and payment in respect of bonds as authorized in Paragraph (C) hereof. Thereafter, the portion of the revenues remaining shall be deposited in the Bond Security and Redemption Fund in the state treasury. After (1) the payment of any obligations for bonds or other evidences of indebtedness in existence on the effective date of this Section which are secured by revenues; (2) payments in respect of bonds authorized in Paragraph (C) hereof; and (3) credit to the Bond Security and Redemption Fund, the treasurer shall deposit in and credit to the trust fund all of the revenues remaining (the "excess revenues") from the avails of all taxes levied on gasoline and motor fuels and on special fuels, as follows: for the fiscal year beginning July 1, 1989, the avails of twelve cents per gallon of said taxes received on and after January 1, 1990; for the fiscal year beginning on July 1, 1990, the avails of fourteen cents per gallon of said taxes; for the fiscal year beginning on July 1, 1991, and thereafter, the avails of all taxes levied on gasoline and motor fuels and onspecial fuels. Purchases of gasoline, diesel fuel, or special fuels which are subject to excise tax under Chapter 7 of Subtitle II of Title 47 of the Louisiana Revised Statutes of 1950 shall be exempt from the state sales tax and any sales tax levied by a political subdivision as defined by Article VI, Section 44(2). All monies appropriated by the Federal Highway Administration and the Federal Aviation Administration, or their successors, either reimbursed or paid directly, shall be paid directly or deposited in and credited to the trust fund.

(B) The monies in the trust fund shall be appropriated or dedicated solely and exclusively for the costs for and associated with construction and maintenance of the roads and bridges of the state and federal highway systems, the Statewide Flood-Control Program or its successor, ports, airports, transit, state police for traffic control purposes, and the Parish Transportation Fund or its successor and for the payment of all principal, interest, premium, if any, and other obligations incident to the issuance, security, and payment in respect of bonds or other obligations payable from the trust fund as authorized in Paragraph (D) hereof. Unless pledged to the repayment of bonds authorized in Paragraphs (C) or (D) of this Section, the monies in the trust fund allocated to ports, airports, flood control, parish transportation, and state highway construction shall be appropriated annually by the legislature only pursuant to programs established by law which establish a system of priorities for the expenditure of such monies, except that the Transportation Infrastructure Model for Economic Development, which shall include only those projects enumerated in House Bill 17 of the 1989 First Extraordinary Session of the Legislature, shall be funded as provided by law. The state generated tax monies appropriated for ports, Parish Transportation Fund. The annual appropriationfor airports shall be a sum equal to, but not greater than, the annual estimated revenue to be derived from the state taxes to be collected and received on aviation fuel. Unencumbered and unexpended balances at the end of each fiscal year shall remain in the trust fund. The earnings realized in each fiscal year on the investment of monies in the trust fund shall be deposited in and credited to the trust fund.

(C) The State Bond Commission or its successor, may issue and sell bonds, notes, or other obligations ("Bonds") secured by a pledge of a portion of the revenues not to exceed the avails of four cents per gallon of the taxes on gasoline and motor fuels and on special fuels received by the state treasurer. Bonds so issued may also be secured by a pledge of all or a portion of excess revenues as additional security therefor, and if so pledged any portion thereof needed to pay principal, interest, or premium, if any, and other obligations incident to the issuance, security, and payment in respect to Bonds may be expended by the treasurer without the need for legislative appropriation. The Bonds may be issued in the manner set forth in this Section to provide for the costs for and associated with construction and maintenance of the roads and bridges of the state and federal highway systems, Statewide Flood-Control Program, ports, airports, and for any other purpose for which monies in the trust fund may be expended as provided by law. Such Bonds shall not be considered to be debt under Article VII, Section 6, unless the provisions of Article VII, Section 6, relative in incurring debt by the state are met, in which case the full faith and credit of the state may also be pledged in addition to the revenues received by the treasurer.

(D) The State Bond Commission or its successor may also issue and sell bonds, notes, or other obligations secured by a pledge of the excess revenues deposited in the trust fund, which shall otherwise be issued in the manner and for the purposes provided for in this Section, and if so pledged any portion thereof needed to pay principal, interest, or premium, if any, and other obligations incident to the issuance, security, and payment in respect thereof may be expended by the treasurer without the need for legislative appropriation.

(E) Bonds, notes, or the obligations issued pursuant to the provisions of Paragraphs (C) or (D) above may be issued in the manner provided by resolution of the State Bond Commission or its successor under the authority of said Paragraphs without compliance with any other requirement of this constitution or law. To that end, said Paragraphs (C) and (D) hereof shall be deemed self-operative. [Section 27 was added by amendment in 1989.]

Section 27 was adopted by amendment in fall 1989. After Governor Roemer's earlier attempt at drastic tax reform failed, this was one of the provisions adopted as a companion to an increase in the tax on gasoline and other motor fuels.

Paragraph A dedicates most of the revenues from those taxes to use for road construction and other purposes related to transportation. It is another example of the continuing trend to dedicating revenues to specific purposes in the constitution, reflecting a distrust in the legislature's assignment of priorities to use of state funds.

Article VIII

Education

PREAMBLE

The goal of the public educational system is to provide learning environments and experiences, at all stages of human development, that are humane, just, and designed to promote excellence in order that every individual may be afforded an equal opportunity to develop to his full potential.

SECTION 1
Public Education System

The legislature shall provide for the education of the people of the state and shall establish and maintain a public educational system:

Educators serving on the Committee on Education and Welfare sponsored the unusual second preamble and the hortatory mandate to the legislature contained in section 1. Both provisions are not self-enforcing and have little substantive effect. In *Simmons v. SOWELA Technical Institute* (1985), a nursing student invoked these provisions to buttress a claim for wrongful dismissal. The court of appeal said they established only moral duties and held they were not the basis for any legal claim against the state.

SECTION 2
State Superintendent of Education

There shall be a superintendent of education for public elementary and secondary education who, subject to provisions for appointment in lieu of election set forth in Article IV, Section 20, of this constitution, shall be elected for a term of four years. If the office is made appointive, the State Board of Elementary and Secondary Education shall make the appointment. He shall be the administrative head of the Department of Education and shall implement the policies of the State Board of Elementary and Secondary Education and the laws affecting schools under its jurisdiction. The qualifications and other powers, functions, duties, and responsibilities of the superintendent shall be provided by law.

The constitution's scheme for elementary and secondary education produced an inevitable tension between the elected superintendent of education provided for in this section and the Board of Elementary and Secondary Education (BESE) established in section 3. The 1974 Constitution simply established the positions and gave them no constitutional powers. The powers of the superintendent and the board would be as "provided by law." The supreme court in *BESE v. Nix* (1977) affirmed the legislature's powers in this regard and held that a statute giving broad powers to the superintendent did not invade the powers of the board. Continuing difficulties in determining the powers of the board and the superintendent led, in 1985, to legislation (Louisiana Revised Statutes 17:21) providing for appointment of the superintendent instead of election, as allowed by Article IV, section 20. The superintendent is now appointed by the BESE.

SECTION 3
State Board of Elementary and Secondary Education

(A) Creation; Functions. The State Board of Elementary and Secondary Education is created as a body corporate. It shall supervise and control the public elementary and secondary schools, vocational-technical training and special schools under its jurisdiction and shall have budgetary responsibility for all funds appropriated or allocated by the state for those schools, all as provided by law. The board shall have other powers, duties, and responsibilities as provided by this constitution or by law, but shall have no control over the business affairs of a parish or city school board or the selection or removal of its officers and employees.
(B) Membership, terms. The board shall consist of eleven members, eight of whom shall be elected from single-member districts, which shall be determined as provided by law, and three of whom shall be appointed by the governor from the state at large, with consent of the Senate. Members shall serve terms of four years, which shall be concurrent with the term of the governor.
(C) Vacancy. A vacancy in the office of an elected member, if the remaining portion of the term is more than one year, shall be filled for the remainder of the term by

> election, as provided by law. Other vacancies shall be filled for the remainder of the term by appointment by the governor.

The powers of the board are determined by the legislature; the constitution provides only for the establishment and composition of the board. Eight elected members serve on the board, with geographic diversity accomplished by providing for one member from each of the state's eight congressional districts. Giving the governor three appointments to the board serves, in part, to provide for representation of minorities.

Continuing the legacy of the independent blue ribbon boards favored by the anti-Long forces during the 1940s and 1950s, the delegates to the 1973 convention sought to ensure the board's independence from the governor by providing for six-year overlapping terms. In 1979, however, an amendment was adopted to reduce the terms to four years and to make them concurrent with that of the governor, giving the chief executive significant additional powers over education. That 1979 amendment also added section 15 to provide for the transition to the new scheme.

Under this section, the state board cannot be given any control over a local school board's business affairs or its power of removal of its officers and employees. Relying on this last limitation, the supreme court in *Johnson v. BESE* (1982) invalidated a statute that gave the state board power to revoke the teaching certificate of a tenured teacher for violation of a code of ethics.

The board's powers are "all as provided by law." The supreme court in *Aguillard v. Treen* (1983) held that this language meant that the board had no unreviewable power to determine curriculum. The legislature had the authority to require the teaching of a designated course or curriculum, in that case a requirement that creation science be taught to balance the teaching of evolution science. Subsequently, in *Edwards v. Aguillard* (1987), the U. S. Supreme Court held the statute unconstitutional as a violation of the First Amendment prohibition of a law establishing religion.

SECTION 4
Approval of Private Schools

> Upon application by a private elementary, secondary, or proprietary school with a sustained curriculum or specialized course of study of quality at least equal to that prescribed for similar public schools, the State Board of Elementary and Secondary Education shall approve the private school. A certificate issued by an approved private school shall carry the same privileges as one issued by a state public school.

Although no significant court litigation has arisen under this section, it has been invoked in a number of political debates as private and parochial schools have sought more state aid and have resisted controls that the state has sought to attach to the aid. An opinion of the attorney general (77–479) stated that the board is limited in its power to approve or disapprove a private school. The board can consider only the question of the school's "sustained curriculum" and not "any other aspect of the operation and conduct of the private school."

COMMENTARY TO SECTIONS 5–8

For many years, legislation outside the constitution governed the management of public institutions of higher education. The Louisiana scandals in the 1930s, which saw the president of Louisiana State University (LSU) jailed for speculating in wheat futures with university funds, prompted a typical Louisiana response: adoption of a constitutional amendment. The amendment sought to take politics out of education by establishing an independent board to govern LSU. As the number of state educational institutions grew, competition for funds and programs arose, and constitutional amendments providing a coordinating council were adopted. By the time of the 1973 Constitutional Convention, governance of higher education was a controversial political issue, one of the most intensely debated subjects in the convention. The convention proposed two alternative versions of the education article to the voters. The voters rejected the centralized one-board alternative for higher education and instead chose the plan with four constitutional boards. LSU continued with its board. Black delegates sought and obtained a similar board for Southern University, a predominantly black institution. A third board of trustees was established to govern the other state colleges. To replace the coordination council, the board of regents was established with enumerated powers related to avoiding duplication and competition among institutions.

One of the early problems this fractured system had to contend with was eliminating the vestiges of prior racial discrimination. A consent decree adopted in 1981 (*United States v. Louisiana,* 1981) appeared to have failed to produce the desired desegregation. When renewed efforts to modify the decree in 1989 failed, the federal court appointed a special master to devise a new desegregation plan. Adopting most of that plan, the district court ordered the centralization of state college governance in one board, thus superseding the provisions of sections 5–8. The plan was also supported by the governor of the state despite the constitutional provisions to the contrary. The U. S. Supreme Court first stayed the lower court order and then dismissed the case for lack of jurisdiction (*Southern University Board of Supervisors v. United States,* 1989). An appeal of the district court order was pending in the U.S. Court of Appeal for the Fifth Circuit as of June 1990.

SECTION 5
Board of Regents

(A) Creation; Functions. The Board of Regents is created as a body corporate. It shall plan, coordinate, and have budgetary responsibility for all public higher education and shall have other powers, duties, and responsibilities provided in this Section or by law.

(B) Membership; Terms. The board shall consist of fifteen electors appointed by the governor, with consent of the Senate, for overlapping terms of six years, following initial terms which shall be fixed by law. At least one member, but no more than two members, shall be appointed from each congressional district.

(C) Vacancy. A vacancy occurring prior to the expiration of a term shall be filled for the remainder of the unexpired term by appointment by the governor, with consent of the Senate.

(D) Powers. The Board of Regents shall meet with the State Board of Elementary and Secondary Education at least twice a year to coordinate programs of public elementary, secondary, vocational-technical, career, and higher education. The Board of Regents shall have the following powers, duties, and responsibilities relating to public institutions of higher education:

(1) To revise or eliminate an existing degree program, department of instruction, division, or similar subdivision.

(2) To approve, disapprove, or modify a proposed degree program, department of instruction, division, or similar subdivision.

(3) To study the need for and feasibility of any new institution of postsecondary education, including branches of institutions and conversion of two-year institutions to institutions offering longer courses of study. If the creation of a new institution, the addition of another management board, or the transfer of an existing institution from one board to another is proposed, the Board of Regents shall report its written findings and recommendations to the legislature within one year. Only after the report has been filed, or, after one year if no report is filed, may the legislature take affirmative action on such a proposal and then only by law enacted by two-thirds of the elected members of each house.

(4) To formulate and make timely revision of a master plan for higher education. As a minimum, the plan shall include a formula for equitable distribution of funds to the institutions of higher education.

(5) To require that every higher education board submit to it, at a time it specifies, an annual budget proposal for operational needs and for capital needs of each institution under the control of each board. The Board of Regents shall submit its budget recommendations for all institutions of higher education in the state. It shall recommend priorities for capital construction and improvements.

(E) Powers Not Vested. Powers of management over public institutions of higher education not specifically vested by this Section in the Board of Regents are reserved to the Board of Supervisors of Louisiana State University and Agricultural and Mechanical College, the Board of Supervisors of Southern University and Agricultural and Mechanical College, the Board of Trustees for State Colleges and Universities, and any other such board created pursuant to this Article, as to the institutions under the control of each.

The board of regents is designed to be a coordinating, policymaking board without direct authority over colleges and universities. The constitution gives it limited, enumerated powers in section 5(D) and then provides in section 5(E) that all other powers of management "not specifically vested by this Section in the Board" are reserved to the three management boards governed by sections 6 and 7.

The board's powers extend primarily to control over the establishment, revision, or elimination of degree programs and departments of instruction. In matters of planning, budgets and establishment of new colleges, it is an advisory body to the legislature.

In *Board of Regents v. Board of Trustees* (1984), the court of appeal held that the regents' powers did not include changing the name of a college. The court also held the power was not in the board of trustees, for that matter was not a power of administration or management. The power to name institutions is thus left to the legislature.

SECTION 6
Board of Trustees for State Colleges and Universities

(A) Creation; Functions. The Board of Trustees for State Colleges and Universities is created as a body corporate. Subject to powers vested by this Article in the Board of Regents, it shall have supervision and management of state colleges and universities not managed by a higher education board created by or under this Article.
(B) Membership; Terms. The board shall be composed of two members from each congressional district and one member from the state at large, appointed by the governor with consent of the Senate. The members shall serve overlapping terms of six years, following initial terms fixed by law.
(C) Vacancy. A vacancy occurring prior to the expiration of a term shall be filled for the remainder of the unexpired term by appointment by the governor, with consent of the Senate.

SECTION 7
Board of Supervisors of Louisiana State University and Agricultural and Mechanical College; Board of Supervisors of Southern University and Agricultural and Mechanical College

(A) Creation; Powers. The Board of Supervisors of Louisiana State University and Agricultural and Mechanical College and the Board of Supervisors of Southern University and Agricultural and Mechanical College are created as bodies corporate. Subject to powers vested by this Article in the Board of Regents, each shall supervise

and manage the institutions, statewide agricultural programs, and other programs administered through its system.
(B) Membership; Terms. Each board shall be composed of two members from each congressional district and one member from the state at large, appointed by the governor with consent of the Senate. The members shall serve overlapping terms of six years, following initial terms fixed by law.
(C) Vacancy. A vacancy occurring prior to the expiration of a term shall be filled for the remainder of the unexpired term by appointment by the governor, with consent of the Senate.

SECTION 8
Boards; Membership; Compensation

(A) Dual Membership. No person shall be eligible to serve simultaneously on more than one board created by or pursuant to this Article.
(B) Student membership. The legislature may provide for the membership of one student on the boards created by Sections 5, 6 and 7 of this Article. The term of a student member shall not exceed one year, and no student member shall be eligible to succeed himself. A student member shall have all of the privileges and rights of other board members.
(C) Compensation. A member of a board created by or pursuant to this Article shall serve without pay, but per diem and expenses may be provided by law. [Amended by Acts 1980, No. 842, approved November 4, 1980, effective December 8, 1980]

Paragraph B originally provided that the student member would not have the right to vote. An amendment adopted in 1980 granted to the student member all the rights of other board members, including the right to vote.

SECTION 9
Parish School Boards; Parish Superintendents

(A) Boards. The legislature shall create parish school boards and provide for the election of their members.
(B) Superintendents. Each parish board shall elect a superintendent of parish schools. The State Board of Elementary and Secondary Education shall fix the qualifications and prescribe the duties of the parish superintendent. He need not be a resident of the parish in which he serves.

The constitution provides no specific powers that must be granted the local school boards. The state legislature thus has plenary power in the field and can determine the power of the local boards. City governments and parish police juries—the general local governing authorities—have no power over the school boards. Article VI, section 5(G) specifically states that no local government charter "shall contain any provision affecting a school board." Article VIII, section 3, however, protects the local boards to a limited extent by curbing the powers of the state board of education. According to that provision, the state board "shall have no control over the business affairs of a parish or city school board or the selection or removal of its officers and employees."

The court of appeal in *Faul v. Superintendent of Education* (1979) held it was not a violation of school board autonomy for the legislature to require the offering of French-language instruction upon petition of 25 percent of the heads of households in a school district. The supreme court in *St. John the Baptist Parish Association of Educators v. Brown* (1985) held that a school board could not, without statutory authorization, conduct a referendum to determine whether it should recognize a teachers' union and bargain with it.

SECTION 10
Existing Boards and Systems Recognized; Consolidation

(A) Recognition. Parish and city school board systems in existence on the effective date of this constitution are recognized, subject to control and supervision by the State Board of Elementary and Secondary Education and the power of the legislature to enact laws affecting them.
(B) Ouachita Parish and Monroe City School Systems; Board Membership. Only persons residing within the jurisdiction of the Monroe City School Board shall be eligible to vote for or be members of the Monroe City School Board. Only persons residing in that portion of Ouachita Parish outside the jurisdiction of the Monroe City School Board shall be eligible to vote for or be members of the Ouachita Parish School Board. The position of a member of either board shall be vacated when he no longer satisfies the requirements of this Paragraph. Notwithstanding any contrary provision of this constitution, this Paragraph shall become operative upon the election of members to the Ouachita Parish School Board taking office in 1977 or upon the first reapportionment affecting the Ouachita Parish School Board, whichever occurs earlier.
(C) Consolidation. Subject to approval by a majority of the electors voting, in each system affected, in an election held for that purpose, any two or more school systems may be consolidated as provided by law.

In most Louisiana parishes, one school board was established to govern all public schools. The unique situation in Ouachita Parish, with its separate boards for the city of Monroe and for the rest of the parish, was continued by paragraph B, with paragraph C prohibiting a change without approval of the voters in both jurisdictions.

SECTION 11
Appropriations; State Boards

The legislature shall appropriate funds for the operating and administrative expenses of the state boards created by or pursuant to this Article.

This section contains another of the constitution's many mandates to the legislature. The mandates are not enforceable, however, because the courts lack power to order appropriation of funds.

SECTION 12
Appropriations; Higher Education

Appropriations for the institutions of higher education shall be made to their managing boards. The funds appropriated shall be administered by the managing boards and used solely as provided by law.

The powers of the higher education management boards (LSU and Southern boards of supervisors and the board of trustees) are solidified by the requirement that appropriations be made to them rather than to the board of regents.

SECTION 13
Funding; Apportionment

(A) Free School Books. The legislature shall appropriate funds to supply free school books and other materials of instruction prescribed by the State Board of Elementary and Secondary Education to the children of this state at the elementary and secondary levels.
(B) Minimum Foundation Program. The State Board of Elementary and Secondary Education, or its successor, shall annually develop and adopt a formula which shall be used to determine the cost of a minimum foundation program of education in all public elementary and secondary schools as well as to equitably allocate the funds to parish and city school systems. Such formula shall provide for a contribution by every city and parish school system. Prior to approval of the formula by the legislature, the legislature may return the formula adopted by the board to the board and may recommend to the board an amended formula for consideration by the board and submission to the legislature for approval. The legislature shall annually appropriate funds sufficient to fully fund the current cost to the state of such a program as determined by applying the approved formula in order to insure a minimum foundation of education in all public elementary and secondary schools. Neither the governor nor the legislature may reduce such appropriation, except that the governor may reduce such appropriation using means provided in the act containing the appropriation provided that any such reduction is consented to in writing by two-thirds

of the elected members of each house of the legislature. The funds appropriated shall be equitably allocated to parish and city school systems according to the formula as adopted by the State Board of Elementary and Secondary Education, or its successor, and approved by the legislature prior to making the appropriation. Whenever the legislature fails to approve the formula most recently adopted by the board, or its successor, the last formula adopted by the board, or its successor, and approved by the legislature shall be used for the determination of the cost of the minimum foundation program and for the allocation of funds appropriated. [Amended by Acts 1987, No. 948, approved November 21, 1987, effective December 23, 1987]

(C) Local Funds. Local funds for the support of elementary and secondary schools shall be derived from the following sources:

First: Each parish school board, Orleans Parish excepted, and each municipality or city school board actually operating, maintaining, or supporting a separate system of public schools, shall levy annually an ad valorem maintenance tax not to exceed five mills on the dollar of assessed valuation on property subject to such taxation within the parish or city, respectively.

Second: The Orleans Parish School Board shall levy annually a tax not to exceed thirteen mills on the dollar of the assessed valuation of property within the city of New Orleans assessed for city taxation, and shall certify the amount of the tax to the governing authority of the city. The governing authority shall have the tax entered on city tax rolls. The tax shall be collected in the manner, under the conditions, and with the interest and penalties prescribed by law for city taxes. The money thus collected shall be paid daily to the Orleans Parish School Board.

Third: For giving additional support to public elementary and secondary schools, any parish, school district, or sub-school district, or any municipality or city school board which supports a separate city system of public schools may levy an ad valorem tax for a specific purpose, when authorized by a majority of the electors voting in the parish, municipality, district, or subdistrict in an election held for that purpose. The amount, duration, and purpose of the tax shall be in accord with any limitation imposed by the legislature.

(D) Municipal School Systems. For the effects and purposes of this Section, the municipalities of Monroe in Ouachita Parish, and Bogalusa in Washington Parish, and no others, shall be regarded and treated as parishes and shall have the authority granted parishes.

As adopted by the 1973 convention, paragraph B simply provided, "The legislature shall appropriate funds" for the minimum foundation program. The supreme court in *Louisiana Association of Educators v. Edwards* (1988) recognized that this mandate to appropriate was not enforceable by court order. The court ruled that it was within the legislature's discretion to appropriate less than had been recommended pursuant to a complex minimum foundation formula used by the board.

Anticipating the court's decision, education forces procured adoption of an amendment to paragraph B in 1987 to reduce legislative discretion and to force appropriation of the sum required by a formula. Under the amendment, once the legislature approves the formula, it shall appropriate sufficient funds. The legislature, however, has the power to disapprove of the formula submitted by the Board of Elementary and Secondary Education. If the two groups are unable to agree on a new formula, the old one remains in place. As John Devlin has indicated, "It seems at least possible that . . . 13(B) will still not be interpreted to require the legislature to appropriate whatever funds the [board] deems necessary."[18]

SECTION 14
Tulane University

The Tulane University of Louisiana in New Orleans is recognized as created and to be developed in accordance with Act No. 43 approved July 5, 1884.

Delegates to the 1973 Convention recognized that section 14 was probably unnecessary because it merely confirms the existence of a contract executed in the nineteenth century that transferred the public University of Louisiana to the Tulane University of Louisiana, a private institution. Among the continuing effects of the contract is a tax exemption for the university and the right of each legislator to select a student to receive a tuition waiver at the university.

SECTION 15
Members of State Board of Elementary and Secondary Education; Beginning and End of Terms

In order to effectuate the terms of office as provided in Article VIII, section 3(B), the successors in office to the elected members whose terms end in 1980 and 1982 shall be elected for terms which shall end at noon on the second Monday in March in 1984, and thereafter the successors in office to those members shall be elected and shall take office at the same time as the governor. The successor in office to the elected member whose term ends in 1984 shall be elected for a term which shall end at noon on the second Monday in March in 1988, and thereafter the successor in office to that member shall be elected and shall take office at the same time as the governor. The successors in office to the appointed members whose terms end in 1980 and 1982 shall be appointed for terms which shall end at noon on the second Monday in

[18] John Devlin, "Developments in the Law—Louisiana Constitutional Law," *Louisiana Law Review* 49 (1988):400.

> March in 1984, and thereafter the successors in office to those members shall be appointed for terms which shall be concurrent with the term of the governor making the appointment. The successor in office to the appointed member whose term ends in 1984 shall be appointed for a term which shall end at noon on the second Monday in March in 1988, and thereafter the successors in office to that member shall be appointed for terms which shall be concurrent with the term of the governor making the appointment.

When the 1979 amendment to Article VIII, section 3(B) was adopted to shorten the terms of BESE members from six to four years, this new section was adopted to provide for the transition to the new terms. The terms of the current members were not shortened.

Article IX

Natural Resources

SECTION 1
Natural Resources and Environment; Public Policy

> The natural resources of the state, including air and water, and the healthful, scenic, historic, and aesthetic quality of the environment shall be protected, conserved, and replenished insofar as possible and consistent with the health, safety, and welfare of the people. The legislature shall enact laws to implement this policy.

As its title indicates, section 1 is only a statement of policy; it is a nonbinding mandate to the legislature to protect the environment. Attempts to adopt a stronger provision first in the Committee on Natural Resources and the Environment and then on the convention floor were defeated.

In *City of New Orleans v. State* (1983), the state attempted to use section 1 to support its power to take over a city-owned park. The court rejected the argument stating, "While the park contributes to the healthful, scenic and aesthetic quality of the environment, the legislature cannot assume its ownership and regulation merely by declaring it a natural resource."

SECTION 2
Natural Gas

(A) Public Policy; Regulation. Natural gas is declared to be affected with a public interest. Notwithstanding any provision of this constitution relative to the powers and duties of the Public Service Commission, the legislature shall provide by law for regulation of natural gas by the regulatory authority it designates. It may designate the Public Service Commission as the regulatory authority.
(B) Pipelines. No intrastate natural gas pipeline or gas gathering line shall be connected with an interstate natural gas pipeline, and no interstate natural gas pipeline shall be connected with an intrastate natural gas pipeline, without a certificate of public convenience and necessity issued as provided by law after application for the connection and hearing thereon.

Paragraph A allows the legislature to establish any regulatory authority it chooses to regulate natural gas. The Natural Resources Committee has recommended allocation of that power to the Public Service Commission, but a floor amendment was readily adopted to provide otherwise, conforming the proposal to legislation that had been adopted during a recent special session of the legislature.

Paragraph B prohibits connection of an intrastate gas pipeline with an interstate pipeline without state approval in an attempt to keep gas from being removed from the state and thus subject to federal price regulation under existing federal law. The attempt was ineffective, for any state action to keep the privately owned product out of interstate commerce would be a violation of federal constitutional law, as determined by a federal district court in *Tenneco, Inc. v. Sutton* (1981).

SECTION 3
Alienation of Water Bottoms

The legislature shall neither alienate nor authorize the alienation of the bed of a navigable water body, except for purposes of reclamation by the riparian owner to recover land lost through erosion. This Section shall not prevent the leasing of state lands or water bottoms for mineral or other purposes. Except as provided in this Section, the bed of a navigable water body may be reclaimed only for public use.

A strong Louisiana Civil Code policy against private ownership of the beds of navigable water bodies was made a constitutional rule in Article II, section 2 of the 1921 Constitution. This development was in reaction to prior transfers of valuable mineral rights in such properties to private individuals. The basic policy is continued in this section. The state itself cannot alienate the bed of a navigable water body. Any attempt by a state agency or subdivision to do so is null by virtue of the language that the state also cannot authorize such alienation. More broadly, such property is insusceptible of private ownership and cannot be acquired by private persons through acts of possession for long periods of time.

New to the constitution is the exception that permits the state to transfer part of the bed to a riparian landowner reclaiming land lost through erosion. The legislature has adopted Louisiana Revised Statutes 41:1702 allowing reclamation of land lost through erosion occurring after July 1, 1921.

Although it broadened reclamation by private riparian landowners, the constitution limited the power of governmental units to reclaim and otherwise fill in the beds of navigable water bodies. Prior law allowed the state to alienate land for purposes of reclamation. This section allows alienation only for reclamation for public use. As the chairman of the committee told the convention, the practice of filling in the bed of a water body and then selling lots to private owners, as was done with Lake Pontchartrain, is no longer permitted. Indeed an amendment supported by delegates from Orleans and Jefferson parishes to allow more development along the lake was rejected. As the debate on residential development indicates, the reference is not to public purposes, the concept often used in expropriation matters and broadly construed to include private ownership under urban renewal plans; rather the reference is to a narrower public use concept borrowed from the civil code.

The court of appeal in *Save Our Wetlands, Inc. v. Orleans Levee Board* (1979) held that an airport runway available for public use, for a fee, was a permissible use under the section and that land could be reclaimed for such use.

SECTION 4
Reservation of Mineral Rights; Prescription

(A) Reservation of Mineral Rights. The mineral rights on property sold by the state shall be reserved, except when the owner or person having the right to redeem buys or redeems property sold or adjudicated to the state for taxes.
(B) Prescription. Lands and mineral interests of the state, of a school board, or of a levee district shall not be lost by prescription.

Paragraph A is also devoted to protecting the state's economic interest in oil and gas revenues; the state must reserve the mineral rights to land it sells. More important in this regard is Paragraph B. Normally a mineral interest or mineral servitude is a temporary right that is lost by ten years nonuse, but this section holds that the state's interests last indefinitely. The 1974 Constitution enlarged the scope of this protection by extending it to school boards and levee districts.

The section goes beyond mineral interests. Title to land owned by the state, school boards, and levee districts cannot be acquired by third persons through acquisitive prescription or adverse possession. This section does not address the issue of whether a private person can in fact physically possess land owned by the state and does not prohibit such a possessor from being presumed the owner. The supreme court in *Todd v. Department of Natural Resources* (1985) allowed such an action to protect possession to proceed against the state, at least as to land in the state's private domain.

Land owned by other governmental entities is not protected by this section; in such cases the general civil code provisions on acquisitive prescription still apply. Those rules would allow land owned by these entities in their private capacity to be acquired by possessors over time but not land owned by them in their public capacity (Louisiana Civil Code Articles 450, 453, 3485).

SECTION 5
Public Notice; Public Bidding Requirements

No conveyance, lease, royalty agreement, or unitization agreement involving minerals or mineral rights owned by the state shall be confected without prior public notice or public bidding as shall be provided by law.

Section 5 is a provision new to the 1974 Constitution, an attempt sponsored primarily as an anticorruption device by a delegate who was a former member of the state's Mineral Board.

SECTION 6
Tidelands Ownership

Revenues and royalties obtained from minerals located beyond the seaward boundary of the state belong to the state.

Although delegates to the 1973 Constitutional Convention knew that federal law governs claims to offshore minerals, it continued this claim from the prior constitution out of an abundance of caution. Louisiana's claim to ownership of the bed of the sea beyond three miles from the coast had been denied by the U. S. Supreme Court in *United States v. Louisiana* (1960).

SECTION 7
Wildlife and Fisheries Commission

(A) Members; Terms. The control and supervision of the wildlife of the state, including all aquatic life, is vested in the Louisiana Wildlife and Fisheries Commission. The commission shall be in the executive branch and shall consist of seven members appointed by the governor, subject to confirmation by the Senate. Six members shall serve overlapping terms of six years, and one member shall serve a term concurrent with that of the governor. Three members shall be electors of the coastal parishes and

representatives of the commercial fishing and fur industries, and four shall be electors from the state at large other than representatives of the commercial fishing and fur industries, as provided by law. No member who has served six years or more shall be eligible for reappointment.
(B) Duties; Compensation. The functions, duties, and responsibilities of the commission, and the compensation of its members, shall be provided by law.

Although the commission is established by this section and thus exists independent of legislation, paragraph B provides that its "functions, duties, and responsibilities" shall be provided by law. Thus, the legislature has virtually complete freedom to determine its powers.

SECTION 8
Forestry

(A) Forestry; Acreage Taxes. Forestry shall be practiced in the state, and the legislature may enact laws therefor. It may authorize parish governing authorities to levy acreage taxes, not to exceed two cents per acre, for the purposes of this Section. The provisions of this constitution exempting homesteads from taxation shall apply to forestry acreage taxes.
(B) Forestry Commission. The practice of forestry is placed under the Louisiana Forestry Commission. The commission shall be in the executive branch and shall consist of seven members. The head of the Department of Forestry at Louisiana State University and Agricultural and Mechanical College and the director of the Wildlife and Fisheries Commission shall serve ex officio as members. The governor shall appoint the remaining five members, subject to confirmation by the Senate, for overlapping terms of five years, as provided by law.
(C) State Forester. The commission shall appoint a state forester. He shall be a graduate of an accredited school of forestry and have at least four years of forestry experience, as provided by law.

The Forestry Commission and the state forester are constitutional officers in the sense that the office is established in the constitution; however, the constitution gives them no powers, which depend on legislation for their establishment.

SECTION 9
First Use Tax Trust Fund

(A)(1) Creation. The First Use Tax Trust Fund is hereby created and established in the state treasury as a special and irrevocable trust fund for the deposit of the proceeds, and interest derived therefrom, of the first use tax imposed by law in 1978 or thereafter and any other tax imposed by law which would have the effect of imposing any new or alternative tax on uses of those resources subject to the tax levied by the first use tax. The treasurer shall pay into the state general fund, from the total proceeds of the first use tax, as imposed by law in 1978 or thereafter such amounts as are necessary to fully reimburse the state general fund for tax credits granted in 1978 against that tax pursuant to Part I-B of Chapter 6 of Title 47 of the Louisiana Revised Statutes. The remainder of such tax proceeds shall be credited to the following accounts within the First Use Tax Trust Fund and shall not be deposited into the Bond Security and Redemption Fund or the general fund.

(2) Distribution; debt accounts. Seventy-five percent of the proceeds, and interest derived therefrom, shall be deposited into the following accounts:

(a) Initial Proceeds Account. From this portion of the initial proceeds of the tax, the sum of five hundred million dollars shall be maintained in an account within the First Use Tax Trust Fund in the state treasury to be known as the "Initial Proceeds Account". Monies in the Initial Proceeds Account shall be invested, and the investment earnings shall accrue to that account. Except for investment and except as provided in Paragraph (C), monies on deposit in the Initial Proceeds Account shall not be used. If the balance of the Initial Proceeds Account at any time is less than five hundred million dollars, then an amount from the next proceeds of the tax shall be credited to the Initial Proceeds Account until there is a balance therein of five hundred million dollars.

(b) Debt Retirement and Redemption Account. All proceeds of this portion of the tax over and above the amount required to be maintained in the Initial Proceeds Account shall be maintained in an account in the First Use Tax Trust Fund to be known as the "Debt Retirement and Redemption Account". Monies in the Debt Retirement and Redemption Account shall be invested and the investment earnings shall accrue to that account. Except for investment, monies on deposit in the Debt Retirement and Redemption Account shall be used only to purchase, in advance of maturity, on the open market any outstanding obligations of the state, or to call, pay or redeem in advance of maturity any outstanding bonds, notes or other evidence of state debt, or both. No purchase or redemption of state debt shall occur with the monies unless the purchase or redemption results in interest savings to the state. The methods used for retiring such future debt shall be determined by the state treasurer, with concurrence of two-thirds of the members of the State Bond Commission acting in open session.

(3) Distribution; conservation account. Twenty-five percent of the proceeds, and interest derived therefrom, shall be deposited into the following account:

(A) Barrier Islands Conservation Account. Twenty-five percent of the proceeds of the tax shall be maintained in an account in the First Use Tax Trust Fund to be known as the "Barrier Islands Conservation Account". Monies in the Barrier Islands Conservation Account shall be invested and the investment earnings shall accrue to that account. Except for investment, monies on deposit in the Barrier Islands Conservation Account shall be used exclusively to fund capital improvement projects designed to conserve, preserve and maintain the barrier islands, reefs, and shores of the coastline of Louisiana. Only such capital improvements contained in the comprehensive capital budget adopted by the legislature each year shall be funded.

(B) Investments. The state treasurer shall invest all monies on deposit in the accounts established under Paragraph (A) in accordance with the law governing the investment of idle funds of the state.

(C) Use of Investment Earnings of Initial Proceeds Account. If in the judgment of the state treasurer the best interest of the state would be served, and only if the Debt Retirement and Redemption Account is depleted or otherwise not funded, the treasurer may, with concurrence of two-thirds of the members of the State Bond Commission, acting in open session, expend the investment earnings which have accrued in excess of five hundred million dollars in the Initial Proceeds Account for any purpose for which the Debt Retirement and Redemption Account may be used.

(D) The funds deposited in the First Use Tax Trust Fund shall be considered escrowed and shall not be used for the purposes enumerated herein until the proceeds of the first use tax are determined to be available for such uses by the treasurer with concurrence of two-thirds of the members of the State Bond Commission, acting in open session. During the time these funds are escrowed such funds may be ordered remitted upon final action by a court of last resort, with the interest earned thereon, as provided by law, if the tax is held to be invalid as to any taxpayer who has paid the tax. [Added by Acts 1978, No. 797, adopted November 7, 1978, effective December 11, 1978]

Added as an amendment in 1978, section 9 is a constitutional dedication of part of the proceeds of the state's first use tax on natural gas produced offshore and shipped through pipelines in the state. The U. S. Supreme Court in *Maryland v. Louisiana* (1981) found the tax to be an unconstitutional violation of the commerce clause because it discriminated against gas entering interstate commerce. Although the section has no effect, an effort to clean up the constitution by removing the provision was defeated by the voters in 1982.

SECTION 10
Louisiana Investment Fund for Enhancement

(A) The Louisiana Investment Fund for Enhancement is established as a special fund in the state treasury. All revenues received by the state from the production of oil and gas within the state shall be deposited in the state treasury and credited to the Bond Security and Redemption Fund in accordance with the provisions of Article VII, Section 9, and shall be remitted to the political subdivisions of the state pursuant to Article VII, Section 4. In each fiscal year out of the funds remaining in the Bond Security and Redemption Fund, after a sufficient amount has been allocated for the payment of obligations secured by the full faith and credit of the state which become due and payable within the fiscal year, the treasurer shall credit an amount equal to the windfall revenues from oil and gas price deregulation to the Louisiana Investment Fund for Enhancement.

(B) As used in this Section, "windfall revenues from oil and gas price deregulation" means those revenues received by the state in a fiscal year which are in excess of the base for that particular fiscal year, as calculated in accordance with this Paragraph. The base for fiscal year 1981–1982 shall be the estimated level of collections for oil, gas, and other severance taxes and from oil and gas production royalties in fiscal year 1980–1981, which for the purposes hereof shall be one billion eighty-five million dollars, calculated as follows:

(1) Seven hundred sixty million dollars from oil, gas, and other severance taxes; and

(2) Three hundred twenty-five million dollars from oil and gas royalty payments, excluding bonuses and rentals.

In each subsequent fiscal year, the state treasurer shall calculate the windfall revenues from oil and gas price deregulation for that fiscal year by determining a new base as follows: The base for the previous fiscal year shall be multiplied by the most recent annual change in the consumer price index and then the product shall be added to the base for the previous fiscal year.

(C) The state treasurer shall invest the monies in the Louisiana Investment Fund for Enhancement in the manner provided by law. Interest from the investment shall be credited to the general fund.

(D) Monies credited to the Louisiana Investment Fund for Enhancement may be expended only pursuant to an appropriation enacted by the vote of two-thirds of the elected members of each house of the legislature.

(E) The legislature shall have the authority to enact any legislation with regard to the Louisiana Investment Fund for Enhancement not inconsistent with the provisions of this Section.

Adopted by amendment in 1983, section 10 continues to display the public's distrust of the legislature. The section was designed to limit the legislature's use of windfall oil and gas revenues coming from declining oil and gas reserves. Such revenues were to be deposited in a special fund, and appropriations from the fund would require a two-thirds vote of the elected members of each house. The section has yet to be applied because of the decline in oil and gas revenues but remains in force and susceptible of being applied when oil and gas revenues to the state exceed those collected in 1980–1981, after adjustment for inflation.

Article X

Public Officials and Employees

Article X is a good example of how political forces interacted to produce long and detailed Louisiana constitutions. The statutory civil service system adopted by the anti-Long forces of Governor Sam Houston Jones during his 1940–1944 term was a major reform that was seen as an attack on the traditional patronage system. After Earl Long won the election for governor in 1948, he was able to promote legislation that gutted the civil service system. When the anti-Long candidate, Robert F. Kennon, became governor in 1952, he restored the earlier system, protecting it from change by placing the whole text of the provisions in the constitution. That attitude on civil service remains, and the 1974 Constitution continues to contain lengthy, detailed regulations of the civil service system. Not only is the state civil service system established in the constitution but also the system for New Orleans.

Debate in the 1973 convention was not so much devoted to removing the system from the constitution or to returning to a patronage system. Rather, opposition to the committee proposal was led by labor union interests who wanted more flexibility in the system, which would also provide for more union influence. For the most part, the opponents failed, and the traditional rules remain, although now one of seven members of the state commission is elected by state employees.

This commentary will not attempt to cover the detail of the provisions in parts I and II, which are devoted more to matters of labor law than to basic constitutional principle. It will address some of the broader concerns, most of which are in part III.

PART I STATE AND CITY CIVIL SERVICE

SECTION 1
Civil Service Systems

(A) State Civil Service. The State Civil Service is established and includes all persons holding offices and positions of trust or employment in the employ of the state, or any instrumentality thereof, and any joint state and federal agency, joint state and parochial agency, or joint state and municipal agency, regardless of the source of the funds used to pay for such employment. It shall not include persons holding offices and positions of any municipal board of health or local governmental subdivisions.
(B) City Civil Service. The city civil service is established and includes all persons holding offices and positions of trust or employment in the employ of each city having over four hundred thousand population and in every instrumentality thereof. However, paid firemen and municipal policemen may be excluded if a majority of the electors in the affected city voting at an election held for that purpose approve their exclusion. The election shall be called by the municipal governing authority within one year after the effective date of this constitution.

SECTION 2
Classified and Unclassified Service

(A) Classified Service. The state and city civil service is divided into the unclassified and the classified service. Persons not included in the unclassified service are in the classified service.
(B) Unclassified Service. The unclassified service shall include the following officers and employees in the state and city civil service:

(1) elected officials and persons appointed to fill vacancies in elective offices;
(2) the heads of each principal executive department appointed by the governor, the mayor, or the governing authority of a city;
(3) city attorneys;
(4) registrars of voters;
(5) members of state and city boards, authorities, and commissions;
(6) one private secretary to the president of each college or university;
(7) one person holding a confidential position and one principal assistant or deputy to any officer, board, commission, or authority mentioned in (1), (2), (4), or (5) above, except civil service departments;
(8) members of the military or naval forces;

(9) teaching and professional staffs, and administrative officers of schools, colleges, and universities of the state, and bona fide students of those institutions employed by any state, parochial, or municipal agency;
(10) employees, deputies, and officers of the legislature and of the offices of the governor, lieutenant governor, attorney general, each mayor and city attorney, of police juries, school boards, assessors, and of all offices provided for in Article V of this constitution except the offices of clerk of the municipal and traffic courts in New Orleans;
(11) commissioners of elections, watchers, and custodians and deputy custodians of voting machines; and
(12) railroad employees whose working conditions and retirement benefits are regulated by federal agencies in accordance with federal law.

Additional positions may be added to the unclassified service and those positions may be revoked by rules adopted by a commission.

The general rule is to place in the classified service, and thus subject to the detailed merit system provided in Article X, all employees except those specifically excepted. Paragraph B then lists the exceptions, making those officials and employees part of the unclassified service. The final paragraph of the section allows the Civil Service Commission to make additional exceptions.

Smith v. Division of Administration (1978), true to the purpose of the convention, gave a narrow reading to the "office of the governor" exception to the classified service. The supreme court held that employees of the Division of Administration were not within the constitutional exception, although legislation made the division part of the office of the governor. The division, employing more than a thousand persons, was responsible for the mechanics of state administration–budget control, payrolls, purchasing, data processing—rather than formulating public policies. The court reasoned that the exception of paragraph B(10) refers to the governor's personal staff and policy advisers and that it is not a device that enables the legislature to transfer any state department into the office of the governor and thus out of the classified service.

SECTION 3
State Civil Service Commission

(A) Composition. The State Civil Service Commission is established and shall be domiciled in the state capital. It shall be composed of seven members who are electors of this state, four of whom shall constitute a quorum. No more than one appointed member shall be from each congressional district.
(B) Appointment. The members shall be appointed by the governor, as hereinafter provided, for overlapping terms of six years.
(C) Nominations. The presidents of Centenary College at Shreveport, Dillard University at New Orleans, Louisiana College at Pineville, Loyola University at

> New Orleans, Tulane University of Louisiana at New Orleans, and Xavier University at New Orleans, after giving consideration to representation of all groups, each shall nominate three persons. The governor shall appoint one member of the commission from the three persons nominated by each president. One member of the commission shall be elected by the classified employees of the state from their number as provided by law. A vacancy for any cause shall be filled by appointment or election in accordance with the procedure or law governing the original appointment or election, and from the same source. Within thirty days after a vacancy occurs, the president concerned shall submit the required nominations. Within thirty days thereafter, the governor shall make his appointment. If the governor fails to appoint within thirty days, the nominee whose name is first on the list of nominees automatically shall become a member of the commission. If any nominating authority fails to submit nominees in the time required, or if one of the named institutions ceases to exist, the governor shall make the appointment to the commission.

Although the governor appoints six commissioners, his power is limited to selecting from the nominees of a presumably independent, nonpolitical class of individuals: the presidents of private colleges and universities. Two of those schools, Dillard University and Xavier University, are by tradition black institutions. New to the 1974 Constitution is the seat held by a person elected by classified employees. Independence is also promoted by making the terms of the commissioners overlapping. Geographic dispersion is required since no more than one member can be appointed from each of the state's eight congressional districts.

SECTION 4
City Civil Service Commission

> (A) Creation; Membership; Domicile. A city civil service commission shall exist in each city having a population exceeding four hundred thousand. The domicile of each commission shall be in the city it serves. Each commission shall be composed of five members, who are electors of the city, three of whom shall constitute a quorum. The members shall serve overlapping terms of six years as hereinafter provided.
>
> (B) New Orleans; Nomination and Appointment. In New Orleans, the presidents of Dillard University, Loyola University, Tulane University of Louisiana, and Xavier University, after giving consideration to representation of all groups, each shall nominate three persons. In addition, the employees in the classified service of the city of New Orleans shall nominate three persons in the classified service of the city of New Orleans by means of an election called for that purpose. The municipal governing authority shall appoint one member of the commission from the three persons nominated by each nominating authority.

(C) Other Cities; Nomination and Appointment. In each other city subject to this Section, the presidents of any five institutions of higher education in the state, selected by the governing authority of the respective city, each shall nominate three persons, after giving consideration to representation of all groups. The municipal governing authority shall appoint one member of the commission from the three persons nominated by each.

(D) Vacancies. A vacancy shall be filled by appointment in accordance with the procedure for the original appointment and from the same source. Within thirty days after a vacancy occurs, in a seat held by a university nominee, the university president concerned shall submit the required nominations. Within sixty days after this amendment is ratified by the electors of the state of Louisiana, and when a vacancy occurs in a seat held by a nominee nominated by employees in the classified service, there shall be held an election at which the employees in the classified service shall nominate three persons in accordance with this section. Within thirty days thereafter, the municipal governing authority shall make the appointment. If the municipal governing authority fails to appoint within the thirty days, the nominee whose name is first on the list of nominees automatically shall become a member of the commission. If one of the nominating authorities fails to submit nominees in the time required, or if one of the named institutions ceases to exist, the municipal governing authority shall make the appointment.

(E) New Orleans; Implementation of Certain Member. The member appointed from nominations by the classified employees of the city of New Orleans shall be the successor to the member nominated by the president of St. Mary's Dominican College and the initial member so appointed shall take office at the expiration of the term of the member who took office on April 30, 1987. [Amended by Acts 1987, No. 949, approved November 21, 1987, effective December 23, 1987]

As in section 3, the attempt here was to promote nonpolitical nominees by having them made by presidents of private colleges. The peril of such constitutional detail, however, was demonstrated when one appointing institution, St. Mary's Dominican College, ceased to exist. Voters rejected amendments proposed in 1984 and 1985 to replace as the appointing body, first, Our Lady of Holy Cross College, and then the University of New Orleans and Southern University in New Orleans. The third attempt in 1987 was ratified; the amendment allowed that seat to be filled from nominees elected by city classified employees.

SECTION 5
Removal

A member of the state or of a city civil service commission may be removed by the governor or the governing authority, as the case may be, for cause, after being served with written specifications of the charges against him and being afforded an opportunity for a public hearing thereon by the appointing authority.

SECTION 6
Department of Civil Service; Directors

(A) State Department. A Department of State Civil Service is established in the executive branch of the state government.
(B) City Departments. A department of city civil service shall exist in each city having a population exceeding four hundred thousand.
(C) Directors. Each commission shall appoint a director, after competitive examination, who shall be in the classified service. He shall be the administrative head of his department. Each director shall appoint personnel and exercise powers and duties to the extent prescribed by the commission appointing him.

SECTION 7
Appointments; Promotions

Permanent appointments and promotions in the classified state and city service shall be made only after certification by the appropriate department of civil service under a general system based upon merit, efficiency, fitness, and length of service, as ascertained by examination which, so far as practical, shall be competitive. The number to be certified shall not be less than three; however, if more than one vacancy is to be filled, the name of one additional eligible for each vacancy may be certified. Each commission shall adopt rules for the method of certifying persons eligible for appointment, promotion, reemployment, and reinstatement and shall provide for appointments defined as emergency and temporary appointments if certification is not required.

SECTION 8
Appeals

(A) Disciplinary Actions. No person who has gained permanent status in the classified state or city service shall be subjected to disciplinary action except for cause expressed in writing. A classified employee subjected to such disciplinary action shall have the right of appeal to the appropriate commission pursuant to Section 12 of this Part. The burden of proof on appeal, as to the facts, shall be on the appointing authority.
(B) Discrimination. No classified employee shall be discriminated against because of his political or religious beliefs, sex, or race. A classified employee so discriminated against shall have the right of appeal to the appropriate commission pursuant to Section 12 of this Part. The burden of proof on appeal, as to the facts, shall be on the employee. [As Amended by Acts 1982, No. 883, approved September 11, 1982, effective October 15, 1982]

SECTION 9
Prohibitions Agaisnt Political Activities

(A) Party Membership; Elections. No member of a civil service commission and no officer or employee in the classified service shall participate or engage in political activity; be a candidate for nomination or election to public office except to seek election as the classified state employee serving on the State Civil Service Commission; or be a member of any national, state, or local committee of a political party or faction; make or solicit contributions for any political party, faction, or candidate; or take active part in the management of the affairs of a political party, faction, candidate, or any political campaign, except to exercise his right as a citizen to express his opinion privately, to serve as a commissioner or official watcher at the polls, and to cast his vote as he desires.

(B) Contributions. No person shall solicit contributions for political purposes from any classified employee or official or use or attempt to use his position in the state or city service to punish or coerce the political action of a classified employee.

(C) Political Activity Defined. As used in this Part, "political activity" means an effort to support or oppose the election of a candidate for political office or to support a particular political party in an election. The support of issues involving bonded indebtedness, tax referenda, or constitutional amendments shall not be prohibited.

This section, in addition to the specific listing of prohibited activity by classified employees in section 9(A), contains a general prohibition against "political activity," that term being broadly defined in paragraph C to include any effort to support or oppose a candidate for office or to support a political party in an election. The U. S. Court of Appeals for the Fifth Circuit, in *Bruno v. Garsaud* (1979), considered an attack on the limitations on political activity contained in section 9 on the ground they were unconstitutional on their face because of vagueness and overbreadth. The court upheld the limitations, finding neither vagueness nor substantial overbreadth. Although the facts in the case are not clear, since the lower court had decided the issue on summary judgment without a full trial, the appellate court did admit, however, to "strong doubts" that the provision could prevent employees from contributing funds to a political candidate or party. The U. S. Supreme Court decision in *Buckley v. Valeo* (1976) was cited in that regard, the case establishing a First Amendment right to contribute to candidates free of a $1,000 limitation imposed under federal law.

SECTION 10
Rules; Investigations; Wages and Hours

(A) Rules

(1) Powers. Each commission is vested with broad and general rulemaking and subpoena powers for the administration and regulation of the classified service,

including the power to adopt rules for regulating employment, promotion, demotion, suspension, reduction in pay, removal, certification, qualifications, political activities, employment conditions, compensation and disbursements to employees, and other personnel matters and transactions; to adopt a uniform pay and classification plan; to require an appointing authority to institute an employee training and safety program; and generally to accomplish the objectives and purposes of the merit system of civil service as herein established. It may make recommendations with respect to employee training and safety. Nothing herein shall prevent the legislature from enacting laws supplementing these uniform pay plans for sworn, commissioned law enforcement officers of the Division of State Police, Department of Public Safety and regularly commissioned officers of the Enforcement Division of the Department of Wildlife and Fisheries.

(2) Veterans. The state and city civil service departments shall accord a five-point preference in original appointment to each person honorably discharged, or discharged under honorable conditions from the armed forces of the United States who served between the wartime dates of April 6, 1917 through November 11, 1918; or between September 16, 1940 through July 25, 1947; between June 27, 1950 through January 31, 1955; or in the Viet Nam Theater between July 1, 1958 through the date the United States government declares to be the date of termination of service for members of the armed forces to receive credit for the award of the Viet Nam Service Medal; in a peacetime campaign for expedition for which campaign badges are authorized.

The state and city civil service departments shall accord a ten-point preference in original appointment to each honorably discharged veteran who served either in peace or in war and who has one or more disabilities recognized as service-connected by the Veterans Administration; to the spouse of each veteran whose physical condition precludes his or her appointment to a civil service job in his or her usual line of work; to the unremarried widow of each deceased veteran who served in a war period, as defined above, or in a peacetime campaign or expedition; or to the unremarried widowed parent of any person who died in active wartime or peacetime service or who suffered total and permanent disability in active wartime or peacetime service; or the divorced or separated parents of any person who died in wartime or peacetime service or who became totally and permanently disabled in wartime or peacetime service. However, only one ten-point preference shall be allowed in the original appointment to any person enumerated above. If the ten-point preference is not used by the veteran, either because of the veteran's physical or mental incapacity which precludes his appointment to a civil service job in his usual line of work or because of his death, the preference shall be available to his spouse, unremarried widow, or eligible parents as defined above, in the order specified. However, any such preference may be given only to a person who has attained at least the minimum score required on each test and who has received at least the minimum rating required for eligibility.

(3) Layoffs; Preference Employees. When a position in the classified service is abolished, or needs to be vacated because of stoppage of work from lack of funds or other causes, preference employees (ex-members of the armed forces and their dependents as described in this Section) whose length of service and efficiency ratings are at least equal to those of other competing employees shall be retained in preference to all other competing employees. However, when any function of a state agency is transferred to, or when a state agency is replaced by, one or more other state agencies, every preference employee in classifications and performing functions transferred, or working in the state agency replaced, shall be transferred to the replacing state agency or agencies for employment in a position for which he is qualified before that state agency or agencies appoint additional employees for such positions from eligible lists. The appointing authority shall give the director written notice of any proposed lay-off within a reasonable length of time before its effective date, and the director shall issue orders relating thereto which he considers necessary to secure compliance with the rules. No rule, regulation, or practice of the commission, of any agency or department, or of any official of the state or any political subdivision shall favor or discriminate against any applicant or employee because of his membership or non-membership in any private organization; but this shall not prohibit any state agency, department, or political subdivision from contracting with an employee organization with respect to wages, hours, grievances, working conditions, or other conditions of employment in a manner not inconsistent with this constitution, a civil service law, or a valid rule or regulation of a commission.

(4) Effect. Rules adopted pursuant hereto shall have the effect of law and be published and made available to the public. Each commission may impose penalties for violation of its rules by demotion in or suspension or discharge from position, with attendant loss of pay.

(B) Investigations. Each commission may investigate violations of this Part and the rules, statutes, or ordinances adopted pursuant hereto.

(C) Wages and Hours. Any rule or determination affecting wages or hours shall have the effect of law and become effective only after approval by the governor or the appropriate governing authority.

SECTION 11
Penalties

Willful violation of any provision of this Part shall be a misdemeanor punishable by a fine of not more than five hundred dollars or by imprisonment for not more than six months, or both.

SECTION 12
Appeal

(A) State. The State Civil Service Commission shall have the exclusive power and authority to hear and decide all removal and disciplinary cases, with subpoena power and power to administer oaths. It may appoint a referee, with subpoena power and power to administer oaths, to take testimony, hear, and decide removal and disciplinary cases. The decision of a referee is subject to review by the commission on any question of law or fact upon the filing of an application for review with the commission within fifteen calendar days after the decision of the referee is rendered. If an application for review is not timely filed with the commission, the decision of the referee becomes the final decision of the commission as of the date the decision was rendered. If an application for review is timely filed with the commission and, after a review of the application by the commission, the application is denied, the decision of the referee becomes the final decision of the commission as of the date the application is denied. The final decision of the commission shall be subject to review on any question of law or fact upon appeal to the court of appeal wherein the commission is located, upon application filed with the commission within thirty calendar days after its decision becomes final. Any referee appointed by the commission shall have been admitted to the practice of law in this state for at least three years prior to his appointment.
(B) Cities. Each city commission established by Part I of this Article shall have the exclusive power and authority to hear and decide all removal and disciplinary cases, with subpoena power and power to administer oaths. It may appoint a referee to take testimony, with subpoena power and power to administer oaths to witnesses. The decision of a commission shall be subject to review on any question of law or fact upon appeal to the court of appeal wherein the commission is located, upon application filed with the commission within thirty calendar days after its decision becomes final. [Amended by Acts 1982, No. 883, approved September 11, 1982, effective October 15, 1982]

SECTION 13
Appropriations

(A) State. The legislature shall make adequate annual appropriations to the State Civil Service Commission and to the Department of State Civil Service to enable them to implement this Part efficiently and effectively. The amount so appropriated shall not be subject to veto by the governor.
(B) Cities. Each city subject to this Part shall make adequate annual appropriations to enable its civil service commission and department to implement this Part efficiently and effectively.

SECTION 14
Acceptance of Act; Other Cities, Parishes, City and Parish Governed Jointly

(A) Local Option. Each city having a population exceeding ten thousand but not exceeding four hundred thousand, each parish, and each parish governed jointly with one or more cities under a plan of government, having a population exceeding ten thousand, according to the latest official decennial federal census, may elect to be governed by this Part by a majority vote of its electors voting at an election held for that purpose. The election shall be ordered and held by the city, the parish, or the city-parish, as the case may be, upon (a) the adoption of an ordinance by the governing authority calling the election; or (b) the presentation to the governing authority of a petition calling for such an election signed by electors equal in number to five percent of the registered voters of the city, the parish, or the city-parish, as the case may be.
(B) Acceptance. If a majority of the electors vote to adopt this Part, its provisions shall apply permanently to the city, the parish, or the city-parish, as the case may be, and shall govern it as if this Part had originally applied to it. In such case, all officers and employees of the city, the parish, or the city-parish, as the case may be, who have acquired civil service status under a civil service system established by legislative act, city charter, or otherwise, shall retain that status and thereafter shall be subject to and be governed by this Part and the rules and regulations adopted under it.
(C) Rejection. If a majority of the electors vote against the adoption of this Part, the question of its adoption shall not be resubmitted to the voters of the political subdivision within one year thereafter.

SECTION 15
City, Parish Civil Service System; Creation; Prohibition

Nothing in this Part shall prevent the establishment by the legislature, or by the respective parish governing authority, of a parish civil service system in one or more parishes, applicable to any or all parish employees, except teaching and professional staffs and administrative officers of schools, or the establishment by the legislature or by the respective municipal governing authority of a municipal civil service system in one or more municipalities having a population of less than four hundred thousand, in any manner now or hereafter provided by law. However, paid firemen and paid municipal policemen in a municipality operating a regularly paid fire and police department and having a population exceeding thirteen thousand, and paid firemen in all parishes and in fire protection districts, are expressly excluded from such a civil service system. Nothing in this Part shall permit inclusion in the local civil service of officials and employees listed in Section 2 of this Article. No law enacted after the effective date of this constitution establishing a civil service system applicable to one or more parishes or to one or more municipalities having a population of less than four hundred thousand shall be effective in any parish or in any municipality until approved by ordinance adopted by the governing authority of the parish or municipality.

PART II. FIRE AND POLICE CIVIL SERVICE

SECTION 16
Establishment of System

A system of classified fire and police civil service is created and established. It shall apply to all municipalities having a population exceeding thirteen thousand and operating a regularly paid fire and municipal police department and to all parishes and fire protection districts operating a regularly paid fire department.

SECTION 17
Appointments and Promotions

Permanent appointments and promotions in municipal fire and police civil service shall be made only after certification by the applicable municipal fire and police civil service board under a general system based upon merit, efficiency, fitness, and length of service as provided in Article XIV, Section 15.1 of the Constitution of 1921, subject to change by law enacted by two-thirds of the elected members of each house of the legislature.

SECTION 18
Prior Provisions

Except as inconsistent with this Part, the provisions of Article XIV, Section 15.1 of the Constitution of 1921 are retained and continued in force and effect as statutes. By law enacted by two-third of the elected members of each house, the legislature may amend of otherwise modify any of those provisions, but it may not abolish the system of classified civil service for such firemen and muncipal policemen or make the system inapplicable to any municipality having a population exceeding thirteen thousand according to the latest decennial federal census or to any parish of fire protection district operating a regularly paid fire department. However, in a municipality having a population exceeding four hundred thousand, paid firemen and municiple policemen shall be included if a majority of the electors therein voting at an election held for that purpose approve their inclusion. Such an election shall be called by the governing authority of the affected city within one year after the effective date of this consitution.

SECTION 19
Exclusion

Nothing in Part I of this Article authorizing cities or other political subdivisions to be placed under the provision of said Part by election, act of the legislature, or ordinance of the local governing authority shall authorize the inclusion in a city civil service system of firemen and policemen in any municipality having a population greater that thirteen thousand but fewer than four hundred thousand and operating a regularly paid fire and municipal police department paid fire department. Such firemen and policemen and expressly excluded from any such system.

SECITON 20
Political Activities

Article XIV, Section 15.1, Paragraph 34 of the Constitution of 1921 is retained and continued in force and effect.

The contiuned provision contained a long list of prohibited political activities but one not substantially different in substance from the prohibitions of seciton 9.

PART III. OTHER PROVISIONS

SECTION 21
Code of Ethics

The legislature shall enact a code of ethics for all officials and employees of the state and its political subdivisions. The code shall be administered by one or more boards created by legislature with qualifications, term of office, duties, and powers provided by law. Decisions of a board shall be appealabe, and the legislature shall provide the method of appeal.

The legislature complied with the mandate of section 21 and adopted the Code of Governmental Ethics in 1979 (Louisiana Revised Statutes 42:1101–69), which replaced legislation adopted in 1964. Two boards administer the code; one governing public officials and the other governing public employees. On rehearing, the supreme court in *State v. Green* (1990) held that the selection procedure for the Board of Ethics for Elected Officials was constitutional. The composition of the board did not violate the separation of powers doctrine even though the board was composed of members selected by the house and senate. The board members "are not subject to such significant control that the Legislature can be deemed to be performing executive functions through its control of the members of the board in the executive branch."

The reference in section 21 to "officials and employees of the state" is not a limitation that restricts the application of the code to those persons. In *Anzelmo v. Louisiana Commission on Ethics for Public Employees* (1983), the court of appeal held the board could exercise jurisdiction over the children of a public employee.

SECTION 22
Dual Employment and Dual Officeholding

The legislature shall enact laws defining and regulating dual employment and defining, regulating, and prohibiting dual officeholding in state and local government.

All of Louisiana's constitutions have had some type of limitation on dual office-holding, moving from an early concern with federal and foreign officers serving in state government (Art. VI, sec. 14 of the 1812 Constitution) to a modern concern with fraud and financial impropriety. The current provision is a mandate that is not self-executing. Discretion remains in the legislature to define the types of dual employment that are prohibited. The court of appeal in *Bellon v. Deshotel* (1979) upheld the prohibition against a person's holding concurrently the offices of school board member and mayor. It rejected the argument that the statute violated a citizen's First Amendment and equal protection rights and a fundamental right to hold office.

SECTION 23
Compensation of Elected Public Officials; Reduction

The compensation of an elected public official shall not be reduced during the term for which he is elected.

To protect judicial independence, earlier constitutions protected judges from a decrease in salary, and Article V, section 21 of the 1974 Constitution continues that policy. The delegates to the Constitutional Convention of 1973, composed in large part of office-holders, also extended the protection to other court-related officials; the attorney general, district attorney, sheriff, coroner, and clerk of court are protected in Article V, section 32. Section 23 goes further and protects the salary of all elected public officials from reduction during the term for which they are elected.

SECTION 24
Impeachment

(A) Persons Liable. A state or district official, whether elected or appointed, shall be liable to impeachment for commission or conviction, during his term of office of a felony or for malfeasance or gross misconduct while in such office.

(B) Procedure. Impeachment shall be by the House of Representatives and trial by the Senate, with senators under oath or affirmation for the trial. The concurrence of two-thirds of the elected senators shall be necessary to convict. The Senate may try an impeachment whether or not the House is in session and may adjourn when it deems proper. Conviction upon impeachment shall result in immediate removal from office. Nothing herein shall prevent other action, prosecution, or punishment authorized by law.

Louisiana follows the federal pattern in its two-step impeachment procedure. The initial impeachment must be by the house, with trial by the senate. A twothirds vote of the senate is necessary to convict upon the impeachment.

Impeachment results in removal from office. It does not disqualify a person from later holding elected or appointive office, nor does it provide immunity from other criminal or civil penalties.

Impeachment must be based on conviction or commission of a felony or for malfeasance or gross misconduct. *Felony* is not defined in the constitution, but it was used knowing that it was defined in Article 2 of the Louisiana Criminal Code as an offense punishable by death or imprisonment at hard labor. The court of appeal used that definition in *Tucker v. Huval* (1979), which involved Section 25 (removal by suit) and borrows the standards of this section. There, a mayor convicted of a federal felony (attempted income tax evasion) was not subject to removal for conviction of a felony since his conduct was punishable only as a misdemeanor under existing state law.

An official is subject to impeachment if the conduct involved occurred during the term of office or if the conviction is during the term of office, whenever the conduct occurred.

Article V, section 25 also establishes a Judiciary Commission, which, acting with the supreme court, can remove judges from office for improper conduct that is less serious than the grounds for impeachment provided in this section. Judges are also subject to impeachment under this section.

SECTION 25
Removal by Suit; Officials Subject

For the causes enumerated in Paragraph (A) of Section 24 of this Article, the legislature shall provide by general law for the removal by suit of any state, district, parochial, ward, or municipal official except the governor, lieutenant governor, and judges of the courts of record.

The legislature in 1976 adopted Louisiana Revised Statutes 42:11–12 to implement the mandate of this section.

SECTION 26
Recall

The legislature shall provide by general law for the recall by election of any state, district, parochial, ward, or municipal official except judges of the courts of record. The sole issue at a recall election shall be whether the official shall be recalled.

Louisiana Revised Statutes 42:341 et seq. implement the mandate of this section.

SECTION 27
Filling of Vacancies

(A) Gubernatorial Appointment; Election. If no other provision therefor is made by this constitution, by statute, by local government charter, by home rule charter or plan of government, or by ordinance, the governor may fill a vacancy occurring in any elective office. When a vacancy occurs in the office and the unexpired portion of the term exceeds one year, the vacancy shall be filled at an election, as provided by law, and the appointment shall be effective only until a successor takes office.
(B) Qualifications. Nothing in this Section shall change the qualifications for any office, and every appointee must be otherwise eligible to hold the office to which appointed.

Gubernatorial appointment to fill vacancies is still the residual rule that applies in absence of contrary provisions. The 1974 Constitution, however, reduced the governor's power to make appointments to vacancies by providing otherwise for a large number of major offices, including legislators (Art. III, sec. 5), most elected state officials (Art. IV, sec. 16), judges (Art. V, sec. 22), and sheriffs, district attorneys, clerks of court, and coroners (Art. V, sec. 30).

SECTION 28
Definition of Vacancy

A vacancy, as used in this constitution, shall occur in the event of death, resignation, removal by any means, or failure to take office for any reason.

McKenzie v. Edwards (1978) held that a vacancy occurred when a city court judge declared in August his intent to resign effective the following January 1. The court found such declarations to be binding and held that the governor could properly call a special election to fill the judgeship upon receipt of the declaration. In this way, the new judge's term would begin the day following the effective date of the resignation, and no interim appointment would be necessary.

SECTION 29
Retirement and Survivor's Benefits

(A) Public School Employees. The legislature shall provide for retirement of teachers and other employees of the public educational system through establishment of one or more retirement systems. Membership in such a retirement system shall be a contractual relationship between employee and employer, and the state shall guarantee benefits payable to a member or retiree or to his lawful beneficiary upon his death.
(B) Other Officials and Employees. The legislature shall enact laws providing for retirement of officials and employees of the state, its agencies, and its political subdivisions, including persons employed jointly by state and federal agencies other than those in military service, through the establishment of one or more retirement systems. Membership in any retirement system of the state or of a political subdivision thereof shall be a contractual relationship between employee and employer, and the state shall guarantee benefits payable to a member of a state retirement system or retiree or to his lawful beneficiary upon his death.
(C) Retirement Systems; Change; Notice. No proposal to effect any change in existing laws or constitutional provisions relating to any retirement system for public employees shall be introduced in the legislature unless notice of intention to introduce the proposal has been published, without cost to the state, in the official state journal on two separate days. The last day of publication shall be at least thirty days before introduction of the bill. The notice shall state the substance of the contemplated law or proposal, and the bill shall contain a recital that the notice has been given.
(D) Compensation for Survivors of Law Enforcement Officers and Firemen. The legislature shall establish a system, including the expenditure of public funds, for compensating the surviving spouses and dependent children of law enforcement officers, firemen, and personnel, as defined by law, who die, or who died after June 30, 1972, as a result of injury sustained in the performance of official duties or in the protection of life or property while on or off duty.
(E) Actuarial Soundness.

(1) The actuarial soundness of state and statewide retirement systems shall be attained and maintained and the legislature shall establish, by law, for each state or statewide retirement system, the particular method of actuarial valuation to be employed for purposes of this Section.

(2) For public retirement systems whose benefits are guaranteed by this constitution as is specified in Paragraphs (A) and (B) of this Section:

(a) The legislature shall, by law, determine and set all required contributions to be made by members. However, until the unfunded accrued liability referenced in (c) below is eliminated, this determination and setting shall not cause the ratio of employee contributions to total contributions, on the basis of each particular plan or classification within each particular retirement system, to exceed such ratio as it existed on January 1, 1987. Upon elimination of the unfunded accrued liability referenced in (c) below, this determination and setting shall not cause a member's contribution to exceed an amount contributed on his behalf as an employer contribution.

(b) The legislature shall, in each fiscal year, by law, provide an amount necessary to fund the employer portion of the normal cost, which shall be determined in accordance with the method of valuation established under (1) above.

(c) The legislature shall, in each fiscal year, by law, provide for the amortization of the unfunded accrued liability existing as of June 30, 1988, which shall be determined in accordance with the method of valuation selected in (1) above, by the year 2029, commencing with Fiscal Year 1989–1990.

(d) Amounts provided for under (b) and (c) above are hereby guaranteed payable, each fiscal year, to each retirement system covered herein. If, for any fiscal year, the legislature fails to provide these guaranteed payments, upon warrant of the governing authority of the retirement system, following the close of said fiscal year, the state treasurer shall pay the amount guar- anteed directly from the state general fund.

(3) For statewide public retirement systems not covered by Paragraphs (A) and (B) of this Section, the legislature shall determine all required contributions to be made by members, contributions to be made by employers, and dedicated taxes required for the sound actuarial maintenance of the systems, including the elimination of the unfunded accrued liability as of the end of the 1988–1989 Fiscal Year, under the method of valuation selected under (1) above, by. the year 2029, commencing with Fiscal Year 1989–1990.

(4) For all state and statewide public retirement systems, neither the state nor the governing authority of such system shall take any action that shall cause the actuarial present value of expected future expenditures of the retirement system to exceed or further exceed the sum of the current actuarial value of assets and the actuarial present value of expected future receipts of the retirement system, except with respect to the following:

(a) Normal business operating expenses of the retirement system.

(b) Capital outlay expenditures of the retirement system.

(c) Management of investments of the retirement system.

(d) Cost-of-living increases to retirees, as provided by law, provided the retirement system is approaching actuarial soundness as provided by law, and the granting of such increase does not cause an increase in the actuarially required contribution rate.

(5) All assets, proceeds, or income of the state and statewide public retirement systems, and all contributions and payments made to the system to provide for retirement and related benefits shall be held, invested as authorized by law, or disbursed as in trust for the exclusive purpose of providing such benefits, refunds, and administrative expenses under the management of the boards of trustees and shall not be encumbered for or diverted to any other purpose. The accrued benefits

of members of any state or statewide public retirement system shall not be diminished or impaired. Future benefit provisions for members of the state and statewide public retirement systems shall only be altered by legislative enactment. [Added by Acts 1987, No. 947, approved November 21, 1987, effective December 23, 1987]

New to the 1974 Constitution were provisions to assure public employees that benefits due under public retirement systems would be paid. The convention adopted paragraphs A-D in that effort. A further effort produced paragraph E.

Under paragraphs A and B, the state "guarantees" benefits to members of the state teachers and state employees retirement systems. It does not guarantee benefits to members of retirement systems established by political subdivisions. The scope of the guarantee is not specified, but its importance rests on the fact that the state's responsibility goes beyond making contributions to a fund. The aim was to make the obligation to pay the benefits one backed by the full faith and credit of the state so that if the retirement fund is inadequate to pay the benefits, the state must furnish the funds to make up the difference. This protection is no small achievement, particularly in contrast to most private retirement systems. Nevertheless, the guarantee is not self-enforcing, and no mechanism exists to make the legislature appropriate the funds needed to fulfill the guarantee.

The designation in paragraph A of membership in a public retirement system as a contractual relationship was an attempt to invoke the constitutional protection against impairment of the obligation of contracts. Making the relationship a contractual one precludes analogy to the federal social security program, which has been held not to establish a contractual or vested right but one subject to change in benefits so long as minimal due process is afforded (*Fleming v. Nestor*, 1960). The aim was to protect reasonable expectations in accrued rights under a contract. Prospective changes in retirement systems, however, could be made so long as existing accrued benefits were protected.

Representatives of state employees, alarmed at the unfunded liabilities of the state's retirement plans, sought more concrete action and protection through the 1987 amendment that added paragraph E. The legislature is mandated to contribute a sum annually to the retirement funds as part of a long-term process to make the systems actuarially sound. If the legislature fails to make the annual contribution, paragraph E(2)(D) has a self-enforcing mechanism to transfer the funds; upon request of the retirement system, "the state treasurer shall pay the amount guaranteed directly from the state general fund." The amendment also seeks to curb the liberalization of retirement benefits without a financing mechanism to cover those benefits.

In the 1973 convention, a proposal that accrued benefits shall not be "diminished or impaired" was rejected because of its uncertainty. The amendment adding paragraph E resurrected that language and adopted it in (E)(5) despite the continuing problem with the uncertainty of the language.

SECTION 30
Oath of Office

Every official shall take the following oath or affirmation:
"I, . . ., do solemnly swear (or affirm) that I will support the constitution and laws of the United States and the constitution and laws of this state and that I will faithfully and impartially discharge and perform all the duties incumbent upon me as . . ., according to the best of my ability and understanding, so help me God."

The supreme court in *State v. Perez* (1985) used the oath to support a finding of malfeasance by a district attorney and a judge. The court stated, "When the defendants swore to uphold the laws of Louisiana, this oath imposed a specific duty upon them not to obstruct or interfere with the execution of those laws. To intentionally interfere with the execution of any law would be a failure to perform a duty lawfully required of them under their oath and would constitute malfeasance."

Article XI

Elections

The right of citizens 18 years old or older to vote is established in Article I, section 10 of the Declaration of Rights. It represents significant expansion of the suffrage, an issue that was controversial in prior constitutional conventions. The 1921 Constitution contained twelve printed pages of detailed regulations of the right to vote and the method of conducting elections. They included residence, character, and literacy requirements designed to disenfranchise blacks. The constitution even excluded from voting persons who lived in common-law marriages or who were the parents of illegitimate children.

The Constitutional Convention of 1973, however, took place after federal court action and federal legislation expanding voting rights, a development that resulted in twelve black delegates being named to the convention. The old approach to suffrage was quickly abandoned, and Article I, section 10 was adopted with little opposition.

With the substantive issue of the right to vote established early in the convention, the opportunity arose to cleanse the constitution of substantial detail. Although the proposal of the Committee on Bill of Rights and Elections was much longer, the convention delegates voted to reduce Article XI to five articles and fewer than 250 words. It is one of the best examples of how the convention was able to improve the technical aspects of the Louisiana Constitution, and it leaves most matters of election law to the legislature.

SECTION 1
Election Code

The legislature shall adopt an election code which shall provide for permanent registration of voters and for the conduct of all elections.

The legislature complied with the mandate of this section and adopted a comprehensive election code (Louisiana Revised Statutes, Title 18, Chapters 1–13) effective January 1, 1978.

SECTION 2
Secret Ballot; Absentee Voting; Preservation of Ballot

In all elections by the people, voting shall be by secret ballot. The legislature shall provide a method for absentee voting. Proxy voting is prohibited. Ballots shall be counted publicly and preserved inviolate as provided by law until any election contests have been settled. In all elections by persons in a representative capacity, voting shall be viva-voce.

In voting by the people, the secret ballot is the norm. In practice, voting machines are used. The requirement of open or public voting, as viva voce voting requires, applies to public officials who represent voters in legislative assemblies and other governing bodies.

SECTION 3
Privilege from Arrest

While going to and returning from voting and while exercising the right to vote, an elector shall be privileged from arrest, except for felony or breach of the peace.

This section continues provisions contained in nine prior constitutions. In 1910, *Thomas v. Henderson* construed the corresponding language from the 1898 Constitution to prohibit the arrest of a person (for illegal voting) while leaving the voting booth. For making this improper arrest of a political opponent, the sheriff was required to pay $250 in damages.

SECTION 4
Prohibited Use of Public Funds

No public funds shall be used to urge any elector to vote for or against any candidate or proposition, or be appropriated to a candidate or political organization. This provision shall not prohibit the use of public funds for dissemination of factual information relative to a proposition appearing on an election ballot.

An innovation in the constitution, section 4 was proposed by the Committee on Bill of Rights and Elections to end the perceived abuse of some public agencies using public funds to promote election propositions. Prominently mentioned in the debate was the use of such funds by school boards to promote bond issues and tax proposals. The committee draft contained only the first sentence; the second sentence allowing dissemination of factual information was added by floor amendment. The distinction between information urging one to vote and information that is factual is not a precise one, but the convention delegates compromised on that language. The court of appeal in *Godwin v. East Baton Rouge Parish School Board* (1979) held that the section was self-operative and that it was not unconstitutionally vague. The court stated, "We believe the average individual understands 'urge' to mean promote, take a position favorable or opposed to a particular candidate or proposition, or openly and publicly seek the election or defeat of a particular candidate, or the passage or defeat of a proposition submitted to the electorate." Permitted would be dissemination of "all empirical data required by the public to intelligently decide whether to vote for or against the issue," so long as it suggests no position for or against.

SECTION 5
Registrar of Voters

The governing authority of each parish shall appoint a registrar of voters, whose compensation, removal from office for cause, bond, powers, and functions shall be provided by law. Upon qualifying as a candidate for other public office, a registrar shall forfeit his office. No law shall provide for the removal from office of a registrar by the appointing authority.

The duties of the local registrars are left to be provided by the legislature, and their appointment is by local governments. The constitution, however, seeks to ensure independence of the registrars, and thus protect the integrity of the registration process, by prohibiting the local governments from removing registrars from office.

Article XII

General Provisions

SECTION 1
State Capital

The capital of Louisiana is the city of Baton Rouge.

In the nineteenth century, the seat of government moved back and forth between New Orleans and Baton Rouge, but Baton Rouge has been designated the capital city since the adoption of the 1879 Constitution (Art. 150). The 1921 Constitution so provided in Article XIX, section 2, but Article VII, section 14 also directed the supreme court to sit in New Orleans. Although the 1974 Constitution no longer directs the court to sit in New Orleans, the Judiciary Committee action in deleting the old provision was for the sake of brevity rather than to require the court to move.[19] The convention continued the prior law under which designation of a capital city or seat of government did not mean that the supreme court must be located there.[20] The legislature is required (Art. III, sec. 2) to meet in the state capital. Since the legislature is not prohibited from doing so, it could require the court to sit in the capital city.

---

[19] Lee Hargrave, "Statutory and Hortatory Provisions of the Louisiana Constitution of 1974," *Louisiana Law Review* 43 (1983):688.

[20] Louisiana Acts 1972, No. 2. The call for the constitutional convention, in section 4(3), prohibited adoption of a provision whereby "the state capital is removed or may be removed from Baton Rouge."

SECTION 2
Civilian-Military Relations

The military shall be subordinate to the civil power.

This provision continues a truism that has rarely been invoked in modern times, especially with regard to state government, which has virtually no military forces. The section originated in Article 125 of the 1868 Constitution, which ironically was adopted by delegates to a convention called by a U. S. Army general pursuant to the Reconstruction Acts after the Civil War.

SECTION 3
Right to Direct Participation

No person shall be denied the right to observe the deliberations of public bodies and examine public documents, except in cases established by law.

A new provision proposed by the Committee on Bill of Rights and Elections, this section was adopted by a vote of 104–6, it being understood that the exception clause makes the right subject to legislative control. The sponsor of the provision conceded that it establishes only a "presumption of access" and that statutes can limit the rights to observe public bodies and to examine public records.

The supreme court has used the provision as the basis for a strong presumption in favor of access in a number of cases, *Title Research Corp. v. Rausch* (1984) requiring legislation making exceptions to be specific and clear.

Section 3 does not govern access to sessions of the legislature, which are regulated by the more demanding requirements of Article III, section 15. That section does not allow exceptions to be made by statute.

The right established in section 3 is to observe the deliberations of public bodies, not to participate or take part in the meetings.

SECTION 4
Preservation of Linguistic and Cultural Origins

The right of the people to preserve, foster, and promote their respective historic linguistic and cultural origins is recognized.

This provision complements Article I, section 3, which prohibits unreasonable discrimination based on culture. Both sections protect against government action that would discriminate on that basis or prohibit citizens from advancing their interests in preserving their cultural rights and language. Both result from a resurgence of Francophone influence in the 1970s. Louisiana's first constitution was drafted in French, and early charters protected the use of French in legislative and court proceedings. French influence declined, and several constitutions, including that of 1921, provided that instruction in public schools had to be conducted in the English language.

The Bill of Rights Committee considered a section on cultural rights and was generally supportive of the concept, but it rejected the proposal because of its imprecision and ambiguity. In the last hectic days of the convention, however, a delegate from Lafayette, center of Acadian Louisiana, was able to secure adoption of the provision by floor amendment. Passage, by 95–1 vote, was secured in part because of her statement: "I really don't believe that it would give us a right to do anything we don't want to do now."[21] The language, however, is broad, giving an activist court a basis to protect what it will develop on a case-by-case basis as cultural and linguistic rights. The courts, however, have not had the opportunity or the inclination to proceed in that direction.

SECTION 5
Forced Heirship and Trusts

> No law shall abolish forced heirship. The determination of forced heirs, the amount of the forced portion, and the grounds for disinherison shall be provided by law. Trusts may be authorized by law, and a forced portion may be placed in trust.

Legislation adopted in 1920 to authorize trusts, a common law device which separates title and beneficial ownership of property, provoked civil law traditionalists in the 1921 Constitutional Convention to limit trusts (Art. IV, sec. 16). As a corollary, that 1921 provision also required the continuation of forced heirship, an institution in the civil code requiring that a certain portion of one's estate be left to certain heirs. Under Civil Code Article 1493 then in effect, descendants were forced heirs to one-third or one-half of the deceased's estate, and ascendants were forced heirs if there were no descendants.

The limits on trusts were liberalized in a number of amendments over the years, but the provision against abolition of forced heirship remained unchanged. Never did the constitution designate, however, which heirs were forced and what portion they were entitled to receive. Those matters were governed by the Louisiana Civil Code.

During the 1973 convention, civil law preservationist sentiment had some political appeal. Opponents to forced heirship also knew that the rule had minimal practical impact, for the provision allows the legislature almost complete freedom in diminishing the impact of forced heirship. The delegates had before them the language from *Succession of Earhart* (1952): that the constitution

---

[21] Hargrave, "Statutory and Hortatory Provisions," 683.

means "that forced heirship cannot be done away with wholly, wiped out or destroyed. This provision does not prohibit the legislature from regulating or restricting the rights of forced heirs." Delegate Max Tobias stated, "As I presently read Louisiana constitution and statutes, the legislature could very simply say that each child is a forced heir to the extent of one dollar."[22]

Even before 1973, the impact of forced heirship had been diminished. Life insurance proceeds and U. S. savings bonds were not subject to the rights of forced heirs. A surviving spouse could be granted the right to use (usufruct) the forced portion inherited by a child. Also the forced portion could be subject to a trust that effectively denied the heir control over the use of the property. Since the adoption of the 1974 Constitution, the legislature has continued to limit the rights of forced heirs in a number of other ways. Ascendants are no longer forced heirs (Civil Code, Art. 1494, repealed); the mass of assets to which the forced portion applies was changed to exclude sums received under pension or deferred compensation plans (Art. 1505); and the forced portion was reduced from a maximum of two-thirds to one-half of the deceased's estate (Art. 1493). In 1989 the legislature acted to continue as forced heirs only the children of the deceased who are 23 years old or younger or are incompetent at the time of death (Art. 1493).

SECTION 6
Lotteries; Gambling

Neither the state nor any of its political subdivisions shall conduct a lottery. Gambling shall be defined by and suppressed by the legislature.

This provision has the important impact of forbidding government-operated lotteries. This ban reflects a continuation of antilottery sentiment that arose in the latter parts of the nineteenth century because of the corruption of the Louisiana Lottery Company. The 1921 constitutional prohibition was broad, Article XIX, section 8 providing, "Lotteries and the sale of lottery tickets are prohibited in this State." The new provision, however, prohibits government only from conducting lotteries; it does not prohibit licensing or otherwise allowing a private lottery, which is what the Louisiana Lottery Company was.

The 1921 Constitution also provided in Article XIX, section 8, "Gambling is a vice and the Legislature shall pass laws to suppress it." The supreme court, however, concluded that the provision was not self-executing and that the only prohibited gambling was what the legislature defined as such. In *Gandolfo v. Louisiana State Racing Commission* (1954), the court approved parimutuel betting at horse

---

[22] IX Records of the Louisiana Constitutional Convention of 1973: Convention Transcripts, Jan. 3, 1974, 3075.

race tracks. The result was a high-sounding constitutional sermon that nonetheless allowed the gambling the legislature chose to allow.

Debate in the 1973 Constitutional Convention recognized that section 6 would have limited effect and that it gave the legislature unfettered freedom to allow various kinds of gambling activities. The legislature has allowed charitable bingo, nonbusiness gambling, parimutuel betting on horse races and offtrack betting.[23]

SECTION 7
State Penal Institutions; Reimbursement of Parish Expense

The state shall reimburse a parish in which a state penal institution is located for expenses the parish incurs arising from crime committed in the institution or by an inmate thereof.

Prosecution for state crimes committed by prisoners is instituted by the local district attorney, and expenses of trial (for example, witness fees, transcript costs, juror fees and meals, and coroner's fees) are paid by the local governments. Although an opinion of the attorney general (86–736) states that the state cannot limit the amount of the required expense reimbursement, it recognizes also that no money can be paid until a legislative appropriation is made. Article VII, section 10 states that no funds can be drawn from the state treasury except pursuant to an appropriation.

SECTION 8
Welfare, Unemployment Compensation, and Health

The legislature may establish a system of economic and social welfare, unemployment compensation, and public health.

Since the legislature can adopt any law that is not prohibited adopting, this permissive provision allowing social welfare expenditures was unnecessary. It was adopted out of an abundance of caution to ensure that Article VII, section 10(D), which limits appropriations to public purposes, will not be violated by social welfare payments to individuals.

SECTION 9
Exceptions From Seizure and Sale

The legislature shall provide by law for exemptions from seizure and sale, as well as waivers of and exclusions from such exemptions. The exemption shall extend to at least fifteen thousand dollars in value of a homestead, as provided by law.

---

[23] Louisiana Revised Statutes 33:4861; 4:105; 4:141 et seq.; 4:211.

The prior constitution's homestead exemption was limited to $4,000. That meant that a home worth more than that amount could be seized and sold but that the debtor would be guaranteed the right to $4,000 of the proceeds. The 1974 Constitution raised the exempt amount to $15,000; more important, it allows the legislature to raise the exemption.

SECTION 10
Suits Against the State

(A) No Immunity in Contract and Tort. Neither the state, a state agency, nor a political subdivision shall be immune from suit and liability in contract or for injury to person or property.
(B) Waiver in Other Suits. The legislature may authorize other suits against the state, a state agency, or a political subdivision. A measure authorizing suit shall waive immunity from suit and liability.
(C) Procedure; Judgments. The legislature shall provide a procedure for suits against the state, a state agency, or a political subdivision. It shall provide for the effect of a judgment, but no public property or public funds shall be subject to seizure. No judgment against the state, a state agency, or a political subdivision shall be exigible, payable, or paid except from funds appropriated therefor by the legislature or by the political subdivision against which judgment is rendered.

Sovereign Immunity. No Louisiana constitution or statute ever provided that the state or its agencies were immune from suit. The courts, however, borrowed a version of sovereign immunity from the common law and applied it in Louisiana. In response, constitutional provisions were adopted to establish a procedure for waivers of immunity and for enforcement of judgments against governmental units.'[24] Even now there is no constitutional foundation to support a claim of a general governmental immunity from suit, and many areas exist in which it has never been questioned that the state is subject to suit. Before 1973, the courts were enlarging that area.

Sovereign immunity was to no avail, for example, in *City of Natchitoches v. State* (1969), when city officials sued the state and some state officials for declaratory and injunctive relief against enforcement of criminal sanctions. The court reasoned that immunity was limited to claims historically part of sovereign immunity, primarily immunity from payment of damages arising in tort.

Delegates to the 1973 Constitutional Convention seeking to expand the right to sue the state were working with this existing state of the law. Their attempts to abolish all sovereign immunity failed. Some delegates worried that complete

[24] George Pugh, "Historical Approach to the Doctrine of Sovereign Immunity," *Louisiana Law Review* 13 (1953):476.

abolition might also affect the immunity of public officials, judicial and legislative as well as executive, for responsibility for their official conduct. At the same time, the concern of most of the proponents of the section was centered on damage awards in tort and contract, and a compromise proposal that specified those subjects was adopted.

The result is that two categories of suits against governmental entities do not require consent to sue: (1) suits that would traditionally have been allowed without obtaining consent of the state and (2) suits in contract and for injury to person or property. In other matters, consent of the state is required. Distinguishing among the three categories is less than simple, and since the debate focused on such a small part of the overall problem—tort and contract damages—it fails to give much guidance. A court of appeal in *Two O'Clock Bayou Land Co. v. State* (1982) did hold that an action for a declaratory judgment that the bed of a bayou was privately owned was not an action in contract or tort. It was characterized as a title contest with the state, a suit that required the state's consent before it could proceed.

The provision represents an expansion of the right to sue governments that is in accord with prior judicial policy. This would suggest an approach that uses a broad construction of the terms *contract* and *injury to person or property*, especially because the enforcement of judgments is still strictly limited by section 10(C).

Enforcement of Judgments. The apparent liberality in almost abolishing sovereign immunity was offset by the continuation of stringent limitations on a private citizen's ability to enforce a money judgment against the state, a state agency, or a local governmental entity.

The court in *Foreman v. Vermilion Parish Police Jury* (1976) held that a judgment against a police jury was not enforceable by seizure of farmland it owned, even if that land was in the police jury's private domain. The court in *De Laureal Engineers Inc. v. St. Charles Parish Police Jury* (1981) recognized that the courts have no power to compel a police jury to appropriate funds to pay a judgment; mandamus is not available to enforce such a discretionary duty.

Paragraph C is aimed at protecting the public fisc and seeks to avoid governmental priorities' being upset by the payment of substantial money judgments. It is not aimed at limiting the courts in a general manner in dealing with the state in the enforcement of judgments that order something other than payment of money.

Legislation has been adopted to provide a procedure for payment of small judgments against the state and for settlement of some claims against the state.[25] Problems have arisen in collecting money judgments against municipalities and parish governing authorities. No legislation exists to force them to pay their

[25] Louisiana Revised Statutes, 13:5141–57.

judgments, although threats from the legislature to cut off various state appropriations if judgments are not paid have been used.

Other alternatives for ordering payment of judgments against the state or its local subdivisions could come from the Declaration of Rights, especially the equal protection guarantee. Article I, section 3 prohibits all discrimination based on race, religion, or political views, and failure to pay judgments based on these classifications undoubtedly would not be supported by any adequate basis. The remedy of injunction or declaratory judgment would be available for such violations, but a problem would arise with respect to granting relief in the form of a money judgment. It might be possible to read paragraph C in conjunction with other constitutional guarantees and to carve out an exception for violations of constitutional rights that would allow seizure or required appropriations in these cases. If the courts are unwilling to do this, the private litigant's alternative is to pursue an action based on denial of U. S. constitutional rights and recover under federal civil rights statutes. That federal remedy would be available in any event, with the power to enforce by seizure of state funds and property (*Gary W. v. State of Louisiana*, 1977).

This section has also been used to support the argument that limits on medical malpractice awards against the state are permissible; they are laws effecting a procedure for payment of judgments and appropriating only a certain amount to pay such a judgment (*Williams v. Kushner*, 1989; *Sibley v. Board of Supervisors of LSU* 1985; *Williams v. Lallie Kemp Charity Hospital*, 1983).

The waiver of immunity in paragraph A to suit in the state's courts is not considered a waiver of the state's right, under the Eleventh Amendment to the U. S. Constitution, not to be sued in federal court, as recognized by *Voisin's Oyster House v. Guidry* (1986).

SECTION 11
Continuity of Government

The legislature shall provide for orderly and temporary continuity of state government, in periods of emergency, until normal processes of government can be reestablished in accordance with the Constitution and laws of the state; and, except as otherwise provided by this Constitution, for the prompt and temporary succession to the powers and duties of public offices when incumbents become unavailable to perform their functions.

This section continues the substance of a constitutional amendment (Acts 1962, No. 505) adopted in the civil defense-conscious 1960s that mandated and authorized the legislature to provide for government during an emergency following an enemy attack. The current provision was expanded to cover any emergency. The legislature has not enacted comprehensive legislation to respond to the mandate.

SECTION 12
Corporations; Perpetual or Indefinite Duration; Dissolution; Perpetual Franchises or Privileges

Neither the state nor any political subdivision shall grant a perpetual franchise or privilege; however, the legislature may authorize the organization of corporations for perpetual or indefinite duration. Every corporation shall be subject to dissolution or forfeiture of its charter or franchise, as provided by general law.

Concern was expressed by some of the lawyers in the Louisiana State Law Institute that the legality of perpetual corporations would be in doubt if this provision of the 1921 Constitution were not continued. The 1973 Convention, in an abundance of caution, continued the substance of the prior section.

SECTION 13
Prescription Against State

Prescription shall not run against the state in any civil matter, unless otherwise provided in this Constitution or expressly by law.

This section protects only the state; it does not protect other governmental entities from prescription running against them. When the broader protection was desired, as in section 10, the reference was to the "state, a state agency or a political subdivision." If section 13 does not apply, the Louisiana Civil Code provision that prescription runs against all persons unless an exception is made comes into play. The supreme court in *State v. City of Pineville* (1981) reasoned that the term *state* "does not include a state agency which is a body corporate with the power to sue and be sued and which, when vested with a cause of action, is the sole party capable of asserting it." In that case the department lost the ability to sue on a contract and recover funds it had advanced to the municipality because of liberative prescription.

Given the general understanding that *prescription* is a generic term that usually includes preemption, prescription of nonuse of real rights, and both acquisitive and liberative prescription (adverse possession and statutes of limitations in other states), it would seem that the section protects the state against losing its lands through acquisitive prescription (adverse possession) by third persons. Nonetheless, the rule is made clearer and broader by Article IX, section 4(B), which provides that land and mineral interests of the "state, of a school board, or of a levee district shall not be lost by prescription." More important, under section 4(B), the legislature is not allowed to change the rule by law.

Property of other governmental entities, such as municipalities and police juries, the parish governing authorities, can be acquired by third persons by acquisitive prescription under the rules provided in the civil code. Property classified as public things cannot be prescribed, whereas private things can be.

In *Town of Broussard v. Broussard Volunteer Fire Department* (1978), the municipality was not protected against acquisitive prescription of a fire truck by the private volunteer fire department.

SECTION 14
Administrative Agency Codes

Rules, regulations, and procedures adopted by all state administrative and quasi-judicial agencies, boards, and commissions shall be published in one or more codes and made available to the public.

An innovation in the 1974 Constitution, this provision was the result of a delegate proposal designed to make agency rules and regulations more accessible to the public. Debate on the provision, which occupies but five lines in the convention record, indicates that it would be permissible to charge a fee for copies of the rules and regulations.

Article XIII

Constitutional Revision

SECTION 1
Amendments

(A) Procedure. An amendment to this constitution may be proposed by joint resolution at any regular session of the legislature, but the resolution shall be prefiled, at least ten days before the beginning of the session, in accordance with the rules of the house in which introduced. An amendment to this constitution may be proposed at any extraordinary session of the legislature if it is within the objects of the call of the session and is introduced in the first five calendar days thereof. If two-thirds of the elected members of each house concur in the resolution, pursuant to all of the procedures and formalities required for passage of a bill except submission to the governor, the secretary of state shall have the proposed amendment published once in the official journal of each parish within not less than thirty nor more than sixty days preceding the election at which the proposed amendment is to be submitted to the electors. Each joint resolution shall specify the statewide election at which the proposed amendment shall be submitted. Special elections for submitting proposed amendments may be authorized by law.
(B) Form of Proposal. A proposed amendment shall have a title containing a brief summary of the changes proposed; shall be confined to one object; and shall set forth the entire article, or the sections or other subdivisions thereof, as proposed to be revised or only the article, sections, or other subdivisions proposed to be added.

However, the legislature may propose, as one amendment, a revision of an entire article of this constitution which may contain multiple objects or changes. A section or other subdivision may be repealed by reference. When more than one amendment is submitted at the same election, each shall be submitted so as to enable the electors to vote on them separately.

(C) Ratification. If a majority of the electors voting on the proposed amendment approve it, the governor shall proclaim its adoption, and it shall become part of this constitution, effective twenty days after the proclamation, unless the amendment provides otherwise. A proposed amendment directly affecting not more than five parishes or areas within not more than five parishes shall become part of this constitution only when approved by a majority of the electors voting thereon in the state and also a majority of the electors voting thereon in each affected parish. However, a proposed amendment directly affecting not more than five municipalities, and only such municipalities, shall become part of this constitution only when approved by a majority of the electors voting thereon in the state and also a majority of the electors voting thereon in each such municipality.

Amendment of the constitution remains relatively easy: proposal by two-thirds vote of the elected members of each house of the legislature and approval by a majority of those voting on the proposition. The governor's approval is not required.

Because of voter resistance to numerous proposed amendments in the years before the constitutional convention, the convention considered several devices to limit the numbers of amendments that could be presented at one time. What emerged instead was the rather modest requirement for prefiling proposed amendments ten days before a legislative session begins.

Under the 1921 Constitution, a proposed amendment could affect more than one section or article of the constitution if the amendment nonetheless had a single object. The first sentence of paragraph B continues that rule with the general requirement that an amendment can have one object. Similar to the limitations that Article III, section 15 imposes on legislation, it prohibits attachment of riders unrelated to the main proposed amendment.

In *Graham v. Jones* (1941), the Louisiana Supreme Court construed the single object limitation broadly and invalidated an executive reorganization plan that involved changes in several sections of the constitution. Reformers who sought to revise the constitution article by article were successful, in 1964, in adopting a constitutional amendment that provided for greater flexibility; it allowed one amendment to provide for "a revision of any article of this Constitution." During the 1973 convention, a committee proposal sought to provide even more flexibility by allowing one amendment to revise an "entire article or articles." The convention rejected the committee proposal and voted to continue the existing rule. Paragraph B thus states that the legislature may propose as one amendment only "a revision of an entire article of this constitution which may contain multiple objects or changes."

Nothing in this section, however, prevents the adoption of an amendment inconsistent with an existing constitutional provision. In such a case, the superseded provision may remain in the document as a matter of form, but the latest expression on substance will prevail.

SECTION 2
Constitutional Convention

Whenever the legislature considers it desirable to revise this constitution or propose a new constitution, it may provide for the calling of a constitutional convention by law enacted by two-thirds of the elected members of each house. The revision or the proposed constitution and any alternative propositions agreed upon by the convention shall be submitted to the people for their ratification or rejection. If the proposal is approved by a majority of the electors voting thereon, the governor shall proclaim it to be the Constitution of Louisiana.

Section 2, a new provision without a counterpart in the prior constitution, it was designed to restrict the means of revising the constitution by convention. It requires a two-thirds vote of the elected members of each house to call the convention and then requires that the new constitution be approved by a majority of those voting on the proposition. Some of the state's past constitutions, including that of 1921, had been adopted with the voters simply approving the call for the convention; the constitution approved by the convention went into effect without submitting it to a vote of the people.

SECTION 3
Laws Effectuating Amendments

Whenever the legislature shall submit amendments to this constitution, it may at the same session enact laws to carry them into effect, to become operative when the proposed amendments have been ratified.

Article XIV

Transitional Provisions

Part IV (sections 38–40) contained the official ballot to be used in voting on the constitution, including the alternative proposition for a single governing board for higher education. The voters defeated the alternative, but the full text of those alternative provisions are included as part of the official text adopted by the constitutional convention.

The technique used in sections 16, 19, 32, and 34—continuing provisions of the prior constitution as statutes instead of simply discontinuing them—was important to voter approval of the new document. It alleviated possible uncertainty about the status of several agencies and officers no longer regulated in the constitution. The mechanism allowed the convention to delete a number of provisions of the 1921 Constitution that it might not otherwise have been able to remove.

A number of sections in this article protected the terms of office of members of various boards and commissions while also providing for transition to changes in the composition of those entities (sec. 1–5, 8, 15, 20, 27, 28, 31).

PART I

SECTION 1
Board of Regents

On the effective date of this Constitution, each member of the Louisiana Coordinating Council for Higher Education appointed by the governor whose term has not expired shall become a member of the Board of Regents until his respective term expires. The governor shall appoint additional members required to complete the membership of the board in accordance with and to effectuate Article VIII, Section 5.

SECTION 2
Board of Supervisors of Louisiana State University and Agricultural and Mechanical College

On the effective date of this constitution, each member of the Board of Supervisors of Louisiana State University and Agricultural and Mechanical College whose term has not expired shall become a member of the Board of Supervisors of Louisiana State University and Agricultural and Mechanical College until his term expires. The governor shall appoint additional members required in accordance with and to effectuate Article VIII, Section 7.

SECTION 3
Board of Supervisors of Southern University

At the next session of the legislature following the effective date of this constitution, the governor shall submit to the Senate for its consent the names of his appointees to the Board of Supervisors of Southern University and Agricultural and Mechanical College in accordance with and to effectuate Article VIII, Section 7.

SECTION 4
State Board of Elementary and Secondary Education; Board of Trustees for State Colleges and Universities

On the effective date of this constitution, each member of the State Board of Education whose term has not expired may elect to become a member of either the State Board of Elementary and Secondary Education or the Board of Trustees for State Colleges and Universities. He shall serve until the expiration of the term for which he was elected. The legislature shall provide by law the procedures by which this right shall be exercised, the secretary of state notified of those elections which must be held, and the governor notified of the appointments which must be made to complete the membership of the boards. The elections and appointments shall be made in accordance with and to effectuate Article VIII, Sections 3 and 6.

SECTION 5
Boards; New Appointments

In making new appointments to a board created by Sections 5, 6, or 7 of Article VIII, the governor shall consider appropriate representation on the board by alumni of the institutions under the control of the board.

SECTION 6
Mandatory Reorganization of State Government

The legislature shall allocate, within not more than twenty departments, the functions, powers, duties, and responsibilities of all departments, offices, agencies, and other instrumentalities within the executive branch, except those allocated by this constitution. The allocation, which shall not be subject to veto by the governor, shall become operative not later than December 31, 1977.

Executive reorganization was accomplished by legislation (Acts 1975, No. 720; Acts 1976, No. 513) that provided for exactly twenty departments. Since then establishment of new departments has been accompanied by the merging of existing ones to maintain the number at twenty.

SECTION 7
Legislative Sessions

The legislature shall provide, by rule or otherwise, for a recess, during the 1975 and 1976 regular annual sessions, which shall be for at least eight calendar days immediately after the first fifteen calendar days of the session.

For at least two years after adoption of the constitution, the legislature had to take a recess of at least eight days after meeting for fifteen days. The aim was to have an initial period devoted primarily to introducing bills, followed by an opportunity for legislators to return home to consult with constituents before regular deliberations began. The experiment was favorably received, and the legislature has continued the system though it is no longer required to do so.

SECTION 8
Civil Service Commission; State; Cities

(A) State Commission. Each person who, on the effective date of thisconstitution, is a member of the State Civil Service Commission shallcontinue in such position for the remainder of the term to which he wasappointed. Within thirty days after the

effective date of this constitution,the president of Xavier University of Louisiana shall submit three names tothe governor for appointment to the commission as provided in Article X,Section 3. Within ninety days after the effective date of this constitution,one member of the commission shall be elected by the classified employeesof the state from their number as provided by law. The term of these appointees shall be six years. Within thirty days after the expiration of theterm of the present member nominated by the president of Louisiana StateUniversity and Agricultural and Mechanical College, the president of DillardUniversity shall submit three names to the governor for appointment to the commission as provided in Article X, Section 3. The term of this appointeeshall be six years.
(B) City Commission. Each person who, on the effective date of thisconstitution, is a member of the New Orleans City Civil Service Commissionshall continue in such position for the remainder of the term to which hewas appointed. Within thirty days after the effective date of this constitution,the presidents of St. Mary's Dominican College and Xavier University of Louisiana each shall submit three names to the governing body of the cityfor appointment to the commission as provided in Article X, Section 4. Within thirty days after the expiration of the term of the present membernominated by the governing body of the city, the president of DillardUniversity shall submit three names to the governing body of the city forappointment to the New Orleans City Civil Service Commission as providedin Article X, Section 4. The term of these appointees shall be six years.

SECTION 9
Civil Service Officers; Employees; State; Cities

Upon the effective date of this constitution, all officers and employees of the state and of the cities covered hereunder who have status in the classified service shall retain said status in the position, class, and rank that they have on such date and shall thereafter be subject to and governed by the provisions of this constitution and the rules and regulations adopted under the authority hereof.

SECTION 10
Offshore Mineral Revenues; Use of Funds

Funds derived from offshore mineral leases and held in escrow under agreement between the state and the United States pending settlement of the dispute between the parties shall be deposited in the state treasury when received. Upon such settlement, these funds and the interest from their investment, except the portion otherwise allocated or dedicated by this constitution, shall be used by the state treasurer to purchase, retire, or pay in advance of maturity the existing bonded indebtedness of the state or shall be invested for that purpose. If any of these funds cannot be so expended within one year, the legislature may appropriate annually, for capital improvements or for the purchase of land, ten percent of the remaining funds, not to exceed ten million dollars in one year.

The constitution sought to limit the uses of any windfall the state might receive upon conclusion of litigation with the federal government over offshore oil and gas revenues. Those funds could not be used for current expenses but had to be devoted to retiring bonds "in advance of maturity" or for capital improvements. The state collected $136 million in 1975 in settlement of the litigation. Legislation sought to allocate $90 million of that sum to pay bonds coming due that year, thus freeing an equivalent amount of current revenues. The supreme court in *Edwards v. Parker* (1976) ruled that such payments violated this section; the funds cannot be used "to pay currently maturing bonded indebtedness of the State."

SECTION 11
Prescription; Tidelands Taxes

No state, district, parish, or other tax, license, fee, or assessment of any kind, and interest charges and penalties attaching thereto, which are imposed, due, or collectible on any property, minerals or the severance thereof, or due or payable by any person, firm, or corporation on any business operation or activity within the tidelands area in dispute between the state and the United States and within the state's historic gulfward boundary three leagues from coast, as established and defined by the Act of Congress of April 8, 1812, which admitted this state into the Union, and as redefined in Louisiana Act No. 33 of 1954, shall prescribe until three years after the thirty-first day of December in the year in which the controversy existing between the United States and this state over the state gulfward boundary is finally resolved and settled in accordance with law. However, no interest charge or penalty shall be assessed or collected on any such tax, license, fee, or assessment if it is paid within one year after the thirty-first day of December in the year in which the controversy is finally resolved and settled.

This was another transitional provision anticipating settlement of the litigation between the state and the federal government over offshore oil and gas revenues. It preserved the claims of governmental units to taxes and other fees that were not collected from or assessed to private individuals because of the pendency of the litigation. Three years from the year of settlement were granted for them to collect such taxes and other fees.

SECTION 12
Forfeitures Prior to 1880

Whenever any immovable property has been forfeited or adjudicated to the state for nonpayment of taxes due prior to January 1, 1880, and the state did not sell or dispose of it or dispossess the tax debtor or his heirs, successors, or assigns prior to the adoption of the constitution of 1921, it shall be presumed conclusively that the forfeiture or adjudication was irregular and null or that the property has been redeemed. The state and its assigns shall be estopped forever from claiming any title to the property because of such forfeiture or adjudication.

This section continues a provision of the 1921 Constitution that was designed to cure title defects arising out of pre-1880 proceedings to forfeit property for nonpayment of taxes. If the property was not sold by the state or if the tax debtor was not removed from the property, the forfeiture was treated as null, and the property belonged to the tax debtor. Probably unnecessary, the provision was nonetheless continued as a precaution against upsetting stable titles.

SECTION 13
Effective Date of Property Tax Provisions

Section 18 and Section 20 of Article VII shall become effective January 1 of the year following the end of three years after the effective date of this constitution. Until that date, the provisions of the constitution of 1921 governing matters covered by those Sections shall continue to apply, notwithstanding any contrary expiration date stated in any provision thereof concerning the veterans' homestead exemption.

This section gave assessors an additional three years from the effective date of the constitution to reassess property according to the new requirements of uniformity and percentage of value of assessments.

PART II

SECTION 14
Limitation on Transitional Provisions

Nothing in this Part shall be construed or applied in such a manner as to supersede or invalidate, or limit or change the meaning of any provision of the foregoing Articles of this constitution, but only to provide for an orderly transition from the constitution of 1921.

SECTION 15
Existing Officials

A person holding an office by election shall continue to exercise his powers and duties until his office is abolished, his successor takes office or the office is vacated, as provided by law. A person holding an office by appointment shall continue to exercise his powers and duties until his office is abolished, his term ends, or he is removed or replaced under the provisions of this constitution or by law. Each public body shall continue to exercise its powers and duties until changed as provided by this constitution or by law.

SECTION 16
Provisions of 1921 Constitution Made Statutory

(A) Provisions Continued as Statutes. Subject to change by law or as otherwise provided in this constitution, and except as any of them conflicts with this constitution, the following provisions of the constitution of 1921 are continued as statutes, but restricted to the same effect as on the effective date of this constitution:

1. Article IV, Sections 2(c), 12-b, and 12-c.
2. Article V, Sections 2, 7, 18, 20, and 21.
3. Article VI, Sections 1, 1(A-1), 11.1, 19, 19.2, 19.3, 19.4, 22(1), 23 except any dedications contained therein, 23.1, 26, 28, 31, 32, 33, 35,36.1, and 39.
4. Article VI-A, Sections 1 through 14, except any dedications therein contained.
5. Article VII, Sections 7, 8, 9, 12.1, 13, 20, 21, 28, 31, 31.1, 31.2, 33, 46 through 51, 51(a), 52, 53, 55, 80, 81, 82, 83, 85, 89 through 92, and 94 through 97.
6. Article IX, Section 4.
7. Article X, Sections 1, 2, 6, 7, 9, 10A, 15, 16, and 23; except any dedications contained therein.
8. Article X-A, Sections 3 and 4.
9. Article XII, Sections 18, 19 through 22, 25, and 26.
10. Article XIV, Sections 3(b), 3(d) (first), 6, 10, 12, 14, 19, 21, 23, 23.1 through 23.43, 24, 24.2 through 24.23, 25, 25.1, 26 through 28, 30, 30.1, 30.3, 30.4, 30.5, 31, 31.3, 31.6, 31.7, 32, 33, 34, 35, 36, 37.1, 38, 38.1, 39, 39.1, 43, 44, 44.1, 45, 47, and 48.
11. Article XV, Sections 1, 3, and 4.
12. Article XVI, Sections 1, 4, 6, 7, 8, and 8(a).
13. Article XVII, Sections 3 and 4.
14. Article XVIII, Sections 4, 8, and 13.
15. Article XIX, Sections 6, 19, 19(a), 20, and 27.

(B) Arrangement. The provisions made statutory in this Article shall be arranged in proper statutory form and recommendations made for additional laws and modifications as provided in R.S. 24:201 through 256, or as otherwise provided by law.

SECTION 17
Provisions of Constitution of 1921 Repealed

Except to the extent provided in this Article and except as retained in Articles I through XIII of this constitution, the provisions of the constitution of 1921 are repealed.

SECTION 18
Existing Laws

(A) Retention. Laws in force on the effective date of this constitution, which were constitutional when enacted and are not in conflict with this constitution, shall remain in effect until altered or repealed or until they expire by their own limitation.
(B) Expiration of Conflicting Law. Laws which are in conflict with this constitution shall cease upon its effective date.

SECTION 19
Ports; Transition to Statutes

All provisions of Article VI, Sections 16, 16.1, 16.2, 16.3, 16.4, 16.5, 16.6, 17, 29, 29.1, 29.2, 29.3, 29.4, 33.1, 34 and Article XIV, Section 30.2 of the constitution of 1921 shall become statutes subject to amendment or repeal only as provided in Article VI, Section 43 of this constitution.

SECTION 20
Public Service Commission

At its next extraordinary or regular session, the legislature shall divide the state into five single-member districts as required by Article IV, Section 21 (A) and shall provide for a special election at which the two additional members of the commission shall be elected, the initial term to be served by each, and other matters necessary to effectuate said Section 21 (A).

PART III

SECTION 21
References to 1921 Constitution

Whenever reference is made in this constitution to the constitution of 1921, it shall mean the Louisiana constitution of 1921, as amended.

SECTION 22
Effect of Titles

No title or sub-title, heading or sub-heading, marginal note, index, or table printed in or with this constitution shall be considered or construed to be a part of this constitution, but to be inserted only for convenience in reference.

SECTION 23
Continuation of Actions and Rights

All writs, actions, suits, proceedings, civil or criminal liabilities, prosecutions, judgments, sentences, orders, decrees, appeals, rights or causes of action, contracts, obligations, claims, demands, titles, and rights existing on the effective date of this constitution shall continue unaffected. All sentences as punishment for crime shall be executed according to their terms.

SECTION 24
Protection of Existing Taxes

All taxes, penalties, fines, and forfeitures owing to the state or any political subdivision levied and collectible under the constitution of 1921 and valid laws enacted thereunder shall inure to the entity entitled thereto.

SECTION 25
Impairment of Debt Obligations Prohibited

Nothing in this constitution shall be construed or applied in such a manner as to impair the obligation, validity, or security of any bonds or other debt obligations authorized under the constitution of 1921.

SECTION 26
Constitution not Retroactive

Except as otherwise specifically provided in this constitution, this constitution shall not be retroactive and shall not create any right or liability which did not exist under the constitution of 1921 based upon actions or matters occurring prior to the effective date of this constitution.

The new equal protection guarantee of Article I, section 3 was applied as of January 1, 1975, the effective date of the constitution. Thus, in *Succession of Clivens* (1983), an illegitimate daughter claiming an interest in the estate of her father who died in 1971 was unsuccessful. In matters of rights to successions, the equal protection guarantee applies to persons who died after the effective date.

Article V, section 21 provides that the term of a judge shall not be decreased "during the term for which he is elected." A judge elected in November 1974 was elected for a fourteen-year term as provided in the prior constitution (*Calogero v. State ex rel. Treen* 1984). The supreme court held that was the case even though the term of the justice began at the same time the new constitution went into effect. The new document "would not affect any rights or liabilities that arose from events occurring before January 1, 1975, whether or not such rights or liabilities had become vested before that date" (Lemmon, concurring).

The mandatory reargument required for some court of appeal cases (Art. V, sec. 8) did not apply in a suit filed in the district court in 1974 (*Traigle v. P. P. G. Industries*, 1975) even though the court of appeals rendered its decision in the case in 1975.

SECTION 27
Legislative Provisions

(A) President of Senate. The lieutenant governor in office on the effective date of this constitution shall continue to serve as president of the Senate until his term expires in 1976.

(B) First Session. The provisions of Article III of this constitution shall become effective for the first session of the legislature to be held in 1975 and each session thereafter. However, in 1976, the legislature shall convene in regular session at twelve o'clock noon on the second Monday in May, at which time the members elected at the statewide election in 1976 shall take office; otherwise, the legislature shall conduct that session as provided in Article III of this constitution.

(C) Legislative Auditor. The legislative auditor shall continue to exercise the powers and perform the functions set forth in Article VI, Section 26(2) of the constitution of 1921 until otherwise provided by law.

(D) Legislative Reapportionment. The requirement for legislative reapportionment in Section 6 of Article III of this constitution shall apply to the reapportionment of the legislature following the decennial census of 1980, and thereafter.

SECTION 28
Judiciary Commission

The members of the judiciary commission in office on the effective date of this constitution shall serve until the expiration of their terms. Within thirty days after the effective date of this constitution, the additional two citizen members shall be selected as required by Article V, Section 25. A lawyer member, as thereby required, shall be selected to succeed the judge of a court of record other than a court of appeal whose term as a member of the commission first expires. Thereafter, when a vacancy occurs, the successor to the position shall be selected in accordance with Article V, Section 25.

SECTION 29
Repealed By Acts 1986, No. 1082, Section 2, Effective October 29, 1986

As adopted, section 29 postponed for one set of state officials (those elected in 1976) the change of date for taking office (from May to March). A 1986 amendment to Article IV, section 3(A) advanced the beginning of those terms to January. Section 3(D) provided its own transition provisions, making this section moot, and deleted it. It had provided, "Officials elected statewide in 1976 under the provisions of this constitution shall take office on the second Monday in May ofthat year. Thereafter, statewide elected officials shall take office on the second Monday in March as provided in this constitution."

SECTION 30
Commissioner of Elections

The commissioner of elections, as provided by Article IV, first elected under this constitution shall be elected to take office in 1976. The custodian of voting machines in office on the effective date of this constitution shall continue to exercise the functions of that office, without change, until the expiration of his term.

SECTION 31
Pardon Board

Until a pardon board is appointed under the terms of this constitution, the lieutenant governor, attorney general, and presiding judge of the sentencing court shall continue to serve as a board of pardons.

SECTION 32
Levee Districts; Compensation for Property

The provisions of Article XVI, Section 6 of the constitution of 1921 shall be continued as a statute, subject to change by the legislature, and the amount of compensation therein required to be paid for property used or destroyed for levee or levee drainage purposes shall be paid as provided in Section 6 of Article XVI of the constitution of 1921 until the legislature enacts a law to effectuate Article VI, Section 42 of this constitution.

This section continued as a statute the rule governing compensation for riparian property appropriated for levee construction. Compensation was at the assessed value of the property, normally only a small percentage of actual worth. The legislature in 1978 superseded that provision and provided in Revised Statutes 38:281 for compensation at "fair market value to the full extent of the loss," the same standard applied in takings under the eminent domain power. (These matters are discussed at length in the commentary following Article I, section 4.)

SECTION 33
Suits Against the State; Effective Date

The provisions of Article XII, Section 10 waiving the immunity of the state, its agencies, or political subdivisions from suit and liability in contract or for injury to person or property only shall apply to a cause of action arising after the effective date of this constitution.

SECTION 34
Exemption from Seizure and Sale

The provisions of Article XI of the constitution of 1921 shall be continued as a statute until the legislature enacts the law required by Article XII, Section 9 of this constitution, but the amount of the exemption shall be fifteen thousand dollars in value until otherwise fixed by law.

SECTION 35
Effective Date

This constitution shall become effective at twelve o'clock midnight on December 31, 1974. The secretary of state shall promulgate the results of the election by publication in the official state journal on the thirtieth day prior thereto; however, he shall announce the results of the election within thirty days after the date of the election at which the constitution is submitted to the people.

The reference to midnight on December 31, 1974, could refer to the moment before 12:01 a.m. on December 31, 1974, or to the moment before 12:01 a.m. on January 1, 1975. In a number of cases, the supreme court has taken a commonsense approach and has referred to the effective date as January 1, 1975.

SECTION 36
Effect of Adoption

Notwithstanding any contrary provision of any law or the prior constitution, this constitution when approved by the electors of this state shall be the constitution of the State of Louisiana upon the effective date as provided in Section 35 of this Article.

SECTION 37
Severability Clause

If any provision of this constitution is declared invalid for any reason, that provision shall not affect the validity of the entire constitution or any other provision thereof.

PART IV

Section 38 provided the ballot proposition for voting on the proposed constitution and for the alternative proposition on higher education management. Sections 39 and 40 provided the alternative text for Article VIII, Education, and Article XIV, sections 1–5 in the event alternative B was adopted. The proposed constitution was ratified by the people at an election held on April 20, 1974, and alternative A, with four boards to govern higher education, was approved. The provisions of alternative B, which provided for one governing board for all higher education, were defeated. It received 199,985 votes (38 percent), and the four-board proposal received 331,339 votes (62 percent).

SECTION 38
Alternative Proposition

There shall be submitted to the people for the ratification of the proposed new constitution an official ballot containing the following propositions and instructions to voters:

OFFICIAL BALLOT

(Instructions to voters: Place an "X" in the boxes which express your preferences. The full text of the proposed constitution and the alternative propositions are available for inspection at the polling place. If the proposed constitution receives a majority of the votes cast thereon and Alternative A below receives a majority of the votes cast on the alternative propositions, the proposed constitution shall become the Constitution of Louisiana. If the proposed constitution receives a majority of the votes cast thereon and Alternative B receives a majority of the votes cast on the alternative propositions, the proposed constitution shall become the Constitution of Louisiana, except that Article VIII of the proposed Constitution shall be deleted therefrom and Alternative Article VIII shall be inserted in lieu thereof. If the proposed constitution fails to receive a majority of the votes cast thereon, both of the alternative propositions shall also fail.)

Do you favor or oppose of adoption of the proposed 1974 Constitution?

(Vote for one)

FOR adoption of the proposed 1974 Constitution 1 [ ]

or

AGAINST adoption of the proposed 1974 Constitution 2 [ ]

ALTERNATIVE PROPOSITIONS

If the proposed 1974 Constitution is adopted, do you prefer (A) the governance of higher education by a Board of Regents and management boards for the LSU system, the Southern University system, and all other state colleges and universities, or (B) the governance of higher education solely by a Board of Regents?

(Vote for one)

ALTERNATIVE A For governance of higher education by a Board of Regents and management boards for the LSU system, the Southern University system, and all other state colleges and universities 3 [ ]

or

ALTERNATIVE B For governance of higher education solely by a Board of Regents 4 [ ]

SECTION 39
Article VIII. Education

(A) If Alternative B concerning education boards is approved by the electors and if the proposed constitution is approved by the electors, then the following Article shall become Article VIII of the new constitution and Article VIII as set forth in the proposed new constitution shall be null, void and of no effect and shall be deemed stricken from the proposed constitution. Alternative Article VIII shall be as follows:

Article VIII. Education
Preamble

The goal of the public educational system is to provide learning environments and experiences, at all stages of human development, that are humane, just, and designed to promote excellence in order that every individual may be afforded an equal opportunity to develop to his full potential.

Section 1. Public Educational System

The legislature shall provide for the education of the people of the state and shall establish and maintain a public education system.

Section 2. State Superintendent of Education

There shall be a superintendent of education who, subject to provisions for appointment in lieu of election set forth in Article IV, Section 20, of this constitution, shall be elected for a term of four years. If the office is made appointive, the State Board of Elementary and Secondary Education and the Board of Regents shall make the appointment. He shall be the administrative head of the Department of Education and the Board of Regents and shall implement the policies of the State Board of Elementary and Secondary Education and the Board of Regents and the laws affecting schools under their jurisdiction. The qualifications and other powers, functions, duties, and responsibilities of the superintendent shall be provided by law.

Section 3. State Board of Elementary and Secondary Education

(A) Creation; Functions. The State Board of Elementary and Secondary Education is created as a body corporate. It shall supervise and control the public elementary and secondary schools, post-secondary vocational-technical schools, special schools under its jurisdiction and shall have budgetary responsibility for all funds appropriated or allocated by the state for those schools, all as provided by law. The board shall have other powers, duties, and responsibilities as provided by this constitution or by law, but shall have no control over the business affairs of a parish or city school board or the selection or removal of its officers and employees.

(B) Membership; Terms. The board shall consist of eight members elected from single-member districts which shall be determined by law and three members appointed by the governor from the state at large, with consent of the Senate. Members shall serve overlapping terms of six years, following the initial terms which shall be fixed by law.

(C) Vacancy. A vacancy in the office of an elected member, if the remaining portion of the term is more than one year, shall be filled for the remainder of the term by election, as provided by law. Other vacancies shall be filled for the remainder of the term by appointment by the governor.

Section 4. Approval of Private Schools

Upon application by a private elementary, secondary, or proprietary school with a sustained curriculum or specialized course of study of quality at least equal to that prescribed for similar public schools, the State Board of Elementary and Secondary Education shall approve the private school. A certificate issued by an approved private school shall carry the same privileges as one issued by a state public school.

Section 5. Board of Regents

(A) Creation; Functions. The Board of Regents is created as a body corporate. It shall plan, coordinate, and have budgetary responsibility for all public higher education and shall have other powers, duties, and responsibilities provided in this Section or by law.

(B) Membership; Terms. The board shall consist of eight members elected from single-member districts which shall be determined by law and seven members appointed by the governor from the state at large, with consent of the Senate. Members shall serve overlapping terms of six years, following the initial terms which shall be fixed by law.

(C) Vacancy. A vacancy occurring prior to the expiration of a term shall be filled for the remainder of the unexpired term by appointment by the governor, with consent of the Senate.

(D) Powers. The Board of Regents shall meet with the State Board of Elementary and Secondary Education at least twice a year to coordinate programs of public elementary, secondary, vocational-technical, career, and higher education. The Board of Regents shall have the following powers, duties, and responsibilities relating to public institutions of higher education:

(1) To revise or eliminate an existing degree program, department of instruction, division, or similar subdivision.

(2) To approve, disapprove, or modify a proposed degree program, department of instruction, division, or similar subdivision.

(3) To study the need for and feasibility of any new institution of higher education, including branches of institutions and conversion of two-year institutions to institutions offering longer courses of study. If the creation of a new institution, or a management board for an institution or group of institutions is proposed, addition of another management board, or the transfer of an existing institution from one board to another is proposed, the Board of Regents shall report its written findings and recommendations to the legislature within one year. Only after the report has been filed, or, after one year if no report is filed, may the legislature take affirmative action on such a proposal and then only by law enacted by two-thirds of the elected members of each house.

(4) To formulate and make timely revision of a master plan for higher education. As a minimum, the plan shall include a formula for equitable distribution of funds to the institutions of higher education.

(5) To require that every institution of higher education submit to it, at a time it specifies, an annual budget proposal for operational needs and for capital needs of each institution under the control of each board. The Board of Regents shall submit its budget recommendations for all institutions of higher education in the state. It shall recommend priorities for capital construction and improvements.

Section 6. Boards; Membership; Compensation
(A) Dual Membership. No person shall be eligible to serve simultaneously on more than one board created by or pursuant to this Article.
(B) Compensation. A member of a board created by or pursuant to this Article shall serve without pay, but per diem and expenses may be provided by law.

Section 7. Parish School Boards; Parish Superintendents
(A) Boards. The legislature shall create parish school boards and provide for the election of their members.
(B) Superintendents. Each parish board shall elect a superintendent of parish schools. The State Board of Elementary and Secondary Education shall fix the qualifications and prescribe the duties of the parish superin-tendent. He need not be a resident of the parish in which he serves.

Section 8. Existing Boards and Systems Recognized; Consolidation
(A) Recognition. Parish and city school board systems in existence on the effective date of this constitution are recognized, subject to control and supervision by the State Board of Elementary and Secondary Education and the power of the legislature to enact laws affecting them.
(B) Ouachita Parish and Monroe City School Systems; Board Membership. Only persons residing within the jurisdiction of the Monroe City School Board shall be eligible to vote for or be members of the Monroe City School Board. Only persons residing in that portion of Ouachita Parish outside the jurisdiction of the Monroe City School Board shall be eligible to vote for or be members of the Ouachita Parish School Board. The position of a member of either board shall be vacated when he no longer satisfies the requirements of this Paragraph. Notwithstanding any contrary provision of this constitution, this Paragraph shall become operative upon the election of members to the Ouachita Parish School Board taking office in 1977 or upon the first reapportionment affecting the Ouachita Parish School Board, whichever occurs earlier.
(C) Consolidation. Subject to approval by a majority of the electors voting, in each system affected, in an election held for that purpose, any two or more school systems may be consolidated as provided by law.

Section 9. Appropriations; State Boards

The legislature shall appropriate funds for the operating and administrative expenses of the state boards created by or pursuant to this Article.

Section 10. Appropriations; Higher Education

Appropriations for the institutions of higher education and post-secondary vocational-technical training and career education shall be made and ad- ministered as provided by law.

Section 11. Funding; Apportionment

(A) Free School Books. The legislature shall appropriate funds to supply free school books and other materials of instruction prescribed by the State Board of Elementary and Secondary Education to the children of this state at the elementary and secondary levels.

(B) Minimum Foundation Program. The legislature shall appropriate funds sufficient to insure a minimum foundation program of education in all public elementary and secondary schools. The funds appropriated shall be equitably allocated to parish and city school systems according to formulas adopted by the State Board of Elementary and Secondary Education and approved by the legislature prior to making the appropriation.

(C) Local Funds. Local funds for the support of elementary and secondary schools shall be derived from the following sources:

First: Each parish school board, Orleans Parish excepted, and each municipality or city school board actually operating, maintaining, or supporting a separate system of public schools, shall levy annually an ad valorem maintenance tax not to exceed five mills on the dollar of assessed valuation on property subject to such taxation within the parish or city, respectively.

Second: The Orleans Parish School Board shall levy annually a tax not to exceed thirteen mills on the dollar of the assessed valuation of property within the city of New Orleans assessed for city taxation, and shall certify the amount of the tax to the governing authority of the city. The governing authority shall have the tax entered on city tax rolls. The tax shall be collected in the manner, under the conditions, and with the interest and penalties prescribed by law for city taxes. The money thus collected shall be paid daily to the Orleans Parish School Board.

Third: For giving additional support to public elementary and secondary schools, any parish, school district, or sub-school district, or any municipality or city school board which supports a separate city system of public schools may levy an ad valorem tax for a specific purpose, when authorized by a majority of the electors voting in the parish, municipality, district, or subdistrict in an election held for that purpose. The amount, duration, and purpose of the tax shall be in accord with any limitation imposed by the legislature.

(D) Municipal School Systems. For the effects and purposes of this Section, the municipalities of Monroe in Ouachita Parish, and Bogalusa in Washington Parish, and no others, shall be regarded and treated as parishes and shall have the authority granted parishes.

Section 12. Tulane University

The Tulane University of Louisiana in New Orleans is recognized as created and to be developed in accordance with Act No. 43 approved July 5, 1884.

(B) If Alternative B concerning education boards is not approved by the electors but the proposed constitution is approved by the electors then no change shall be made therein.

SECTION 40
Transition to Board of Regents and State Board of Elementary and Secondary Education

(A) If Alternative B concerning education boards is approved by the electors and if the proposed constitution is approved by the electors, then the following Section shall become Section 1 of Article XIV of the new constitution and Sections 1, 2, 3, 4, and 5 of Article XIV shall be null, void, and of no effect. If the alternative proposition is not approved, this Section shall be null and void and of no effect.

Section 1. Educational Boards
(1) On the effective date of this constitution, each member of the Louisiana Coordinating Council for Higher Education whose term has not expired shall become a member of the Board of Regents. The legislature shall provide by law the procedure to effectuate the transition to the board, the secretary of state notified of those elections which must be held, and the governor notified of the appointments which must be made to complete the membership of the board. The elections and appointments shall be made in accordance with and to effectuate Article VIII, Section 5 of the alternative proposition as set forth in sections 38 and 39 of this Article.
(2) On the effective date of this constitution, each member of the State Board of Education whose term has not expired may elect to become a member of either the State Board of Elementary and Secondary Education or the Board of Regents. He shall serve until the expiration of the term for which he was elected. The legislature shall provide by law the procedures by which this right shall be exercised, the secretary of state notified of those elections which must be held, and the governor notified of the appointments which must be made to complete the membership of the boards. The elections and appointments shall be made in accordance with and to effectuate Article VIII, Sections 3 and 5 of the alternative proposition.
(3) On the effective date of this constitution the Louisiana Coordinating Council for Higher Education is abolished, and on such date all powers, duties, and functions thereof not inconsistent with this constitution shall be merged and consolidated into the Board of Regents.
(4) On the effective date of this constitution, all functions of the State Board of Education with respect to the governance, supervision, management, administration,

and direction of institutions of higher education not inconsistent with this constitution shall be transferred to the Board of Regents, and in all other respects the functions of the State Board of Education not inconsistent with this constitution shall be transferred to and be exercised by the State Board of Elementary and Secondary Education.

(5) Subject to change by law and except as in conflict with this Alternative Proposition and Act 2 of 1972, the provisions of Article XII, Section 7A of the Constitution of 1921 are continued as a statute, but the powers of the board shall be limited to the management of the daily operations of the Louisiana State University System.

BIBLIOGRAPHICAL ESSAY

BIBLIOGRAPHIC WORKS

Research into Louisiana history should begin with an excellent recent bibliography edited by Light Townsend Cummins and Glen Jeansonne, *A Guide to the History of Louisiana* (Westport, Conn.: Greenwood Press, 1982). Historians specializing in various historical periods contributed eleven bibliographic essays on the leading works on each period. Another valuable contribution of the book is a description of the major archives and historical collections in the state.

GENERAL HISTORICAL WORKS

A readable and perceptive one-volume history of the state from the colonial period to the 1970s is Joe Gray Taylor's *Louisiana: A Bicentennial History* (New York: Norton, 1976), part of the States and the Nation Series sponsored by the American Association for State and Local History. Although the book does not purport to be a constitutional history, it effectively and succinctly reflects the political forces that influenced the succession of constitutions. A standard college text is Bennett H. Wall, ed., *Louisiana: A History* (Arlington Heights, III.: Forum Press, 1984).

Focusing on developments during the territorial period and during early statehood, especially the controversy over continuation of a civil law legal system, is George Dargo's *Jefferson's Louisiana: Politics and the Clash of Legal Traditions* (Cambridge: Harvard University Press, 1975).

Joseph G. Tregle, Jr., "Political Reinforcement of Ethnic Dominance in Louisiana, 1812–1845," in *The Americanization of the Gulf Coast, 1803–1850*, ed. L. F. Ellsworth (Pensacola, Fla.: 1971), is a good essay on developments between the first and second constitutions.

An excellent analysis of the flow of political developments and the transfer of power from group to group and area to area is in Perry H. Howard, *Political Tendencies in Louisiana* (Baton Rouge: Louisiana State University Press, 1957; rev. & expanded ed. 1971).

Roger W. Shugg, *Origins of Class Struggle in Louisiana* (Baton Rouge: Louisiana State University Press, 1939; reissued in paperback 1968) is, as its subtitle indicates, "A Social History of White Farmers and Laborers during Slavery and After, 1840–1875." Joe Gray Taylor, *Louisiana Reconstructed: 1863–1877* (Baton Rouge: Louisiana State University Press, 1974), is an exhaustive study concentrating on the Reconstruction period. It has especially good coverage of the conventions that produced the 1864 and 1868 constitutions.

The standard resource for Louisiana history in the late nineteenth century is William I. Hair, *Bourbonism and Agrarian Protest: Louisiana Politics, 1877–1900* (Baton Rouge: Louisiana State University Press, 1969). Mark T. Carleton, *Politics and Punishment: A History of the Louisiana State Penal System* (Baton Rouge: Louisiana State University Press, 1971), focuses on one aspect of corruption during that time.

Alan P. Sindler, *Huey Long's Louisiana: State Politics, 1920–52* (Baltimore: Johns Hopkins University Press, 1956), contains a good historical summary of the political forces prior to Huey Long's rise and then concentrates on Long's career and its aftermath. It contains good information about the basic problems in and under the 1921 Constitution. More recent is T. Harry Williams, *Huey Long* (New York, Knopf, 1969), the biography of the Kingfish that won the author the Pulitzer Prize. The book is based extensively on oral histories.

Little has been written on postwar Louisiana developments. The best available is from Taylor's *Louisiana* and Howard's *Political Tendencies*. Of some historical interest are the standard romantic versions of the state's colonial and early statehood history: Alcee Fortier, *A History of Louisiana* (New York, 1904); Charles E. A. Gayarre, *History of Louisiana*, 4 vols. (New Orleans, 4th ed. 1903); and Francois-Xavier Martin, *The History of Louisiana from the Earliest Period* (New Orleans, 1882).

CONSTITUTIONAL HISTORY

The best resource is Alden L. Powell's *A History of Louisiana Constitutions* contained in volume 1, part 1, of *Projet of a Constitution for the State of Louisiana With Notes and Studies* (Baton Rouge: State of Louisiana, 1954), 273–508. The history was part of the materials to be furnished to a constitutional convention that was never called. It is exceptionally well detailed and documented. That virtue is also its drawback; at times the detail overwhelms and masks an analysis of trends and developments. Out of print, the project was nevertheless widely distributed and is available at most academic and law libraries in the state.

Cecil Morgan, *The First Constitution of Louisiana* (Baton Rouge: Louisiana State University Press, 1975), contains facsimiles of both the French and English printed versions of the 1812 Constitution. The introduction by the former dean of the Tulane Law School is a concise and readable survey of the events surrounding the drafting of the document. Especially interesting is the biographical information on the delegates, information confirming the aristocratic nature of the group. Philip D.Uzee, "The First Louisiana State Constitution (master's thesis, Louisiana State University, 1938), is a more detailed account of that convention".

Nine essays on diverse legal historical topics are contained in Edward F. Haas, ed., *Louisiana's Legal Heritage*, Studies in Louisiana Culture (Pensacola, Fla.: Perdido Bay Press, 1983). Especially helpful is information on the early courts and the sources of Louisiana law. Several works on Louisiana law are helpful in constitutional matters, if for no other reason than the constitutions have contained so much statutory material. They include Samuel B. Groner, "Louisiana Law: Its Development in the First Quarter Century of American Rule," *Louisiana Law Review* 8 (1948):350; Judge John T. Hood, Jr., "The History and Development of the Louisiana Civil Code," *Louisiana Law Review* 19 (1958): 18; and Henry P. Dart, "History of the Supreme Court of Louisiana," *Louisiana Historical Quarterly* 4 (1921).

As difficulties with the 1921 Constitution developed, several writers began championing the need for reform. Among the better works are Kimbrough Owen, "The Need for Constitutional Revision in Louisiana," *Louisiana Law Review* 8 (1947):1. (Owen went on to direct the law institute's project for a new constitution.) Thomas W. Leigh, who wrote "Need and Basis for Constitutional Revision," *Louisiana Law Review* 14 (1949):247, became one of the delegates to the 1973 convention. Another active participant in the process, Governor Sam Houston Jones, wrote "Constitutional Revision in Louisiana," *Louisiana Law Review* 26 (1965):78, a printed version of the former governor's address when he was inducted as an honorary member of the Order of the Coif at the Louisiana State University Law School. It is a classic enunciation of the anti-Long position on the need for constitutional revision but keeping restraints on the power of the governor and the legislature.

THE 1973 CONSTITUTIONAL CONVENTION

As the Constitutional Convention of 1973 was underway, Professor Louis E. Newman edited *Focus on CC-73* (Baton Rouge: Louisiana State University Institute of Government Research, 1973), for a special Louisiana State University provost's course on the constitution. It is a compilation of lectures covering historical matters, as well as the main policy questions before the convention. Authors include Governor Edwin W. Edwards, law school dean Paul M. Hebert, and historian Mark T. Carleton.

A concise and readable chronology of the attempts at constitutional reform is J. L. Barnidge, "The Louisiana Constitutional Convention of 1973: The Road to Revision," *Louisiana History* 15 (1974):35. Mark T. Carleton, "Elitism Sustained: Louisiana Constitution of 1974," *Tulane Law Review* 54 (1974):560, is a contemporary analysis of the new constitution which criticizes the failure of the document to produce substantial reform. The article is reprinted in chapter 2 of James Bolner, ed., *Louisiana Politics: Festival in a Labyrinth* (Baton Rouge: Louisiana State University Press, 1982). An analysis of voting patterns in the convention is contained in Richard L. Engstrom and Patrick F. O'Connor, "Restructuring the Regime: Support for Change Within the Louisiana Constitutional Convention," *Polity* 11 (1979):440.

Since the adoption of the 1974 Constitution, a number of participants in the convention have written about the document. Volume 21, number 1 of the *Loyola Law Review* (1975) contains articles by Governor Edwin W. Edwards,

"The 1974 Constitution: A New Beginning" (assisted by David Poynter and Edward Hardin, the clerk and assistant clerk of the convention, respectively); delegate David Conroy," Louisiana Constitution of 1974: Taxation"; delgate R. Gordon Kean, "Local Government and Home Rule"; and delegate Louis "Woody" Jenkins, "The Declaration of Rights." These articles are sympathetic to the new document. Related articles in the symposium are more critical. Ben R. Miller, "The Declaration of Rights: Criminal Provisions," argues that the constitution goes too far in protecting individual rights, and Victor A. Sachse, Jr., "Article VIII: Does It Change the Status Quo?" questions whether adequate provision was made to prevent public funds from being used to aid parochial schools.

I was coordinator of legal research for the convention and have written three major articles on the new constitution in the *Louisiana Law Review:* "The Declaration of Rights of the Louisiana Constitution of 1974," 35 (1974): 1; "The Judiciary Article of the Louisiana Constitution of 1974," 37 (1977):766; and "Statutory and Hortatory Provisions of the Louisiana Constitution of 1974," 43 (1983):647. The *Louisiana Law Review* also publishes an annual survey of Louisiana legal developments, which includes a section on Louisiana constitutional law.

Recent student notes in the *Louisiana Law Review* include Connell Archey, "The Status of Private Searches under the Louisiana Constitution of 1974," 49 (1989):873; Frances Bouillion, "Louisiana Constitution, Article VIII: Education," 46 (1986):1137; James Domengeaux, "Native Born Acadians and the Equality Ideal," 46 (1986):1151; and Robert Stockstill, "Voting and Election Law in the Louisiana Constitution," 46 (1986):1253.

THE DOCUMENTS

Readily accessible and easy to use are the three-volume *West's Louisiana Statutes Annotated—Louisiana Constitution* (St. Paul, Minn.:West, 1977). Annual supplements are available. Volumes 1 and 2 contain the 1974 Constitution and extensive annotations. Volume 3 contains the full text of all the state's prior constitutions.

William F. Swindler devotes all of volume 4-A of *Sources and Documents of United States Constitutions* (Dobbs Ferry, N.Y.: Oceana, 1975) to Louisiana. The book contains the full text of most of the constitutions but only abstracts of those of 1861, 1913, and 1974.

Of more than passing interest is Huey P. Long, comp., *Constitutions of the State of Louisiana* (Baton Rouge: State of Louisiana, 1930). It contains the Constitution of 1921 with the corresponding articles of earlier constitutions. Ascribed to Huey Long and published by the state, it was primarily the work of one of Huey's aides, George Wallace, a Winnfield lawyer brought to Baton Rouge to draft statutes. Some speculation exists as to whether Long saw this as a means of obtaining an honorary degree from Loyola. As T. Harry Williams stated, "It is also possible that he was moved by as simple a motive as personal vanity; he wanted to see his name on a book. He would 'produce' two more books later, and with both of them he displayed an inordinate pride of authorship" (Williams, *Huey Long*, p. 490).

Swindler's *Sources* contains a bibliography (p. 471) that is a good guide to the journals of the constitutional conventions. More detailed references to those printed journals are contained in the bibliography produced by the law institute *Projet*, 4:900–902.

After the adoption of the 1974 Constitution, the legislature established the Constitutional Convention Records Commission to compile and edit the documents of the convention. Included in its fourteen-volume *Records of the Louisiana Constitutional Convention of 1973* (Baton Rouge: State of Louisiana, 1977) are transcripts of the floor debates in addition to committee documents. The editor of the records was A. Edward Hardin, assistant clerk for CC/73.

TABLE OF CASES

A

B

C

D

E

F

G

H

I

J

K

L

M

N

O

P

R

S

T

U

V

W

Y

■ INDEX

About the Author

LEE HARGRAVE is Wex S. Malone Professor of Law at Louisiana State University. He has co-authored *Louisiana Matrimonial Regimes,* and authored *Cases and Materials on Louisiana Criminal Law.* Several of his articles have appeared in the *Louisiana Law Review.*

www.ingramcontent.com/pod-product-compliance
Ingram Content Group UK Ltd.
Pitfield, Milton Keynes, MK11 3LW, UK
UKHW020924170926
475595UK00031B/65

9 780199 779031